restless virgins

restless

love, sex, and survival at
a new england prep school

virgins

abigail jones and marissa miley

WM

WILLIAM MORROW

An Imprint of HarperCollins *Publishers*

RESTLESS VIRGINS. Copyright © 2007 by Abigail Drachman-Jones and Marissa Miley. All rights reserved. Printed in the United States of America. No part of this book may be used or reproduced in any manner whatsoever without written permission except in the case of brief quotations embodied in critical articles and reviews. For information address HarperCollins Publishers, 10 East 53rd Street, New York, NY 10022.

HarperCollins books may be purchased for educational, business, or sales promotional use. For information please write: Special Markets Department, HarperCollins Publishers, 10 East 53rd Street, New York, NY 10022.

FIRST EDITION

Designed by Cassandra J. Pappas

Library of Congress Cataloging-in-Publication Data

Jones, Abigail.
   Restless virgins : love, sex, and survival at a New England prep school / Abigail Jones and Marissa Miley.—1st ed.
    p. cm.
   ISBN: 978-0-06-119205-0
   ISBN-10: 0-06-119205-8
   1. Preparatory schools—New England—Case studies. 2. Preparatory school students—Sexual behavior—New England—Case studies.
  3. Teenage girls—Sexual behavior—New England—Case studies.
  4. Values—Study and teaching (Secondary)—New England. I. Miley, Marissa. II. Title.

   LC58.7.J66 2007
   373.22'20974—dc22   2007021120

07 08 09 10 11 WBC/RRD 10 9 8 7 6 5 4 3 2 1

For our families

contents

preface

Meet the girls and boys of *Restless Virgins*: Annie, Whitney, Jillian, and Isabel; Reed, Brady, and Josh. Classmates at Milton Academy, a prep school near Boston, Massachusetts, they give us a very personal, intimate look at their daily lives in their senior year of high school. This book is about fitting in, taking risks, hooking up, and breaking up. It's about best friends, boyfriends, girlfriends, and parents. It's about settling and survival, and always the search for love. Their stories are laugh-out-loud funny, uplifting, heartbreaking, over the top, and outrageous. While many scenes may seem possible only in fiction, everything that happens here is true.

High school is a monster story; where could it possibly begin? In *Restless Virgins*, it begins in early September 2004, when these seven students arrived on campus for their senior year, and it ends in June 2005, when they stood on the picturesque main quad, girls in white dresses and boys in navy blazers, ready to graduate. They began the year wondering if their personal histories were a divination of what was to come—or if, in their final year of high school, something might change. Yet the 2004–2005 school year was hardly typical at Milton. A sex scandal involving a girl and several boys and a daring on-campus locale splashed the school across the news. As the story unfolded, we were both surprised and intrigued, because we were curious young women who graduated from Milton in the late 1990s.

We weren't so far away from our own high school days. We played sports and musical instruments, studied hard, had lots of friends, even a boyfriend or two. But the scandal was entirely unfamiliar ground for us. Young lives were changed and a prestigious school was publicly embarrassed. The circumstances around the scandal may have been unusual but, as we soon learned, the behavior was hardly an exception. How were we to understand teenage life today? The cultural image of the typical high school student in America runs the gamut from *Prep*'s nerdy and jaded Lee Fiora to the sparkling beauties of the hit TV series *The OC*. But these fictional treatments took us only so far. We sought out students from Milton's class of 2005 to find answers.

For two years, Annie, Whitney, Jillian, Isabel, Reed, Brady, and Josh, along with more than twenty of their classmates, shared their lives with us. All had graduated from Milton when we first met, and some had already started their freshman year in college, from the Ivy League to small New England schools to larger universities. We talked with some for a few months and others for much longer. The students told us stories in great detail, lifting the blanket of silence that shielded their world from parents and teachers. An unimaginable divide emerged: These girls and boys had their own values, rules, and boundaries, a culture that most adults did not grasp.

Milton Academy educates the best and the brightest. Its quintessential Georgian brick buildings and rolling lawns blend with its sleek, contemporary additions, evoking the power and status that define New England tradition. But this book is not just a prep school story, nor is it about the scandal in particular. It's an American story about teenagers surviving high school, confusing lust with love and sex with power, and searching for self-worth. Their experiences are the stories of privileged adolescence, but we hope there is not a single reader who won't identify with some part of this book. In these girls and boys we found captivating, complex individuals, each struggling with who they were in high school, and who they wanted to become. *Restless Virgins* is their story.

a note on methods and sources

Restless Virgins is a work of nonfiction. The experiences and conversations portrayed here are based entirely on interviews with students from the class of 2005 at Milton Academy. We met with 28 out of the 181 students in that class over a period of two years, from the summer of 2005 through the spring of 2007. We conducted some interviews as a team and others separately, some with one person and some with groups of friends, some in person and others by telephone. We also interviewed a few parents and teachers, as well as Milton graduates from other years, but most of the material in this book comes from the girls and boys of the class of 2005. Altogether, we held 280 interviews, ranging from thirty minutes to three hours each.

To protect the privacy of our interviewees, as well as certain other students and individuals who appear in the book and were not interviewed, we changed their names and some of their identifying details and characteristics, including, for example, hair color, physical description, extracurricular activities and hometowns. Despite these changes, we retained the integrity of each person's experience and personality. No one who appears in these pages is a composite portrait. We also changed the names of Milton's dormitories and blurred their locations and descriptions. Any similarity between fictitious names and characteristics and those of real people, living or dead, or fictitious dorms and real dorms, at Milton or elsewhere, is purely coincidental.

School officials and public figures appear as they do in real life. All descriptions of Milton Academy's history, campus, and traditions are real, based on independent research, our own observations of Milton, and the experiences of the girls and boys.

Scenes are re-created from interviewees' recollections. Some scenes are rendered from the account of one individual, and in these cases, we write from the point of view of that person. Others are the product of multiple interviewees' accounts of the same event. Where accounts differed, we did our best to provide the fullest and most comprehensive accounts based on our interviews.

Dialogue passages are written as the students remembered them, and some are direct quotes from conversations students had with one another during our interviews. Dialogue is printed in italics here. Internal thoughts are expressed in the third person. Instant message conversations are either direct quotes from saved conversations the students gave us, or re-creations from the students. Journal and newspaper excerpts are direct quotes. We have retained the original spelling and grammar in instant messages, journals, and newspapers except if needed to clarify meaning. Citations from published sources, such as newspaper articles, are set off or italicized. Quotations from the trial proceedings in the case against the three Milton students are from the tape-recorded transcript obtained from the clerk's office of the District Court of East Norfolk, Quincy, Massachusetts.

september 2004–

june 2005

chapter one

everyone's watchin'

Everyone's watchin', to see what you will do
Everyone's lookin' at you, oh
—Lyrics from "Working for the Weekend," by Loverboy,
   the song chosen by the class of 2005 for Senior Walk In

ighties music blasted from a dorm room down
the hall. Annie could hear it from her own room, where she
sat up in bed and forced her eyes open, her wavy blond hair everywhere.
It was early morning on orientation day at Milton, and she could already hear the other girls in Pryce House clogging the dorm's narrow
hallways. They ran between bathrooms and bedrooms, screaming
about summer romances and hugging as though it had been forever. I
love your haircut! How was your trip? Did you go back to camp? Who
do you wanna hook up with this year? Annie stared at the bare walls of
her tiny single room, wondering how much she'd changed that summer and what would become of her that year.

Her first few days as a senior had been packed with the usual excitements and stresses: younger Pryce girls bombarded her with questions, orchestra and dorm commitments beckoned, and so did senior tasks, like checking in with the college office to continue calculating the ever-looming future. But Annie couldn't even begin to grasp the enormity of what she had to do that year: get good grades; perform with the full orchestra and chamber orchestra; take the SATs; pick a college; apply early to that college, which meant writing essays, filling out forms, and having an interview; wait to find out if she got into that college; prepare additional applications in case she was rejected or deferred; pass exams; love senior year; find a way to drink and party over spring break; perfect her senior solo for the spring concert, which would take up at least three hours of practice a day; relish senior spring; make new friends; change her image; not obsess over boys; find a steady hookup, make him a boyfriend, lose her virginity, fall in love, or at least *in like;* and generally live up to the standards set by her civic-minded parents. Over the first few weeks of school, there were times when Annie came back to her dorm room at night, closed her door, and cried.

But everything always looked better in the morning, so Annie bounced out of bed, stumbling over piles of black-and-white posters of the 1920s and glossy Absolut vodka ads that she hadn't had a chance to hang on the walls. She put on vintage Madonna and riffled through her clothes. In about an hour, Senior Walk In would begin, a coveted rite of passage at Milton that took place at the first morning assembly of the school year, which was held on the basketball courts in the Athletic and Convocation Center (ACC). Seniors charged onto the makeshift stage from behind a curtain, wearing outrageous costumes, pumping their fists, proclaiming the start of the school year in front of the upper school. Annie remembered the first Senior Walk In she saw. She was a freshman and sat on the bleachers with the rest of the underclassmen, watching the seniors in Pryce prance out like confident leaders who knew exactly what they were doing.

Now, after three years at Milton, Annie knew that appearances mattered. She wanted to assemble an outfit with the right blend of appropriateness (for the teachers), hotness (for the guys), and individuality (for herself). She was fleshy, a Rubens girl with a curvaceous body, breasts the size of baby melons since they'd first cropped up in fifth grade. She accepted her full figure. She had even come to terms with her acne, applying foundation over the pimples that marked puberty on her face. She'd always been reticent about her breasts, and still didn't understand how even they never garnered her attention from the guys at school.

She inherently accepted her social status: the aspiring socialite who had yet to expand her celebrity since middle school. Senior Walk In was her last chance to make another first impression at Milton. This was a moment of possibility. Some seniors' reputations already had been made, but change was not impossible. This was also a moment of vanity. Seniors considered who they had become (the jock, the academic, the prude) and what lasting impressions they wanted to leave with their friends and teachers. Because Senior Walk In was, after all, the genesis of their final teenage fate—the last year of high school.

Annie squeezed her thighs into a short black skirt and pulled a simple black shirt over her chest. She shuffled up to the mirror. The dimple in her chin was adorable and her cheeks were, as usual, a shade redder than she wanted. Annie liked her outfit. While some Walk In costumes materialized out of closets that very morning, Annie and the other senior girls in Pryce had started planning their outfits that summer, communicating over e-mail (*Get your bumblebee headbands! Get something crazy!*), and agreeing to be bumblebees because they'd each been willed a perky antennae headpiece with glittery yellow-and-black-striped balls from the girls who'd graduated the year before. Wills were a serious business among boarders. The night before graduation, seniors in each of Milton's eight single-sex dormitories passed down personal tokens to favorite underclassmen. Many boarders waited their entire Milton careers for this ritual, while underclassmen loved receiving coveted bequests that they then carried with them until it was their turn to pass them on.

Annie went to the closet to find the finishing touch to her costume, the bumblebee antennae she'd received the previous spring. They rested on a shelf above her hanging clothes, and were important because they were a status symbol that tied her to a specific dorm and a specific group of girls. On the morning of Senior Walk In, they quivered delicately each time she took a step, bobbing like a marionette, just enough to remind Annie that she, too, belonged.

Milton's 125-acre spread of manicured quads, rolling hills, and prep school charm woke up from desolation just as Annie was getting ready in Pryce. Students arrived by bus or carpool, or from houses and dorms a few minutes away. They headed toward the ACC for Senior Walk In, cutting across various quads and fields, often jaywalking on Centre Street, the main road that cuts the campus in half. With understated elegance, the academy sprawls out in its own cushy corner of Boston's intellectual history and affluent past. The picturesque landscape is a place where the relics of early America still endure, the old stone chapel, white picket fences, and redbrick buildings upholding the New England values of virtue and purity.

Established in 1798, Milton is one of the oldest prep schools in the United States. It's a breeding ground of privilege, where students from all over the country and the world are groomed to go on to some of the best colleges and universities. The girls' and boys' successes feed the school's public image—the elite prep school that has educated luminaries like the Kennedys and Roosevelts; and T. S. Eliot, Buckminster Fuller, and James Taylor. Milton promotes an open approach to education, where teachers lead students in pint-size, seminar-style classes held around large Harkness tables or among clusters of individual desks. Annie was just one of the many talented girls and boys to come through the school, chasing dreams and expectations.

As girls and boys arrived on the morning of Walk In, they dropped their backpacks and shoulder bags in random locations around campus, identifiable only by the make (Eastpak, the North Face, Hervé Chapelier) and the owners' embroidered initials. This was a very Milton tradition. The close-knit community nurtured an environment that made it possible to abandon personal belongings by a tree or in a hallway and trust that they would be there later, when it was time for class, the library, or the bus ride home. But the haphazard behavior also stood in the way of neatness and order. Unlike rival prep schools such as Noble and Greenough (Nobles) and Roxbury Latin, Milton rejected dress codes and seemed to have fewer rules for its students to follow.

Inside the ACC, students walked past sleek glass trophy cases and framed pictures of Milton sports teams. The building was a new and formidable shrine to athletics. Older team photos, dating back to the 1900s, were kept next door, in the Robert Saltonstall Gymnasium, called the Old Boys' Gym, as though Milton's lengthy athletic history had been rewritten when the ACC opened in 1998. Underneath its monstrous roof were three glossy basketball courts, an indoor track, an ice hockey rink that converted into tennis courts, a fully equipped fitness center and training room, individual team locker rooms, and coaches' offices. Yet the cavernous basketball field house, where Walk In took place, was surprisingly bland. There were no images of Milton's mascot, the mustang, or murals painted in the school colors, orange and blue. The only noticeable details were the banners from the fifteen other prep schools in Milton's athletic league, the Independent School League (ISL). Thayer Academy, jocks. Belmont Hill School, all boys. St. Paul's School, snobs. Nobles, archrival. The banners hung lifelessly from the high ceiling and seemed only inches long, like misplaced dollhouse decorations.

A white-netted curtain fell like a petticoat from the rafters between the first two basketball courts. On one side, freshmen, sophomores, juniors, and faculty members took their seats on bleachers, facing nearly two hundred fold-up seats, arranged in rows for the senior class. A wood podium stood center stage, another dollhouse trinket, with Milton's insignia painted on the front, an orange-and-blue shield with the message "Dare to Be True." As the school year went on, students would roll their eyes at the sight of this setup, an ominous signal that a required formal event or assembly was coming.

On the other side of the curtain, seniors loitered in a swarming mass, waiting eagerly or fretfully for Walk In to begin. They were on the lookout for what the summer months had done to their exes and crushes, and hugged friends they hadn't seen since the summer or the end of junior year, simultaneously checking each other out.

I love her costume.

She looks like a whore.

Is it almost time?

Ohmygod, did Reed just smile at me?

I think he said hi to me.

Is my shirt too low-cut?

Did that teacher just give me a look?

Can't this all be over?

The seniors were supposed to be having the time of their lives, because in just a few more minutes they would finally burst onstage— behold the happy, talented, united class of 2005. But this was no romantic movie. Any insider knew that this mob was in fact a complex teenage creature all of its own, governed by a distinct social and academic hierarchy, sustained by friendships and crushes, lust and desire, well versed in the art of dicking someone over. The social divisions among the seniors had been brewing since freshman year, when one's social status was based largely on looks, first impressions, interests, and personality (probably in that order). At Walk In, what you wore was intrinsically tied to who you were, and reminded everyone who was in, who was out, and who was not even worth considering.

Annie's blond hair was gorgeous—past her shoulders, filled with movement—and she stood with her dorm mates, dressed up in her short skirt and bumblebee antennae, hoping to God no one noticed the overwhelming size of her chest. Her bright purple heels added extra inches to her height, but she blended in more than she wanted to. On the outside she was all smiles, saying *ohmygosh hi!* to anyone she could. But everywhere she looked was another senior girl flaunting her perfectly proportioned body, or standing next to a boy, arm in arm, laughing.

There were the popular girls dressed up as scantily clad rock stars. They always looked as if they'd been born beautiful, with perfect hair and perfect smiles from the day they'd come screaming into this world. Wandering nearby was a boy dressed as Hugh Hefner. The football guys sported black spandex shorts, complete with a pair of socks shoved down their pants in just the right spot. Annie also spotted pirates, cowgirls, and farmers. Six girls were dressed like pumpkins and strawberries. They weren't sexy like the popular girls, but goofy, with fake white leather boots, pink or orange wigs, and matching A-line velvet dresses straight off the rack at iParty. Annie wasn't impressed by the idea of a store-bought costume, but she would have worn one if it meant she could have been a strawberry, a pumpkin, or anything else, just to be in their group.

A senior in Pryce cruised past Annie on a skateboard—or, more realistically, was tugged by another senior girl. These two were part of the Pryce Girls, a popular clique of seniors in the boarding community. They both had bumblebee headbands, though their matching head-to-toe tie-dyed outfits were far more noticeable, especially to Annie, who couldn't believe they'd tried to upstage their dorm's chosen costume theme. But the Pryce Girls were confident and daring. From time to time they ran around topless on campus at night, and once attended chapel services wearing nothing but their winter coats. Annie thought they always looked like they were having the time of their lives.

Annie regarded the two girls thoughtfully, somewhat resentfully, knowing there was once a time when she was set to become one of them. She and the Pryce Girls were now pretend friends, but Annie had been part of the clique when she first started at Milton. Most of the girls were just like her: white, upper-middle class, and obsessed with boys, magazines, appearances, and kissing. The similarities were comforting, but Annie had watched the gulf grow larger between the Pryce Girls and her after freshman year.

When I was drunk I did this, the girls would say.

Oh, I love doing this sort of alcohol.

Oh, I love tequila shots!

What's tequila? was all Annie could think to add.

She realized that there were social milestones and she'd already missed a big one. By junior year, most of these girls had been to parties, smoked weed, had boyfriends, and lost their virginity. Over time, Annie wanted more than a group of friends who looked and spoke and sounded just like she did. The friends she had senior year were quieter and interesting. They were white, black, and Asian, some from countries she'd never been to, and had life perspectives and experiences that were completely different from her own. Her best friend, Ida, held a prestigious leadership role at school. She was better than a Pryce Girl— a unifying force in the senior class and friendly with everyone, or at least that's how Annie saw it. Annie genuinely loved Ida, but she never quite got over the loss of a well-defined friendship circle. Even at a school where students were raised to believe in their unique talents, there was always the desire to be associated with a particular clique— to be tagged as a jock, a popular girl, or an artsy boy, even if it wasn't the identity you preferred. Having a group was better than having no group at all.

The ultimate achievement, of course, was being singled out from that group—the popular one, the pretty one, the most kissable one. Despite her efforts, Annie had spent all of high school perfecting the art of contentment. To her classmates, she was nice and sweet, and she could accept that fact—to a certain extent. Now, on the eve of her senior year, she couldn't face another year without a Milton boyfriend, or at least a boy in her life. Annie knew how reputations worked. They can be based on friends, sports, and accomplishments, but they're intrinsically tied to who you date, who you hook up with, and how far you go.

While growing up in Lenox, Massachusetts, Annie got attention from boys for all the wrong reasons. They pinched her butt and liked her body, but they also made fun of her for being ambitious and hardworking. Annie grew up taking honors classes and studying flute. Lenox is a creative environment, the year-round home to Tanglewood and the summer home to the Boston Symphony Orchestra; it was here, under the steady guidance of her stay-at-home mom and her doctor dad, that Annie excelled wildly. She couldn't wait to go to Milton. From what she understood, it was a place where it was cool to be smart and an individual; where she wouldn't have to balance her studious and ditzy sides depending on who she was with.

Sometimes Annie couldn't believe that she had yet to have a single Milton boyfriend. Despite her accomplishments as a musician, leader, and dorm confidante, nothing distracted from this personal social failure. More than anything—more than standout SAT scores, a top-tier college, or straight As—Annie wanted to be pursued, adored, and desired. It didn't make sense. She was pretty, wasn't she? Maybe not drop-dead gorgeous, and certainly not as thin as the more popular Milton girls, but she was definitely pretty. A talented flutist. A devoted friend. Everything about her screamed, I'm a nice girl, I have a cheery personality, and I work hard.

Annie wasn't completely inexperienced, either. She'd had boyfriends before, so she'd been validated as a girl who could have a boyfriend, and understood what it meant to kiss a boy, hold his hand, and do a little more. For two long years, she'd been hooking up with Scott, a public school guy from her hometown. She'd first noticed him when they were in middle school; he was a year older, had great hair, and played on two middle school boys' varsity teams. He was also dating the prettiest girl in Annie's class. She didn't think she had a chance. But rumors circulated that he actually liked her back, and during her years at

Milton—over summer breaks and school vacations—Scott and Annie hooked up. For kids at Milton, a hookup meant many things: a kiss, groping, no shirt, no pants, underwear on or off, everything but sex. For Scott and Annie, hooking up usually involved oral sex (on him, not her).

Even though Scott didn't call enough, like her enough, or treat her well enough, his limited affections made Annie feel wanted. But what she longed for most was attention from a desirable boy at Milton. As a senior, she realized she had one final chance to find social success. On this morning, behind the curtain, she twirled the starfish necklace her mother gave her when she graduated from middle school and waited for something to happen to her. She felt at once empowered and invisible. She loved the girl she was—honest, moral, hardworking—but guys weren't attracted to these qualities. Nothing seemed to be changing.

Whitney wrapped her long, shapely arms around her best friend's waist, leared in toward her cheek, and squealed. It was their favorite picture-taking pose. Either that or the one where they palmed each other's breasts, opened their mouths in false alarm, and hung there, two beauties pressed into one, all skin and limbs, swathed in silver Elsa Peretti, the accoutrement that came with being popular, pretty, and someone's girlfriend. While waiting behind the curtain in the ACC, Whitney admired her vintage-style red halter dress, the black tulle spilling out from underneath. She was supposed to look like a rock star, and she did wear chunky knee-high boots and leather gloves, both in black. But she was pleased she also had the sexiest costume of all her friends. The fitted bodice and full skirt gave her a touch of Hollywood; add blond hair extensions and a Southern twang, and she would have been channeling her idol, Britney Spears, premotherhood. The dress wasn't actually Whitney's, which was comforting information since she would have died if anyone found out it was from Hot Topic, a cheap knockoff store. Later, when she wore the same dress to a wedding, she gushed in agreement when a fellow guest complimented her on it, calling it a fabulous red Armani.

Anyone could see that Whitney was an unusual combination of beauty and grace, slim and delicate after a decade devoted to figure skating. She was tall, less like a skater and more like a model, with almond-shaped eyes, a pointed chin, and bright white teeth. Her natural beauty didn't require the time she devoted to her appearance every day. That morning, her long brown hair was stick straight after a session with the flatiron. Her eyebrows were pencil-thin. Whitney liked standing out, and planned on commanding the spotlight that morning at Senior Walk In. At this very event each year before, she'd paid attention to the popular senior girls, mesmerized by their soaring confidence and sparkling eyes. Now, as one of the popular senior girls herself, she knew it was her duty to look hot. Not necessarily slutty, but close enough so that all the boys' eyes started popping. In just a few more minutes it would be Whitney's turn to parade onstage and claim her long-awaited throne. She was, at last, a senior. A big shot. Maybe the coolest girl in school.

In the film *Mean Girls,* the popular girls are called the Plastics. In the film *Heathers,* they are the Heathers. At Milton Academy, they are the Day Student Girls, known to students, parents, teachers, and even administrators as the DSGs. Being a day student was not a prerequisite for membership in this clique, but the majority of members were, in fact, day students. Some were athletic stars (Whitney skated at the national level), while other girls glided into such status on their personalities, beauty, or money, and often all three. According to both stereotype and fact, DSGs partied, drank, and hooked up, and were the most likely girls to befriend and date the most popular guys. Some of Whitney's friends had steady boyfriends and others had random hookups. Whitney had both, often at the same time.

Though many DSGs were bright, they were not known for their intelligence. Some students believed they played up their indifference to intellectual curiosity, but who needed academics when the DSGs were the school's chief arbiters of taste and fashion, defining for everyone else what was in, like Coach or ribbon belts, and what was out, like L.L. Bean backpacks and American Eagle. At a school where there was no formal dress code, the DSGs defined a whole new level of style. They also functioned as pretty trimmings for the popular boys, who used the attention they received from the DSGs as a way of confirming their own status on the social ladder.

Chatting with her girlfriends, Whitney stood with exemplary posture, exuding a sense of privilege and confidence that grew out of her social position. But she was far from the prototypical popular girl when she'd first stepped on campus freshman year. Her face was round with baby fat, she had never heard of designer jeans, and she admits she was a total prude. She was Mommy's little girl, and despite her parents' rocky marriage, she grew up in relative normalcy, which really meant rules, expectations, and affection. But looks are deceiving, especially among Milton's student body, where a nerd can be beautiful, a jock can earn a degree cum laude, and a popular girl with everything—someone just like Whitney—can come close to throwing it all away.

From the moment she slipped on a tiny pair of white figure skates at age six, she showed natural talent. She'd always loved her sport, but competing in one competition a month in the New England region, as well as a handful of summer competitions up and down the East Coast, took relentless commitment. Her coach was tough. Three mornings a week, she woke up at four fifteen A.M. to drive from her home in Dedham, Massachusetts, to her skating club. She'd train for an hour, shower, get dressed, and then jump back in the car for the hour-long drive to school. After classes each day, she went back to the club for afternoon practice, which lasted a few hours more, and then went home to scarf down dinner, fudge some homework, and fall into bed. The hard work paid off. She'd qualified for the national championships the last three years, and was ready for the senior division coming up in January.

But all those practices meant missing parties and avoiding the mind-set her friends adopted on the weekends: *I need to get fucked up and I need to get ass.* Her mother probably thanked God for that, but by senior year, rebellion was growing. Whitney was now one of those girls who had a boyfriend, girlfriends, and lust crushes. Beneath her good-girl facade, resentment festered. A lifetime spent sacrificing nearly every morning, evening, and weekend for figure skating was taking its toll.

While waiting for Walk In to begin, Whitney shifted her weight from one hip to the other. She wondered where Tripp would be sitting in the audience. She thought he was hot—amazing, in-your-face, I-want-to-fuck-you hot. He was tall, muscular, and cut, just like an athlete should be, with smooth, baby-soft skin. His hair was brown and wavy, and his speech had just a touch of the American South. He didn't always shave, but the scruffiness added to his sex appeal, and everywhere he walked he left a trail of Old Spice deodorant.

This wasn't the first time Whitney had desired someone other than Nick, her famously aloof, on-again-off-again boyfriend. They'd been together for years, but she justified cheating on him because the guys she picked were hot and athletic like she was—not like Nick. Whitney knew her friends thought he was overweight, unattractive, and a druggie, and she agreed. Nick didn't care about his grades or listen to the Dave Matthews Band like most of her friends. He didn't even play sports. He and Whitney were an unlikely match, polar opposites in looks, interests, and values. There was little crossover between the tightly knit cliques at Milton. For her to admit she liked a guy outside her social group (even if he went to a different school, which Nick did) was to make a potential faux pas that girls like her were simply not supposed to make. But Nick was a bad boy. He didn't follow rules or respect authority, and introduced Whitney to a life on the edge. His recklessness became her drug, and her mother's disapproval was the ultimate high.

That morning she and Nick were off. In a few weeks they'd be back on. But Whitney wasn't thinking about him as she prepared for Walk In. She wasn't thinking about the boy she'd been hooking up with from

New Hampshire, either, who adored her unconditionally. He was a real sweetheart, overflowing with nice-guy potential, but Whitney had reservations. Distance and his virginity were both problems, and he really would have been so much more attractive had her mother only disapproved. Cheating aside, her mom couldn't have grasped the extent of Whitney's arsenal of wild-child behavior. But there was no preparing for what was to come. There on the basketball court, standing in her red halter dress, Whitney imagined Tripp's face the moment he saw her, and was confident she could have him whenever she wanted.

As Jillian wandered slowly into the ACC, she worked her light brown hair up into a messy bun, placed a silver plastic tiara on top, and looked the rest of the seniors up and down. Her big hazel eyes paused on a few slender girls who wore fishnet stockings and studded belts.

What's your theme? she asked.

Oh, we're rock stars.

They looked more like sluts to Jillian. Her own costume consisted of the tiara. Period, end of story. Jillian knew she should have been excited to dress up for Walk In, but she couldn't have cared less. She was sick of school. There were two kinds of people at Milton, those who loved it and those who hated it. Being one of the latter, Jillian couldn't wait to graduate and leave behind the annoying classmates she'd put up with over the years. All that stood between her and the rest of her life were nine months, five classes, a week of exams, two breaks, a prom, and one lucky college acceptance letter. She expected the stresses of classes, homework, and college applications, but there were so many other reasons to dread the coming year: her mother, a beauty who obsessed over Jillian's weight and was known to drink coffee for lunch; her father, her hero, who insisted that his naturally unathletic daughter play sports; her friends, whom she found to be catty and tiring; and her boyfriend, who didn't exist. Underneath her chintzy tiara, Jillian was a complete wreck, but she revealed that side of herself only in the journal she kept on the computer.

the beginning of school always gets me so high strung. first impressions are a bitch, even with people you already know, because everything is based on such superficial stuff. i also freak out because i always get really anxious and think that if i don't talk to all these people that i'm going to be abandoned by all my friends. and i want to make new friends and like, branch out. but it's hard. and i don't know how. and i'm so shy i want to crawl in a toilet and flush myself.

Under normal circumstances, Jillian loved dressing up. In preschool, she cried and hit her teachers when they made her take off a bride costume she'd coveted from the dress-up trunk. Later in childhood her romance with make-believe blossomed on Halloween, when she wore a tutu with blue sequins, went trick-or-treating with a boy, ran into a shrub, got upset, and then discovered her love of men when he turned to her and said *It's okay, you still look beautiful.* Jillian grew up near Harvard Square in Cambridge, Massachusetts, in a house with rooms that were off-limits to kids. Her mother's walk-in closet was the ultimate shrine, a gaping temple of style where remnants of the past few decades hung from hangers and leather pumps in every color lined one of the walls. The bathroom was bigger than Jillian's bedroom, and she'd sit in her mother's sink (her dad had his own), stare at herself in the mirror, and watch the movie star lights cast shadows across the makeup she spread on her face.

Now seventeen, Jillian was not glamorous and hated looking in the mirror. She was "average," meaning 5 feet 5, wore a size 8 sweater and a size 10 trouser, and had big hazel eyes and a quirky nose that had never been straight. She styled her stringy hair like artwork, swept into a messy ponytail, braided, or secured in some inventive way with various hair clips and elastic bands. Though she had exaggerated features that were put together in an unusual way, Jillian had smooth olive skin and a rare self-awareness that most teenage girls wouldn't know for years. She wore bohemian, funky clothes, and wanted everyone to think she didn't care what they thought, including her parents.

Jillian considered her mom and dad to be stereotypical baby boomers. They wanted a perfect family and a perfect child, and expected intellectual success. Both came from tough backgrounds. There was alcoholism, extreme wealth, and extreme poverty, and all the baggage that came along with each. And they probably had no idea that Jillian considered her own upbringing, which was easy in comparison, to be just as difficult. She was an only child, so being out in public with her parents was less stressful than being with them at home, where they could ambush her at any moment about classes, sports, or her social life. By senior year, Jillian almost expected to find articles about sex, drugs, or alcohol cut out and laid delicately on her bed: *This is really interesting,* the note might say. The message was clear: You better not be doing this.

Jillian's mother affected her the most. Her mom had once been extremely thin and extremely gorgeous, the type of girl everyone dreamed about and Jillian wanted to become. Her mom was also a strong woman with opinions, and strived to create in Jillian a miniversion of herself—a feminist, a confidante, a beauty, a talent. But she was imperious and oversentimentalized every aspect of Jillian's coming-of-age experience, crying at Bloomingdale's when they bought her first bra, and begging to take Jillian out to dinner to celebrate the arrival of her period. Jillian tried to keep secrets. She had her first kiss and tried to shave by herself, but somehow her mom always knew.

As a child, Jillian imagined herself as a beautiful girl with a hot boyfriend, a car, amazing friends, huge breasts, and a thin body. Then puberty happened. With her breasts and hips came weight. One day she decided she would try to stop eating. At first she ate an apple during the day and dinner with her parents at night. By eighth grade she ate hardly anything, and when she did, she exercised obsessively. If she was home alone, she'd only drink tea for breakfast. Her mom was heartbroken that Jillian was growing too thin. She moved the scale out of Jillian's bathroom and into the basement. Every morning before school, she laid out breakfast spreads like scrambled eggs and peanut butter English muffins, hoping Jillian would eat something, trying to feed her like a baby. She bought parenting books and took her daughter to nutritionists and psychologists. Jillian had friends who dieted throughout high school, but for them it was a three-week task; for Jillian it was a way of life.

In elementary and middle school, Jillian had boyfriends, best friends, alcohol parties, and enemies—all the signs of a highly successful social life. When she'd first learned about the DSGs at Milton, she decided she would become one of them. She thought she had it figured out: The idea was to actively pursue the title while simultaneously denying the fact that you were pursuing the title. After all, being popular was supposed to be effortless, something you were born with, like old money and a fast metabolism.

When Jillian arrived at Milton freshman year, she walked onto campus knowing she was the shit. She wore a little dress, had a lithe body, and harbored high hopes: She was going to be popular. Jillian became a DSG before Whitney did, but Jillian and her best friend had a major falling-out during their freshman year. The tension lasted for months, and eventually her best friend, who was now her ex–best friend, turned the DSGs against her. At least that was how Jillian saw it. The first day of sophomore year she sat in the car with her mom, moaning *Please don't make me go in there, I don't want to go in there.* She spent the next two years losing her old friends, making new ones, gaining fifteen pounds, and accepting the fact that she was never going to be the most popular girl in school.

Over time, Jillian distanced herself from the mainstream and cultivated an independent identity. She also kissed girls and became a talented writer and editor for the *Milton Paper,* one of the school's many student newspapers. Eventually, four years after her anorexia began, she inhaled tomato soup as though she was tasting it for the first time. She ate grilled-cheese sandwiches and vegetable pad thai and puffed up like a balloon. Her mom was heartbroken all over again. She sat with Jillian at breakfast to make sure she didn't eat too much, and sent her to an exercise specialist. When senior year began, Jillian was running an hour a day and lifting at the gym.

> *i also can't—simply CAN'T—lose weight and it's driving me insane. i think i've lost two pounds since july. depressed and disgusting. and i'm not going to get into college. and this summer has proved romantically fruitless and barren. . . . i'll be a fat, ill-educated writer, who doesn't write, and who nobody loves so she just sits alone with her poodle and renders opinions about things. which is what i'm doing right now.*

Writing was Jillian's escape. She did it everywhere: in journals, which she'd been keeping since kindergarten, on notebooks in coffee shops, at school in the small *Paper* office where her parents would never find her. The *Paper* had always been interested in controversy. Jillian couldn't possibly have known what her senior year had in store, but there were many insular Milton idiosyncrasies to laud or criticize. The head of school, Dr. Robin Robertson (affectionately—mockingly—called Doc Robs by students), was a prime target. Soon after she took her post as Milton's eleventh head of school in 1999, changes seemed to sweep across campus. Outfitted in what seemed to be her daily school uniform, a solid-colored suit jacket, she spearheaded the construction of the student center and the new dormitories, renovated academic buildings, and increased the size of the boarding community, but these additions came with a cost. Favorite student traditions and locales disappeared. Many current and former students and faculty believed that the Milton of past decades, even as recently as the mid- to late 1990s, was slowly settling into its grave.

Jillian was entirely committed to the *Paper*'s cause, in part because she cared about its reputation but mostly because she considered writing to be her one true gift in life. After Jillian's rocky fall from social starlet freshman year, she forged a new identity with writing and academics. She wasn't necessarily a straight-A student (French was the bane of her existence), but she was an intellectual in every sense of the word, so she sought out similar girls, developing a whole new clique with Caroline, Isabel, Phoebe, and a few others. They were all artsy and intelligent. They took honors classes and were expected to go on to Ivy League schools. Jillian loved these girls, but by senior year she grew tired of always belonging to a group. Then, for reasons that were a bit vague even to her, she learned that some kids in her class referred to them as the Hysterics.

Jillian admitted that she and her friends were emotional. They weren't embarrassed to show their feelings in public or talk openly about being unhappy. But the Hysterics seemed a bit extreme. They didn't channel the Goth look, with dark makeup, facial piercings, and long black capes. No, these girls were fairly preppy, except for Jillian, who wore layered skirts, leggings, and funky shirts. And the girls were hardly hysterical. In fact, their costumes that morning were the perfect antidote: faded orange life jackets they'd pulled out from the basement of one of their summer homes, complete with frayed white straps and oversize arm holes. The puffy vests said it all: We may be your overly emotional artists, your academic success stories, but we can be crazy and ridiculous; we know how to have fun.

Jillian was the only one not wearing a life jacket. She didn't mind. She didn't want to be so publicly associated with the Hysterics, and besides, Walk In was a colossal waste of time. While seniors gathered together for photographs Jillian dipped into the women's bathroom, only to find her ex–best friend from freshman year primping with some of the DSGs. Jillian was trapped. Though the two girls stood only a few feet apart, they were separated by years of drama and petty girlhood jealousies. Ever since their fallout, the girls had obeyed an unspoken rule that they were not to talk to each other. Jillian knew the encounter was overwhelmingly symbolic, something a seventh-grade English student would've been able to deduce. Suddenly she understood: Wow. If this were two years ago, she'd be dressing up with them.

Jillian decided to play nice. Opening the bathroom door to leave, she turned to the girls and chimed in her sweetest voice, *You guys look great!* It was a saccharine lie, but she said it anyway because this was the start of a new school year. By the time both girls reached college, Jillian would remember the interaction as if it was yesterday.

Isabel stood near Jillian with a life jacket strapped around her chest and a dab of zinc oxide on her nose, feeling as goofy as she looked. In her striped leggings and retro sneakers, she entertained a string of split-second assumptions and biting remarks. There were the popular girls dressed up as rock stars (*Slutty rock stars*, she thought) and over there, another group looking like freshmen with pigtails and lollipops (*typical*). Isabel's comments were mildly amusing, but they were probably made out of insecurity more than anything else. As much as she made fun of the other girls' exposed bodies, she had to admit they were the ones with pretty faces, enviable bodies, and sexual experience. Of course they dressed up that way for Walk In. Wouldn't she, if given the same genes? Instead, Isabel had cropped red hair and skin so pale she almost blended into white walls. She loathed the freckles that peppered her nose, barely passed five feet, and had a soft body that came from a disinterest in exercise. But she was adorable. Her features were delicate, just like a doll's—one of those perfectly upturned noses, dewy eyes, and a look that most girls admired and most boys didn't appreciate.

At Milton, Isabel was, in some ways, an unnoticeable girl. She wasn't a talented musician, like Annie; a superstar athlete, like Whitney; or an aspiring writer, like Jillian. Isabel was a well-rounded student. She did her homework, participated in class, and joined organizations because she knew she was supposed to: Milton students were, by definition, active and engaged. At the academy, however, joining was not enough. Students were expected to excel and lead in at least one, if not multiple areas. And so Isabel trailed behind. She was a good student, but not at the top; a staff photographer for the yearbook, not editor in chief; a volunteer tutor at a Dorchester high school, not head of community service; a member of the public issues board on campus, not the head; and a frequent PE class attendee, not an athlete on any team.

Friends like Jillian, Caroline, and Phoebe knew another side of Isabel. She was sharp and witty. She was a culture critic and film connoisseur, and loved classics like Alfred Hitchcock's *Rebecca* as well as what she called *junky* movies like *Face/Off* and *Trainspotting*. Few people at Milton saw these hidden qualities or attached value to them, and senior year, Isabel's academic ambitions usually appeared as shapeless clouds, ill defined and uninspired. She would continue to pursue her B-plus average. She would carry on with her photography, tutoring, and public issues board involvement because she thought they would look good on her college applications. Only one objective truly stuck out: She wanted to get some ass. But she hadn't excelled at Milton when it came to guys, either.

In middle school at Milton, Isabel had weathered nicknames like carrot top and hung out with the fast crowd. She was friendly with boys like Church, who grew up to become one of the biggest senior jocks, along with Brady, Reed, and the other hockey players. In ninth grade, though, she felt bombarded by the new crop of freshmen. Girls like Whitney were the competition because they radiated confidence and seemed to monopolize the attention of the popular boys. Girls like Jillian were intimidating because they seemed to have everything figured out. Friends like Church were destined to fall for these hotter, more sexual girls. Isabel worried. What if these new girls stole her guy friends? What if Church and his buddies ignored her? Over the next three years, that's exactly what happened.

It's not so surprising, then, that Jillian and Isabel found each other. But it was the guys, not the girls, whom Isabel missed.

This is totally our time, her friends heard her say.

Girls are supposed to be in their prime at eighteen!

Regardless of what she said, the reality was that Isabel remained in the shadows. Guys didn't pay attention to her, and if they did, they weren't the right guys. Few students formally dated at Milton; if a girl and a guy were in a relationship, it probably started with random hook-ups that eventually grew less and less random. Isabel was okay with that assumption, and would have settled for a couple of random hook-ups. Yet even those were difficult to initiate because she didn't hang out with the popular kids, whom she associated with hooking up. How was she supposed to finally give head and lose her virginity if she never even went to parties? She spent nearly every weekend with her girl-friends or at home in Lexington, Massachusetts, a quaint, historic town with beautiful homes. Hanging out in the dorms or going to parties in towns like Dedham or Milton was difficult because of the long drive from home. Of course she wasn't often invited, either.

At times she wondered if her life would have been better had she been a boarder. Hooking up seemed so much easier when girls and guys lived in the same place and could sneak into each other's rooms. At least that's what Isabel gathered from her twin sister who boarded at Phillips Exeter Academy, a prep school in New Hampshire. Isabel's sister was perfect. She had a boyfriend who adored her, got amazing grades, and possessed exceptional talent in math. She was a certifiable genius and intimidated nearly everyone, including Isabel.

On the morning of Senior Walk In, Isabel glanced around and realized there wasn't a single senior guy she knew she might like—or one she didn't know whom she wanted to get to know. The hard reality was that Isabel was a prude by default. She didn't want to be one any more than Jillian wanted to be unpopular and Annie wanted to be ignored. But virginity was a sort of cruel fate attached to certain girls at random in high school. Isabel didn't know how she would ever get to have sex.

She fastened and unfastened a hook on her life jacket while waiting for Walk In to begin. She may not have felt desirable, but her freckles were more charming than she realized, and her porcelain face was probably one of the few without makeup, and that was a good thing. Isabel must have noticed Brady, Reed, Church, and the rest of the popular boys. She'd taken to hating them, because rejecting dumb jocks was easier than the alternative—letting herself like them, knowing all along she could never gain their attention. Self-protection was the key to surviving. Though she told herself she was better than the jocks and DSGs, Isabel, soft, sarcastic Isabel, wondered why she couldn't be slutty, too.

The gym suddenly grew quiet. Seniors gathered together behind the curtain, waiting for their debut, when they would storm the stage with pounding hearts and anxious eyes, ready to proclaim their collective leadership and, in a single gasping breath, begin their final year of high school. Annie stood with the Pryce Girls and the rest of her dorm mates at the very front of the mob, just feet from the curtain.

Annie, you should walk out first, the girls said, their bumblebee antennae trembling as they talked.

No! she pleaded.

There wasn't actually a line, but Annie did not want to be the first person from Pryce, never mind the senior class, to parade on stage. Ida marched beside her wearing a pink wig and a wide smile, and proclaimed that they would walk out together. Annie was saved.

A voice blasted through the microphone.

Please welcome the class of 2005!

The speakers sounded. Music filled the gym.

> *Everyone's watchin', to see what you will do*
> *Everyone's lookin' at you, oh*

The entire school waited to witness the senior class burst forward, a balance of school spirit, class unity, intelligence, and beauty colliding with who you admitted you were and who you wished you could be. Despite their differences, the seniors were all lusting after more perfect versions of themselves. Annie's cheeks flushed with excitement. In a moment she'd be onstage, a senior leader just like the ones she remembered watching when she'd first arrived at Milton. She couldn't believe underclassmen would now look up to her. She couldn't believe there were no longer older boys to secretly adore. Annie hoped she was on the cusp of another life, and it all began at this very moment, on the far side of the curtain.

the man

reed lounged in his dorm room's brown leather chair, wearing his velvet smoking jacket, clenching a cigar between his teeth. He'd just settled into Hanley House for senior year, and the jacket was the perfect projection of the life he wanted for himself, one with women (well, girls), style, and wealth, all with rather little effort. The jacket was a relic Reed believed came from a one-of-a-kind shop in France, and he loved everything about it. The deep burgundy color. The crisp collar. The material. The equestrian horse embroidered on the pocket. Everything. He glanced at himself in the mirror, looked into his deep-set eyes, and admired the line of his jaw, clenching his teeth so that the muscles protruded on either side. Yes, he was good looking. Not in the stereotypically prep school way, as though he'd just returned from a weekend sailing, with sun-kissed hair, freckles, and a tan, but with buzzed jet black hair and pale porcelain skin. He had a dark mystery about him, and that wasn't just his own opinion.

Girls had deemed Reed the new "it boy" when he first arrived at Milton. Part of this identity was his overall appearance. He wasn't as tall as he wanted to be, but he held his own against girls in heels. And after years as a pudgy dumpling, he had a chiseled body that he worked hard to maintain. He'd learned how to evoke the New England WASP image with pink and yellow Polos, cable-knit sweaters, and anything else that looked like it had walked off the ferry from Martha's Vineyard. He instituted his own personal dress-up days, wearing oxfords, sporting multiple collars, and paying attention to how cocked each one was. Reed was eternally grateful when a teacher taught him how to hang his just-washed shirts with clothespins clipped to the collars so that they dried stiff as cardboard.

But part of his "it boy" identity was his association with Milton's boys' varsity hockey team. All he had to do was stand there, hips cocked, one leg forward, left arm bent with his hand above the thigh— pure high school sex appeal. Reed's social identity came from an assumed coolness bestowed upon such athletic stars. Being a member of the hockey team catapulted him to the top of Milton's social pecking order, where he and many of his teammates benefited from the spoils of popularity regardless of looks, intelligence, or financial status. They were guaranteed entrance into the popular crowd, just as certain girls—the attractive, extroverted, and wealthy kind—constituted the female equivalent: potential girlfriends, random hookups, or, more likely, what everyone called "friends with benefits."

Milton hockey players didn't achieve their social status because they were athletes. Over the past few years, the guys hadn't won many games, and they knew that their record was laughable. Yet the team still competed in the Keller division of the ISL, what most recruiters deemed the country's top prep school hockey league. In the approximately thirty games Reed and the guys played each season, they received ample exposure to recruiters and coaches. It was rare for ISL athletes to go on to professional sports teams or take bids for the Olympics, but the Keller division was arguably the most formidable prep school league in the country; players were often the top picks at division I and III colleges and universities.

Reed believed he was the total package. He was handsome and

smart. He hooked up. He had access to parties and alcohol, and was the object of crushes. He had cool friends who drove cool cars and had cool parents who let them throw parties. Yet the fact that his athletic prowess alone could generate attention from girls was a stunning revelation to him.

Back home in Farmington Hills, Michigan, Reed was often relegated to what he called the "friend zone." Of course he was admired: Most knew he was one of the area's star hockey players. Of course he had friends: not just a few friends, but the right friends in the right social groups who invited him to the right parties. Yet he rarely drank and rarely had girlfriends, thanks, in part, to his mother, Carol. She believed that there was a time for girls (after high school), and that Reed should focus on his activities and homework if he wanted to go to a great college. Reed agreed: *Okay, Mom, you're right, that's what I'm doing.* So his life was about hockey, school, and tormenting his siblings.

While growing up in a house of rambunctious boys, with a mother who held her own with her sons and a father who was often distant, Reed started calculating his transition into extravagance. As a boy he'd walk up to his parents, eyebrows furrowed, and ask, *Why can't I have a Bentley as a first car?* Reed sensed there was a world beyond his family's middle-class lifestyle. *I want to play hockey and go away to a boarding school and then go to an Ivy League school,* he'd say. His parents humored him, nodding their heads in encouragement, rolling their eyes at this precocious little man and his grand plans. Private school wasn't on their agenda.

Carol had graduated from an Ivy League school with the distinct impression that private school kids were different from public school kids, and not in a favorable way. Reed's father, a first-generation immigrant, just wanted him to be the first in his family to graduate from any high school, never mind a private school. But Reed insisted, and when he was accepted to Milton with a financial-aid package (tuition costs $32,725 a year for boarders as of Reed's senior year), his parents understood that something exceptional had just happened.

On that early September day when they helped him move to Milton,

Reed looked out the window of his mom's old SUV, staring at the majestic buildings and campus rising up around him. As they made their way down Centre Street, Reed saw a school that belonged in a movie. On one side of the street was Ware Hall, a tall beauty with elegant lines, and on the other side was Warren Hall, Wigglesworth Hall (Wigg), and Straus Library, looking equally proud. The buildings, sidewalks, and scenery were flawless, evocative of a time and place that didn't seem to belong to the real world. This was a fairy tale unfolding.

Reed was overwhelmed by what Milton offered. It consisted of an upper school, middle school, and lower school, spanning kindergarten through twelfth grade. There were twelve sports fields, seventeen tennis courts, and seven squash courts. Nearly fifty student-run organizations, a dozen student publications, a handful of singing groups, and ten major theater productions each year. There was a Jim Dine sculpture, a theater funded by Stephen King, an observatory, and a bookstore. Even Doc Robs had her own large house, set between two lush playing fields. Reed was enthralled by the legacy of famous speakers: President Bill Clinton, Senator Edward Kennedy, Maya Angelou, and David McCullough. And he knew that with an endowment approaching $145 million in 2005, Milton gave millions of dollars in financial aid each year, and could, of course, afford much more.

Prep schools have long been criticized for their exclusivity. They educate only the nation's elite. They are too expensive and white. They are bona fide country clubs. Reed embraced the stereotypes, but underneath Milton's surface a diverse community thrived. He lent validity to the assumption that boarders received more financial aid than day students, who often lived locally in Boston and in upper-middle-class communities like Milton, Wellesley, Weston, and Newton, some from old Boston families with old Boston money. Boarders came from faraway places like Jamaica, Hong Kong, England, and California. Students of color comprised roughly one-third of the student body during Reed's senior year, and day and boarding students were split nearly in half.

The first day of Reed's Milton career, over three hundred boarders flooded the campus in packed cars, toting parents, siblings, and personal belongings. Redbrick dormitories flanked the main quad, and when Reed stepped out of the car he saw the words HANLEY HOUSE painted in neat black letters above the entrance to his dorm. The outside was handsome with white trim, four stories, and dozens of square windows punctuating the flat brick face. A row of neat shrubs stood in front, and older Hanley guys waited for him at the entrance, the obligatory greeting committee. In the main lobby Reed saw a large chalkboard, his mailbox, and a plaque of boys' names that honored previous student dorm leaders. One of the Hanley guys showed him around. Reed expected to find more plaques and historical paintings, and there they were, hanging in the study room above the cushy couches and dark wooden desks that sat on sophisticated rugs. He could hardly believe he was there, a freshman at one of the most exclusive prep schools in the country. Milton wasn't just a high school; it was a new world—paradise.

As Reed lugged his suitcases upstairs, he watched boys arrive with fathers who seemed to know one another from business or college or both; with mothers who dressed alike in sleeveless sweaters and silk scarves, who spoke in hushed tones, as if they were sisters. Some of these parents glided from cars to dormitories to a hug and a kiss good-bye, as though they'd done it a million times, so casual about everything, yet so refined at the same time. It wasn't hard to sense the disparities between these and other families. Range Rovers and luxury SUVs lined up next to Hondas and Buicks. Golf buddies from Greenwich chatting about the stock market next to someone with a broad New Yorker's accent calling out, *It's just like Disneyland!* New money, old money, experience, and inbred opportunity mingled with looks of overwhelming wonder and dreams of upward mobility.

Reed wanted to be both athletic and academic at Milton. In public school he was known as the typical hockey player who, by definition, was not smart. Now he wanted to stand out from the masses, the nice guy in the popular kid's clothes, the student in the hockey player's uniform. He would take honors classes, win over his teachers, and receive awards. He expected success and wouldn't be surprised when he got it—at least that's what he wanted people to believe. The truth was that he worked hard to achieve his nonchalance. Beneath his favorite salmon-colored cashmere sweater from Polo Ralph Lauren, buried in his short black hair, the real Reed was just another teenage boy, his mother's panicky little kid.

During his first few months of school, he called home constantly.

How do I iron a shirt?

What setting do I wash my clothes on?

Where do I get a taxicab?

What do you think about . . . was his constant refrain. It would take time for him to conquer boarding school life, but there was one thing he saw quickly: Wealth was everywhere.

Everybody has money, he told his mom.

Everybody wears this.

Everybody has that.

This girl's a billionaire.

Her father started this.

Reed quickly learned that his future success depended partly on who he knew. He often sized up his friends based on their parents and second homes, and how closely his buddies' summer social lives mimicked HBO's *Entourage.* He also modeled himself after his idol, James Bond. Reed wanted to save the world, steal women's hearts, be fabulously rich, wear dapper suits, and flaunt washboard abs poolside on enormous private estates, which he owned. He knew Milton was his halfway ticket. The rest was up to him.

The air was chilly and damp when Reed moved back into Hanley for his senior year. He set up his single dorm room carefully. The institutional wood furniture matched the interiors of every other room in Hanley—a desk, bed, chair, and dresser. He called his leather chair his throne. He hung predictable posters of the Red Sox and the movie *Scarface,* and carefully folded his clothes into drawers. He made his bed with the gray blanket and floral pillowcases he'd taken from home, purposely omitting a top sheet, because he used only the finest kind he found in fancy hotels. Though smaller than his bedroom at home, Reed's dorm room legitimized his transformation into a Milton Academy student each year, and linked him to an esteemed tradition of boys who lived in that very room, slept in that very bed.

Throughout the day, Reed caught up with underclassmen and welcomed the new boys, who were just as nervous and excited as he'd been his first year. But all he really cared about was reconnecting with Cushman, his good friend and dorm mate. Cush, as everyone called him, had a model's face. He wasn't tall, but he had muscles and definition, sharp facial features that softened when he smiled, and pink lips. He came from monied Los Angeles, wore vintage T-shirts and designer jeans, and rarely left his dorm without his pin-striped blazer that had a patch on the shoulder. Most of all, Cush coexisted in all of Reed's worlds; he played hockey, strived to be a connoisseur of culture, cared about fashion, and had a girlfriend. When Reed and Cush saw each other, they hugged guy style, arms tense and robotic, and started talking immediately, shooting the shit about summer, girls, and senior year.

In Hanley, if Reed wasn't wearing his velvet robe or channeling James Bond, he and Cush often ran around the dorm dressed up like ninjas. Around midnight, they'd put on the kung fu shoes they'd bought for five bucks on the Internet, adorn themselves in all black, and stalk the hallways with toy bats, ready to harass the freshmen. When make-believe got old, there was always porn to watch. Many boarding guys traded videos or DVDs, like Valentine's Day notes in elementary school. And when watching porn got old, there was always the real thing. Reed was a teenage boy living with some thirty other hormone-driven, pimple-popping, mischievous boys whose voices were changing. Schemes were always in the works. Reed heard rumors that, before his time, a male boarder ran a fledgling porn industry from his dorm room, taking orders, working out a mailing system, and reportedly making a fortune. (He was caught and later expelled.)

On the first day of senior year, Reed looked forward to seeing Mr. Carr, his favorite dorm parent in Hanley. He was a good guy, tough in a protective way, and Reed believed he was a favorite, especially when Mr. Carr pulled him aside and explained that if he got in trouble for drinking that year, he should contact him before anyone else. There were other dorm parents living in Hanley, some with their families, and they all offered varying levels of the same responsibilities, acting as parents, teachers, and disciplinarians, providing academic advice, and maintaining order. They also regulated social lives and off-campus activities.

Though the school is located just eight miles south of Boston, it was one of few attractions in the town of Milton, which was primarily upper-middle-class and residential, save for a few small commercial pockets. Boarders often grew restive on campus. East Milton Square, about five minutes away by car, had a grocery store, nail salon, Starbucks, and other uninspired shops. The movie theater was a bit farther, and so was the South Shore Plaza (known as the SSP), a predictable middle-class mall with chain restaurants and stores like Abercrombie & Fitch. Then there was the Blue Hills Reservation, roughly seven thousand acres of natural woodland where people could walk, bike, and ski. Milton students also knew it as a secret hideaway for hanging out, drinking, smoking, and hooking up. But boarders weren't permitted to have cars, and local spots within walking distance eventually grew old. Tedeschi's was little more than a run-down convenience store. Bent's was a favorite deli, yet there were only so many times students could order "the Academy," a special chicken sandwich with cheese and bacon. Boarders needed permission from their dorm parents to walk around town at night or go somewhere outside the town of Milton. The restrictions could become unbearable.

If Reed wanted to stay over at a friend's house, getting permission was more complicated. He not only had to ask a dorm parent, but he also needed verbal consent from the outside adult who would presumably look after him. What the school didn't want was, of course, what

Reed usually tried to orchestrate: signing out to a day student's house to attend an unchaperoned party. Reed had an easy solution. Whenever he wanted to go to a party or stay off campus, he relied on Brady, his friend from the hockey team, even when Brady wasn't around.

Hey, what are you doing? he'd ask, calling Brady by phone.

I'm in Somerville (or some other town in Massachusetts that was nowhere near Reed).

Can your mom sign me out?

Yeah.

So Reed called Brady's mom: *Hey, can you sign me out?*

Okay, she said, agreeing to call one of Reed's dorm parents. Half the time Reed didn't even show up at Brady's house, but Brady's mom never cared. She was one of those "cool" parents who seemed happy to help boarders on the weekends.

Getting caught for being at a party—or worse, for hosting the party—usually led to disciplinary action. But students at Milton could get in trouble for all sorts of offenses: cheating, plagiarizing, wearing a T-shirt with a cannabis leaf, cutting too many classes, missing too many assemblies, smoking, drinking, doing drugs, having sex on campus, and then, of course, committing an act *prejudicial to the academy,* which happened, for example, when a Milton student, while wearing a school T-shirt or logo, drank a beer at a barbecue on a beach on Martha's Vineyard, did something embarrassing, and got caught by a faculty member who just so happened to be attending the same barbecue. The scenario, ridiculous as it may sound, had the potential to tarnish the academy's reputation, and was therefore grounds for disciplinary action.

A turn before the Dean's Committee usually led to work hours, and an appearance before the Disciplinary Committee, a select group of faculty, administrators, and students, usually resulted in suspension or expulsion. A hearing before the Disciplinary Committee was called, by students, a DC, and receiving two DCs for the same offense, or three for different offenses, often led to expulsion. The *Milton Academy*

Student Handbook, which every student received and few actually read from cover to cover, explained that Milton was responsible for boarders around the clock, and all students when they were either in school or at school events. Rules about signing out to friends' houses may have looked good on paper, but parents had no idea that the dorm experience was, at times, as open and freewheeling as summer camp.

Regardless of school rules, persistent students usually found a way to sneak off and hook up. Reed's first opportunity to hook up, have sex, and be an asshole—a vital moment in his development into James Bond—happened a month into his first year at Milton. The girl was an adorable thing who caught his attention when she walked up to him at a dance and asked him if he wanted to leave. *Am I supposed to answer that?* Reed thought to himself, nodding his head and walking her out the door. Here was a girl who approached him, propositioned him, and then, hidden somewhere on the Milton campus, gave him a blow job. She behaved like girls he'd only heard about back home, who formed the Blow Job Club and serviced guys in public locations. Reed wasn't surprised that such girls attended Milton, but suddenly he was part of their prime clientele. He loved not having to do any of the work.

Then the girl had to spoil it by saying she wanted to sleep with him. Reed was a virgin at the time, and despite numerous offers from girls who wanted to have sex, he'd never said yes. He wasn't concerned about pregnancy, STDs, or HIV, and he wasn't swayed by religious belief or moral theory. He was concerned about his image. Having sex with this particular girl would have been cool, but doing so on his own terms (casual and noncommittal) would get only him one thing: a reputation for being an asshole. When senior year began, Reed was still a virgin. Half the time he wanted to embody the hockey jock stereotype, but half the time he wanted to play nice, talking with less popular classmates, participating in class, being his mother's son. He wanted to prove that he was different. Hockey players aren't all shitheads, he wanted to say.

His friends probably called him crazy for turning down sex, but

Reed had yet another reason: Most girls bored him. Reed loved the chase but lost interest easily. He was like a little boy, pursuing a girl just because he could, waiting for that single look: I am intrigued by you, I like you, I want you. Once he got it, he was ready to move on. In Reed's mind, some girls were good for decoration. Others were too intelligent to toy with. And then there were girls like Lily, a type that guys like Reed would hook up with and then keep a secret. Lily was decently pretty, and she did have big breasts, but she wasn't girlfriend material, which is why Reed decided to get a good story out of her.

One night they were "watching a movie" in her dorm room. This act, in and of itself, took patience and time because they had to get parietals—official permission from a dorm parent to have a student of the opposite sex in one's dorm room at certain hours of the day. Reed had to hunt down Mr. Carr, introduce his guest, and formally ask for permission. When Reed went by the book, he opened the door a shoe's width and kept the lights—and his clothes—on. Thankfully he wasn't a freshman and didn't have to keep his door wide open, but all boarders feared random checks by dorm parents, who could walk into students' rooms at any time. Some teachers had good reputations: They understood that students wanted privacy when a girl or boy came over. Some had bad reputations: They barged in every twenty minutes with little more than a knock. Timing was everything, and a degree of caution was necessary, because there was always a teacher walking in on so-and-so doing you-know-what to you-know-who.

When Reed was a junior, some guys he knew rebelled against a particularly fastidious dorm parent who walked into their rooms after little more than a light knock. The boys gathered in their dorm rooms, stripped, and waited until the teacher, per usual, barged in. Reed thought the story was hilarious, but he never would have disrespected his own dorm parents. Still, he loathed parietals and thought they restricted his social life (they did). He and the rest of his buddies constantly invented ways to circumvent the system. That time with Lily, they left the movie playing in her dorm room, sneaked down to a spare room in the basement, and hooked up in private. Reed quickly got her down to just a bra. Her panties were off. He kissed her everywhere, her mouth, her neck, her stomach, and then further still, until he pushed his face between her legs. But what if someone walked in? More important, this was kinda gross. He lasted ten seconds, stopped, then lay down on the sofa and waited for Lily to give him head.

He assumed she would. Hookups were largely guycentric. Girls gave guys hand jobs or blow jobs until they had an orgasm. Guys, however, didn't necessarily have to return the favor, because it was not part of the contract. Lily behaved just like Reed expected she would; she performed oral sex on him. Reed lay back, pushing his black hair against the couch, and thought: *How can I make this into a good story?*

As a hockey player, Reed had heard his teammates tell hundreds of stories, revealing the dirty details from a hookup, painting the scene with such precision that everyone could see and feel and smell the girl. Among Reed's friends, coming all over a girl would have been legendary, so that's what he decided to do to Lily.

He was seconds away, so close, almost there, when the door suddenly banged against a chair.

Um, hold on! they yelled.

Both of you, a voice barked. *See me upstairs.*

Reed couldn't believe it. Of all possible moments, the dorm parent on duty had to find them right as he was about to get his story. He knew what it was like to walk into his dorm or the hockey locker room and tell a story. First the questions would go flying.

Did you go at it?

Did you knock it out?

So what happened, did you do it?

Eventually, at someone's urging or the storyteller's behest, the dirty details would seep out.

Apparently so-and-so's got a little problem down there.

I've heard it's gross.

Sloppy.

Oh God, someone come listen to this.

As for reactions, if the girl was hot: *nice.*

If the girl was not: *oh ho ho.*

If the story was impressive: The storyteller automatically became *the man.*

Reed wanted to be more than *the man.* He wanted sexual conquests as well as respect. He wanted to impress friends, girls, and teachers all at once. He wanted to exist in two worlds—the popular one where jocks get off, girls get reputations, and guys kiss and tell, and the respectable one where teachers like you, parents raise their eyebrows at you, and girls think you're dreamy.

Every morning of high school, at 6:26 A.M., Josh woke up to applause churning out from the speakers of his alarm clock. He lay there listening to Dave Matthews and Tim Reynolds sing a live version of "One Sweet World," and then lay there for a couple more songs, lingering until 6:36 A.M., when he popped out of his brother's bed to take a shower. Josh was a day student at Milton and hadn't slept in his own room for at least a year. It was small and impersonal, while his brother's room, abandoned ever since his brother went to a different boarding school, was spacious and welcoming, with all the signs of a young man's personal space—the handsome brown and neutral decor, a large sofa, a wireless keyboard and mouse, Gucci sunglasses conveniently left behind. Josh thought his older brother was a total *man,* and idolized him for being athletic, popular, and aggressive.

At home in Wellesley, a tony Boston suburb with wrought-iron lampposts lighting driveways and boutiques enticing couples to dress their children in ribbon belts and fashionable jeans, Josh grew up in an overachieving family, with a brother who strapped him into hockey pads and fired pucks at his head, and parents who raised him to be a good boy. Josh wore his seat belt. He opened doors for girls. He said *please* and *thank you.* He believed the guy should pay for dinner. He had little desire for random hookups. Instead of sleeping off hangovers on the weekends, he woke up early to participate in a local community-service program before going to his basketball games. He grew up in a big house, with lots of land and a family of Ivy League graduates. He didn't get it. What about him could a girl *not* like?

The problem was obvious: Josh struggled to parlay his success with basketball into success with girls. At seventeen, he was neither handsome nor unattractive. Just tall and unassuming, with a mop of brown hair, and a bump on his nose. Josh hadn't yet grown into his body or his face, and wore T-shirts and hooded sweatshirts to school that cloaked him in perpetual boyhood. But on the basketball court he was graceful and controlling, attractive in the most unexpected way. You could see his ripped thighs and defined arms beneath his orange-and-blue uniform. He was the kind of boy who would grow into a handsome and gentle man. The kind that girls would want to date and marry in another ten years. What he lacked at age seventeen was talent with the opposite sex, and he had no idea why.

The truth was that Josh had never been *the man*. He'd had only one girlfriend (in seventh grade), and he hadn't even kissed a single girl at Milton. In middle school he cried before going to dances, begging his mother not to make him go. She sprayed cologne on him, told him to get in the car, and sent him off into manhood. By high school, Josh thought he knew how to flirt and ask girls out, and he even practiced, in the attic among his brother's stash of *Playboy* magazines. But failure seemed inevitable. He accepted his routine of disappointment, yet he always found the courage to ask another girl out, or flirt with her online, or do something to show his interest. He looked up to his older brother, who threw the greatest parties, rented hotel rooms, and had fashion shows. His brother wouldn't have been himself without his extravagant lifestyle, and Josh wouldn't have been Josh without an unrequited love.

Diana looked like many other Milton girls: athletic, with a ponytail, not thin but not overweight. Josh had liked her since freshman year, when a buddy told him that she thought he was cute. They were at the Jessups Open House, a weekend event when students could visit the dorm and hang out in boarders' rooms without parietals. Josh and Diana ended up in someone's room together. She lay on the bed. He stood nearby. He took a few steps in her direction and sat down awkwardly, telling himself over and over again that Diana liked him, Diana liked him, Diana liked him. Then she pushed Josh off the bed. Persistent, he gave her a romantic CD on Valentine's Day freshman year, and then learned she promptly asked out his best friend.

As Josh anticipated senior year, he trusted that he would get into a good college, do a senior project, and graduate. But who would he take to the prom? It was nine months away, and he already worried about finding a date who actually wanted to go with him. If only he had a viable crush. If only he had a girlfriend. If only he had Diana.

What Josh did have, however, was instant messaging (IM). He sat at his computer for hours, talking about absolutely nothing with his friends and being an entirely different person with girls. He could act confident and cocky, or funny and sensitive, tailoring his comments to each one. Saving online conversations was typically a girl's preoccupation, but Josh did it for the same reasons they did; exciting IMs with crushes were validating, and even disappointing IMs with exes made trophies out of gravestones.

Josh: still seeing that kid?
Girl: ya . . .
Josh: how long have you been going out with him
Girl: 9 months
Josh: wow
Girl: ya
Josh: are you feeling more comfortable with him
Girl: yep
Josh: so youve moved to the next step i take it
Girl: if u want to put it that way ya

Josh: well i have to be polite

Girl: but i dont really wanna talk about it.

Josh wanted to talk about it. He was curious. What did sex feel like? What did it sound like? What did this girl look like? Did she have orgasms—and if she did, what did she whisper to her boyfriend right before she came? Whenever Josh thought about girls, his mind drifted to his last and only hookup. It had taken place all the way back in eighth grade, but the worst part was that the credit went to his friend, who generously invited him over to hang out with two girls, one of whom was designated for Josh.

We gonna do anything or what? the girl asked, sitting next to him on the couch.

Did a girl really just ask him to hook up? Was she serious? Wasn't she nervous? Josh was nervous. But he started making out with her right away. The girl seemed more experienced than he realized, sliding off his pants and undoing her own belt buckle. He followed her cues and reached behind her back to undo her bra. The seconds ticked by like hours. Where were the hooks? Shouldn't there be a clasp? He blushed when she explained that there are no hooks on sports bras. The mistake was a minor blip, because Josh persevered. He wedged his fingers between her legs, wondering the entire time where all her hair came from. Why was everything wet? What was going on down there? Josh was relieved when she reached for his groin. She seemed to know as little about his body as he knew about hers; whoever had told her to treat penises like Play-Doh was seriously misinformed.

Her hand job didn't work, but Josh stretched out on the bed while she went to the bathroom, delighting in his newfound sexuality. He wanted to know what he had to do to make it happen again. Was hooking up always so easy? Did guys just designate girls for their friends? How could he ensure that this girl—or any girl—would hook up with him again? Should he ask her out? He needed answers to these questions.

The next four years went by in an instant, and, at the same time, the next four years seemed like forever. Josh made the boys' varsity basketball team and was cut from the varsity hockey team. His older brother had been a star player on his high school hockey team, and his mother wanted Josh to repeat that feat. She called the coach, furious, but he wouldn't budge. Josh's athletic failure—and he did see it as a failure—was symbolic: By the fall of his senior year, Josh was the same boy with the same social identity that he had had at Milton years before. Change seemed impossible.

The final proof that Josh would never be able to seal the deal with a girl materialized junior year, when he turned seventeen. His mom gave him tickets to see Jerry Seinfeld. Fantastic. Perfect. But not really: He had to find a date. Few guys he knew actually took girls out on dates, and if they did, it was usually after they'd already hooked up. Josh liked traditional courtship. He wanted to get to know a girl and have intimacy, not just the sexual act. He was, in this sense, a very different type of man. But who would he take to the show? Caroline, his childhood buddy and current classmate, had a boyfriend, and he knew her like a sister. Diana had a boyfriend, too. After much debate and anxiety he mustered up the courage to ask a crush from another school. The girl said yes. The girl actually said yes.

Seinfeld was hysterical. His date laughed all night (Josh listened to make sure), and on the way home he played the CD he'd burned specifically for that night, hoping she liked Dave Matthews and John Mayer as much as he did. Josh walked her to the house like any gentleman would, and with one arm outstretched, he opened the door and waited for the critical moment. *I had a really nice time tonight,* he said. He wanted to hold her hand or touch her skin, anything, as long as it was part of her. But he only leaned forward and hugged her limply, detesting the feeling of her cheek. Josh instinctively knew the magnitude of his missed opportunity. Even when romance was there—dinner, a show in Boston, a long drive home—he couldn't follow through; he was the kind of guy who didn't have the guts to make a move.

Josh was not naive going into senior year; he didn't expect any more luck with girls than he'd had before. He resigned himself to the role of spectator, watching the other jocks dominate the social scene, as though it was some innate ability that was simply missing from his DNA.

The only time Josh was at ease was with the basketball team. Here was a world in which he rarely second-guessed his decisions. He had confidence and strengths (height, quick feet, good hustle), and knew how to use them in games. His favorite part of the season was his one reliable social plan: team dinner every Friday night. After practice and in preparation for Saturday's game, the basketball guys descended upon a local restaurant for a night of bonding. There was nothing better than pulling out of the ACC parking lot after practice on a Friday night, his windows rolled down, Michael Jackson's *Thriller* blasting, guys sitting in the back. Sitting around the tables at the restaurant, he and the guys played games with the coasters and goofed around about some movie or some girl. Josh was his most comfortable self.

After dinner, younger teammates usually went straight home while Josh's group of friends retreated to one of the dorms to watch movies or play video games. Dorms were like twenty-four-hour playrooms to Josh, so much more fun than life in his own house, which was staid and quiet with his brother away at school. Boarders had vibrant flags and tapestries hanging in their rooms, not the boring framed paintings his mom picked out for his own walls. Sometimes Josh felt like staying the night in the dorms, but he quickly remembered the quality of breakfast at school.

As dorm check-in time approached, at 11:00 P.M., Josh left to drive home. The car was silent without his friends. Sometimes he sang out loud, amused by his terrible deep voice. Eighteen minutes later he pulled into his driveway. He had to be up early the next morning for a community-service program and then Saturday's game, but before going to bed he signed onto IM and flipped on *Letterman,* snacked on a cookie and a glass of juice, and then slumped into his brother's bed. Between the sheets, surrounded by a masculinity that was not his own, he slipped into sleep.

There on the computer screen, in the featured photograph on the main page of a now-defunct hockey Web site, a boy lay on top of a pool table with a hockey stick cradled between his hands, and muscles that looked as if they'd come from your local Gold's Gym. His limbs appeared limp, and they were, because he was passed out from a night of drinking. This mountain of flesh—strong yet soft, and tan—extended over six feet, and on the boy's head was a ski helmet and a pair of ski goggles strapped over his eyes. Tight blond curls spilled out from underneath the helmet, and clouds of alcohol-stinking breath rose from his mouth. The boy was absolutely shitfaced. It couldn't have been anyone but Brady, a Milton Academy varsity hockey player, legendary party boy, and one of Reed's good friends.

Brady's rugged good looks and laid-back demeanor had helped him become one of the most popular guys in school—at least among certain guys (jocks) and certain girls (the freshman, sophomore, and junior DSGs, who were known as young DSGs). He was the social director among his friends, a self-professed go-to guy for help and advice, and the designated driver, though not always 100 percent sober. A teammate remembered him as a leader who walked around campus with big muscles and drove around town with small, dainty girls in the back of his big car, a mid-90s Volvo wagon, maroon, boxy, a hallmark of understated old money. Brady moved through the world with the self-assurance of one who never experienced an awkward stage, never suffered from braces, and never felt undesirable. At school he walked around like the biggest man on campus. At home in Duxbury, Massachusetts, he had no curfew. In the Volvo, he drove from party to party, friends crammed in, a couple of beers deep, a thirty-pack in the back. These were the benefits of being Brady's brand of day student: He had no dorm parents (like Reed) and no nagging parents (like Josh).

Brady exuded the confidence and entitlement that went along with his social position, and his appearance often reinforced this air: broad shoulders, the backward Red Sox hat, and the cheeky, boyish face. He wore collared shirts to parties, but wouldn't have been caught dead in Reed's salmon-colored cashmere sweater. He favored old jeans that he'd had forever, and the kind of worn-in, old school T-shirts that now come ready-made at stores like Urban Outfitters and sell for $40. As a hockey and football player, Brady was thick and muscular by necessity, but he was soft as well, especially around the middle, as though he'd already gained his freshman fifteen. At the top of his formidable body, jutting delicately from the pale skin around his eyes, were long eyelashes that made him look vulnerable. Girls couldn't get enough of his curly locks and irresistible smile.

Brady is a type of boy who has gone to Milton for generations. Men in his family graduated from the academy, and some went on to Harvard. His parents' wedding was announced in the *New York Times*. Many students recognize that there is an invisible yet definite connection between boys like Brady and Milton's longtime lineage among the privileged elite. He feeds the school's public image—the private institution that has existed since the eighteenth century and educated world-famous leaders.

But Brady did not carry on this tradition of academic excellence. His pedigree aside, he didn't keep up with Milton's intellectual reputation. He wasn't a standout student or an exceptional athlete. He wasn't the head of any student groups or organizations. Rumor had it that he wasn't well liked by teachers, advisers, and certain groups of students. Still, it was hard to feel bad for him. He had his own extracurriculars (partying, driving the Volvo) that some fellow classmates would never experience. He was the kind of guy who received nicknames in the *Milton Paper* simply because he was a popular, well-known social creature. His stories were hysterical and his storytelling ability renowned. He could make friends laugh so hard they cried. He was popular and good looking, and couldn't remember a single moment when he'd lacked confidence. Brady was clearly *the man*.

His long line of sexual conquests had begun back in eighth grade, when his first girlfriend gave him his first hand job, blow job, and gossip story. His stories grew in force and number. By the end of sophomore year, he'd hooked up with at least fifteen girls. By the beginning of junior year, he was no longer a virgin. By the time he was a senior, he estimated that the majority of his sexual experiences involved alcohol, a party, and a casual acquaintance. By the time he graduated, he'd slept with eleven girls.

A strong if dangerous alliance had been growing between Brady's crew and the young DSGs. As senior fall began, small parties held in Caitlin Lane's basement became a weekend staple, with beer, TV, hookups, parents upstairs without a care. She was a stunning young DSG and had the kind of parents most teenagers dreamed about: They let older boys come over, left the group alone, and either had no idea about the alcohol or purposely turned their heads. There in the basement, or in cars parked in empty parking lots, these girls offered themselves to Brady and his friends.

Whitney thought the situation was pitiful. These darling younger girls, who were so perfectly stenciled and outfitted, didn't realize what was really going on in the guys' minds. So Brady drove hot younger girls around in his car. So he hooked up. So he bought beer and made a scene. Few senior girls were going to say, *Brady, you're the greatest, you have a car!* But younger girls seemed to.

Hookups involving one girl and several guys—or at least one girl, one guy, and an audience—were not unusual at Caitlin Lane's parties. Though Reed believed that every guy's fantasy involved two girls, his friends seemed to prefer the reverse scenario. One day junior year, Brady and Quinn, a buddy from the hockey team, decided to convince Emma, a young DSG, to have a threesome with them. Brady was mildly interested in her, not as a girlfriend, but as a girl who was a friend he happened to hook up with from time to time. He'd heard she'd ski-poled Quinn and another guy earlier that year (which meant she'd given them hand jobs simultaneously), but persuading her to do a threesome would be challenging because she was furious with Brady and Quinn for the ways they treated her friends.

Emma, let's go drink somewhere, the guys said.

No, she began.

We know you're mad at us. We should just hook up.

I can't do it, I can't do it.

Come on, let's get serious. Get over it.

She did.

The three of them piled into Quinn's car and drove to the parking lot at a local hockey rink. While Quinn drove, Brady hooked up with Emma in the backseat. When they parked the car, the three of them went at it for fifteen minutes, until Brady said, *All right, all right, we gotta get outta here* as people walked by. On the way home, Quinn took a turn with Emma in the backseat, then Brady pulled over so the boys could switch places again.

Emma, you can't be mad at us anymore, Brady said when the hookup was over, trying to talk seriously through his goofy grin. *Because obviously you're not.*

He and Quinn knew they couldn't tell anyone about what had happened, but keeping secrets implied they would at least tell all their friends. The hockey guys had a special bond, like brothers, impenetrable and unabashed. They felt they could—and should—do everything together. Brady and his teammates had seen each other naked, probably more often than their girlfriends—when they had girlfriends. Group sex acts were just like showering together after practice.

Senior year, Brady wasn't looking for a relationship. Girlfriends, he believed, were good for one thing: sex. The rest of the time they got in the way. Brady had only one serious relationship at Milton; it had extended almost two years, minus the summer, minus the fights, minus that time he'd cheated on her. Commitment was not something he generally thought about or practiced. When his relationship was going well, he and his girlfriend talked on the phone, ate meals together, met each other's parents, and crashed at his house after parties. Brady knew how to be sweet when he wanted to, like the time he bought her a necklace from Tiffany (she got him all three *Mighty Ducks* movies and he couldn't have loved anything more). They said *I love you,* and though he doesn't remember the circumstances of the confession, it was mostly meaningful, because he rarely expressed emotion, even to his parents.

Junior year Brady's girlfriend claimed she hated his friends and dumped him. He understood why. He was a true guys' guy and couldn't dream up a better night than one with Church, Quinn, and the rest of the crew. The guys shared similar characteristics: They were attractive, athletic, and preppy. Junior year they spent most of their time in Brady's Volvo, the latest 50 Cent hit blasting as they cruised around Milton's back roads for at least an hour, drinking Budweiser, telling stories, killing time just because they could. Sometimes they drove into Dorchester, past its gray streets and tattered storefronts, to fill up at a shady convenience store that casually sold alcohol to high-schoolers who were in the know and looked as close to twenty-one as any teenager could. Dorchester and its neighbor, Mattapan, surround Milton, and are racially diverse neighborhoods known for frequent crime-related appearances on the local news.

Amid this patchwork of working-class life, Brady spent Friday nights during his senior year much like Josh did—having dinner with his teammates. There were three discernible differences. First, Brady played football; second, he ate at Wendy's; and third, the meal was hardly the highlight of his week. For him, Friday nights were about gearing up for the weekend. Brady wolfed down a double cheeseburger, fries, and a Coke, and if he had anything left over he'd save it, like the rest of the guys, to chuck at one another's cars on the way back to school. Josh heard they'd once dumped milk shakes on a friend's car just to give him a hard time; Brady thought the stunt was hilarious.

The night after Senior Walk In, Brady and his friends arrived at the First Dance as though they owned the place. The event was a highlight of the back-to-school weekend, and took place in the newly constructed Schwarz Student Center, an all-glass tribute to modern architecture.

Literally squeezed between Wigglesworth and Warren halls, two late-nineteenth-century brick buildings, the student center is conspicuously out of place on campus. It towers above the ground, an iceberg of glass. The lower level isn't visible from the Centre Street entrance, but downstairs, not far from the snack bar and bookstore, freshmen descended upon the dance as the first major event of their high school careers.

Brady and his friends didn't stay long. There was always, without fail, something better to do, and that night it was fighting a group of Milton townies (the term commonly used to describe teenagers in the town of Milton who did not go to the academy). The soldiers were ready: just drunk enough after having beers at a friend's house nearby. And their cause was noble: Punish the local kids who had started trouble with some of their friends the night before, at the all-school cookout held on the main quad. The plan was that Brady would charge first, and the rest of his buddies would follow.

Brady believed his desire to fight was perfectly rational. He and his friends had each other's backs and were willing to go the limit. He didn't know how many other people could say something like that about their best friends. Brady thought fighting was about loyalty to his boys; if there was anyone he truly loved, it was them.

At some point that night, what seemed like twenty-five guys left the First Dance. Teachers must have noticed. The guys weren't all seniors, but they were popular, identifiable, and impossible to ignore. They crashed into the brisk autumn night and crossed Centre Street, trying to look normal, pausing in front of the cars parked in front of Ware Hall. Brady spotted a few teachers following them outside. A teacher who'd been at Milton for decades walked by, and at that very moment, one of the guys opened Brady's car door, turning on the interior light that illuminated the thirty-pack of beer in the back. Brady saw his high school career flash before his eyes—decent athlete, good son, best friend, occasional boyfriend, college bound.

Shut the door! Brady yelled.

His friend didn't understand what was going on.

Shut the door!

But Brady knew it was too late. He watched the teacher look straight into the car and straight at the beer, which was right there in plain sight. It was so obvious and so illegal. Brady knew he could get DCed.

At practice that very afternoon, he and a few other seniors told their coach that they were imposing a no-drinking rule for the entire season. Later, when their coach was gone, they clarified the rule for the under-classmen on the team: Drinking was forbidden during the week; the guys were expected to use discretion on the weekend. Brady figured that if he couldn't even make it a few hours . . .

Just as suddenly as the car light flicked on, the teacher glanced away and kept on walking. Many faculty members were sticklers for the rules, but some were famous for being lenient. As Brady watched the man dis-appear down the sidewalk, he couldn't believe how lucky he was. Then again, this wasn't the first time he'd dodged unwanted consequences. This was merely an impressive stroke of providence that meshed neatly with the rest of his enviable social life. Breathing deeply, Brady eased into the driver's seat and waited for his friends to pile in. He turned the key in the ignition, changed gears, and pulled onto Centre Street, not thinking twice about the beers he'd already had that night.

chapter three

awkward little virgins

high school is all about measurements. How many As or Cs you get. How many friends you have. How many upperclassmen say hi to you in the hallway. How many parties you go to. How many times you avoid curfew. How many times you drink alcohol. How many boys ask you to dance, and how many of those boys are the ones you want to ask you to dance.

When you are a student at Milton Academy, where the pressure to perform and succeed at the highest level affects all areas of your life, the measurements can be even more specific. If you are an athlete, how often your name makes the *Milton Paper*. If you are an academic, how many honors science classes you take, and how soon in your high school career you take them. If you are a writer, how many Persky Awards you receive. If you are anyone, what kind of car you drive, how many vacation homes you have, and whether they're on Cape Cod or Martha's Vineyard. If you are a jock, how many DSGs you sleep with. If you are a DSG, how many guys think you're hot. For some, it's about how many of those guys play sports, and of that number, how many play ice hockey, and of that number, how many you've hooked up with.

For others, it's how many times the most popular guy in school smiles at you. And then of course, how many times you contemplate hooking up with him, admitting to yourself that you would sleep with him if that's what he wanted.

By the time Whitney became a senior, she was highly aware of the unspoken and often arbitrary calculations that had determined her rank in Milton's social hierarchy. She knew what it meant to be a girlfriend, a hookup, a slut; loved, wanted, used. She knew about extremes—late-night studying or late-night partying. And sexual temptations—a kiss, a boyfriend, sex in a dorm room. But there'd been a time when she was not so well informed, and life had been simpler.

When Whitney thought about her first week as a freshman, she remembered herself as an eager fourteen-year-old filled with promise and youthful optimism, a well-bred girl who had been told she could do and become whatever she set her mind to. That first week of school teemed with expectations. A friend could become a crush. A crush a boyfriend. A new it girl could be made. A nobody could be discovered. Technically, anyone could become popular. But that, of course, is not how it works. Whitney and the other freshmen girls may not have known at the time that their high school identities hung in the balance, to be determined by immediate and mostly superficial judgments. Yet on some level they understood that first impressions counted; that Milton's annual First Dance was the opening skirmish in a battle for popularity and recognition that would determine their respective social paths.

On the night of her first First Dance, Whitney was still adjusting to life as a new day student. She may not have been familiar with the histories of Milton's mythical buildings, or known that many of their names honored the distinguished New England families who'd donated them. What she did know was that on this particular evening, she would begin her own Milton history. The First Dance sealed Whitney's status as true teenage royalty. In retrospect, she saw that she owed this achievement, at least in part, to a single gesture. Even now, years later, she can recall that moment when Preston asked her to dance to the very first slow song. In front of his friends, too.

Whitney had been sure to position herself near him throughout the evening, chest out, lips glossed, eyes smiling even when she caught him talking with other girls. She thought he was the hottest freshman boy, and the two had been flirting all week. When he asked her to dance, she hoped everyone noticed; it meant Preston really liked her. Even at fourteen, she knew that displaying public affection like that didn't happen to just any girl, especially when a guy like Preston was involved. But Whitney was primed for the role as Preston's latest female pastime: bubbly, effortlessly slender, and flirtatious. And he was an obvious go-to guy: a social leader, handsome, and a complement to her identity as a leading lady-in-training.

Beneath Wigg's dimmed lights, Whitney looked up at Preston when he asked her to dance. Of course she said *yes*. It felt like the biggest moment of her life. And when he leaned in, ever so slowly, almost unnoticeably, pressing his lips against hers, she was the happiest she thought she would ever be—until he slobbered all over her chin. *Way too much tongue, buddy,* she thought silently, persevering, kissing him back until she couldn't take it anymore.

Whitney was willing to forgo the kissing problem, because she wanted to fall in love and get swept off her feet. That's exactly what was happening until one of Preston's friends passed on a message.

Preston might ask you to go on a walk, the friend said.

Really? Whitney asked, pushing her shoulders back.

Yeah. Like, he wants head.

Whitney was appalled. She didn't have that kind of experience, and knew she didn't want to get it in such an impersonal way, with someone she barely knew. She may have been young, but she knew about STDs and was concerned with the social and emotional repercussions. Kissing was still a big deal to her, and oral sex was still like sex: unimaginable. Whitney's mom had always warned her against boys like Preston. *If they're not going to like you for who you are, and they're just going to expect that, just think what kind of guy [he must be].* Whitney hadn't met guys like that until the First Dance. She knew she was in high school now.

Preston was smooth and confident when he proposed the idea.

Let's take a break from dancing, he said. *Let's go outside.*

Um, I can't, Whitney stammered, thankful she'd been warned. *I can't find my shoes.*

And then she'd walked away, her long brown hair moving from side to side.

It was a daring move for a new freshman girl, such a public rejection of a desirable freshman boy. Whitney knew there were plenty of girls who would have jumped at the opportunity to go on a walk with Preston. Not because they thought he would have given them oral sex in return—he was popular; he didn't have to—but because the act would have aligned them with the right guy, making them, potentially, the right girls. But she gave her mother a reason to be proud when she turned down Preston. The social consequences of Whitney's decision were obvious. Preston told everyone she was a bad kisser, and they never hooked up again. But Whitney ultimately achieved popularity without his help. Crushes from older guys and friendships with certain girls secured her future as a DSG. She didn't have to put out—unless she wanted to.

Whitney had been raised to be a good girl. Her mother taught her that having sex with one man—her future husband—was part of being a lady and respecting herself. Weekly church attendance supposedly reinforced a religious upbringing, but when skating left no time for formal religion, her mom took the reins—or at least tried. Whitney's coming-of-age unfolded in the backseat of the car during all those trips to and from skating practices and competitions. Nearly every day for twelve years, her mother made Whitney's skating career possible. But the trips also brought them together. The car was where Whitney received her very first razor and bottle of shaving cream, and pulled her first thong around her narrow hips in seventh grade. Then, one day, the inevitable occurred.

Mom, I think I pooped in my pants, Whitney blurted out as she changed into her skating outfit in the backseat.

What?

I don't know how this happened!

But it was only her first period. Whitney learned immediately how to use a tampon and her mother stressed the importance of consequences. Just because Whitney knew a guy from school didn't mean she knew his sexual history. Just because he said he didn't have an STD didn't mean it was true. Just because he said he loved her didn't mean she had to give him her virginity. Whitney listened, wondering what it would feel like to have oral sex or sex. Would she have to take off her underwear? What if she was too hairy? What if she smelled? What if she had discharge? Would she bleed—did that even happen? A vagina wasn't like a penis, so functional in its construction, even to an innocent like Whitney. Vaginas had folds of skin, multiple openings, and beneath it all was a clitoris, something many girls knew they had but did not intimately understand. She loved her mother like a best friend, but knew she couldn't possibly ask her these questions.

When Whitney entered freshman year, she may have been more sexually naive than some of her fellow classmates, but she knew all about popularity. She wanted to be the prom queen and worshipped films like 10 *Things I Hate About You* and *She's All That*, paradigms of the ideal teenage life, where the nerd gets the cheerleader, the rocker gets the misfit, and the parents rekindle their own love, too. Back at her old school, Whitney's friends were superficial, and she liked them that way. Arriving on the Milton campus, she knew what she wanted: attention from the hottest boy in her class.

After Preston, various boyfriends followed. Whitney made out with them in the backseat of her mom's car while her mom asked questions like, *Can you do that some other time?* Everything changed when she met Nick at a basketball game later freshman year. He went to another local private school and didn't look like he belonged near a sporting event any more than Whitney looked like she belonged with a boy like him. A fake diamond earring sat squarely in his left earlobe, and he always had a cleanly shaven head.

Ohmygod, he's looking at me, Whitney whispered to a girlfriend when she noticed Nick looking at her from a few seats away. *Oh, God, that's gross!*

Later that night, and then over the next few weeks, Whitney and Nick hung out when their friends got together. She heard he fell in love with her right away, but she had one word for him: *ew.*

I would never go out with Nick, she told her girlfriends.

He's not my style.

I like the preppy boyfriend totally decked out in Abercrombie.

But somehow, by a stroke of luck or an excruciating effort on Nick's part, Whitney gave him a chance. He was outgoing. He made her laugh. She didn't have to wear makeup. She felt comfortable enough to cry in front of him. She could be herself, and in the process of becoming herself, she fell for him. But their differences emerged in neon lights. Whitney was devoted to skating, while Nick's passions included smoking marijuana and slacking off. Whitney had never thought about drinking, smoking marijuana, or having sex until Nick came into her life. It all started one afternoon in the library during the early days of their relationship, when Whitney still turned to her mother for everything, and Nick pulled out a small bag.

Oh, Mom, Nick showed me weed! she confessed later that night.

Whitney's mother wasn't stupid. She sensed this boy was bad for her daughter, and set out to cautiously guide Whitney into womanhood and contain her budding sexuality. One day she informed Whitney that they were going to a concert. Whitney was psyched. She was a self-professed teenybopper who listened to Britney Spears and 'NSync, and religiously followed Hollywood stars in *CosmoGirl* and *Seventeen.* When they arrived at the concert, though, Whitney was confused. There was a stage. There were performers and speakers. There was music. But this was no ordinary concert. This was an event for the Silver Ring Thing, a religious youth program preaching faith-based abstinence to teens. The Silver Ring Thing wasn't popular at Milton (nor, really, were any prominently religious programs). Whitney was skeptical, but in her usual easygoing style, she rolled with it.

She learned that her future husband was out there somewhere. Didn't she want to give all of herself to him, pure and virginal? Her answer: yup. Didn't she want to abstain? Her answer: sure. Didn't she know it was cool to be a virgin? Her answer: okay! Even if she'd already had sex (she hadn't), she could still participate, because the Silver Ring Thing taught that everyone deserved a second chance. If Whitney was ever unsure about whether a particular sexual act was inappropriate, the program offered clear advice: *What would you NOT want your husband or wife to do with a member of the opposite sex? You probably shouldn't do that either right now.*

At the end of the concert, anyone committed to the program accepted a ring and made a pledge to god to remain a virgin until marriage. Whitney looked around and saw everyone putting on rings, so she did, too. Her mother was thrilled. Whitney wore the ring on her left ring finger for about a week, but after she and Nick had been a couple for two full weeks, they decided to lose their virginity to each other. She already knew how to shave her pubic hair so that only a thin strip remained. And she'd already tried everything but sex with the boy she dated before Nick. So Whitney and Nick planned the time (after school), the place (his dorm room), the location (his couch), and the method of birth control (condoms). When Whitney saw Nick the very next day, she kept giving him cute smiles, loving their secret, anxious to do it all over again. Two times later, after she told her best friends every detail, Whitney and Nick stopped using condoms. They did not have STD tests. They did not use the pill. *We are awkward little virgins,* she thought to herself, *but we love each other.*

She wore the ring for at least eight more months, but she eventually hid it in her jewelry box, taking it out only when she was sure her mother would notice its absence. Whitney did not believe she was sinful or slutty, and wasn't ashamed of her behavior. As she got older, she became more cavalier, embracing the hookups she had with random boys.

By the start of her senior year, Whitney had slept with four guys, including Nick, all during her relationship with Nick. On the night of her senior year First Dance, Tripp's was likely to be the fifth. It was a hectic Saturday evening on the Milton campus, the first weekend of the school year, and Whitney was relieved to be a senior, free of the entanglements and dangers she now considered silly underclassmen ordeals. She was older and wiser. Since she'd already achieved the coveted popular-girl status, she was out for pleasure, not perfection. Whitney felt free to enjoy herself without limits, on her own terms. Whitney at the First Dance was Whitney in her element. No one was going to stand in her way.

Whitney's short, frilly white skirt sashayed back and forth as she shook her body against Tripp's on the dance floor. They were only partially visible in the crowd of girls and boys grinding together in tight circles on the lower level of the student center, where the event was held. Hip-hop songs roared from the speakers. Underclassmen were everywhere. Whitney's tousled brown hair seduced Tripp with every move she made toward him. She knew she was head-turning, jaw-dropping, weak-in-your-knees hot. And she knew he noticed. Her green top was cut low and her face was beautiful: bronze with golden hues, shimmering whenever she stood in the right light. And he looked good, too, in faded jeans and a button-down shirt he did not tuck in.

Tripp had been a romantic idea in her mind for roughly twenty-four hours. The day before the First Dance, at the all-school cookout held on the main quad, they'd found a spot on the grass and talked. The topics were harmless—sports, school, family—but when she got home that night she went to bed with one thought: *I'm definitely hooking up with him tomorrow night.*

There was no denying that Tripp meshed well with the social image Whitney had been perfecting since her freshman year. Her first year at Milton, she studied her wealthy friends and the older girls for clues on fashion, language, and behavior. At first she failed to notice the disparities between her American Eagle outfits and their designer clothes. The Kate Spade insignias on their black bags were meaningless to her, as were the "7s" stitched on the back of their Seven jeans, slung low on their hips. Whitney's hometown, Dedham, was a middle-class suburb with a middling reputation. After visiting various friends' homes—most of them enormous—she'd realized that there was a difference between girls like herself, who probably thought Izod was related to iPod, and girls like some of her new friends, who would have been shocked had she asked how a Pink shirt could be blue.

As the years went by, Whitney's mother tried to understand her daughter's developing taste for luxury. She was a strict woman who believed in tradition, family, her Catholic faith, and the imperative of understatement. She never made sense of her daughter's desire for designer clothes. Wouldn't she rather get five shirts or a couple of pairs of pants on a birthday shopping spree instead of one pair of Seven jeans for $200? Whitney's answer: a casual *nope*.

Of course, not all Milton students were wealthy. The school was a diverse community of trust-fund babies, financial-aid dependents, and everyone else in between. Yet displays of wealth were constant. Whitney eventually grew numb to the BMW convertibles and Hummers she saw on campus, driven by students, not teachers. She wasn't surprised when a friend jetted to Florida for the weekend or showed up to a dance in $400 Jimmy Choo shoes. By the time she became a senior, she also recognized that she was fortunate, for her parents were comfortable. They took her on vacations, drove nice cars, and sent her to private school. Whitney tried to remember that some of her friends had nothing. *This school is so ridiculous, people complain about their cleaning people,* a friend on financial aid once said after overhearing a DSG bitch about her housekeeper. But Whitney couldn't tame her fascination with an inner circle of old-money Milton families who seemed to own the world, or at least private planes, gigantic homes, and companies.

At the First Dance, Whitney pulled Tripp off the dance floor. For a brief moment, as they climbed the very public staircase, they were a couple on display. Anyone paying attention would have seen their silhouettes, a girl, a guy, lust growing between them. Reed noticed. He'd stopped by the dance for only a few minutes, but he couldn't miss Whitney. The day they'd first met, he thought she was beautiful. He was disappointed when he heard about Nick, and then utterly baffled when he met Nick—how in the world did this grungy guy who smoked weed wrap Whitney around his finger? Reed watched Whitney and Tripp together, knowing Tripp was what he called a good kid, wondering, like anyone else there, what would become of them.

Upstairs, Whitney and Tripp leaned over the railing by the stairs and amused themselves with the drunk freshmen who thought alcohol made them cool. The lower level was packed, but this time, unlike recess, which took place in the student center each morning after second period, social divisions temporarily merged as girls and boys shared a single space on the dance floor. Cliques were seemingly inconsequential, though most students knew better than to believe everyone was equal. Whitney and Tripp were a clear reminder. They were laughing, flirting, naturally getting along—until a girl who didn't go to Milton walked up to Whitney and Tripp, shoved them, and then called Whitney a bitch.

Whitney had never spoken to this girl before, but Tripp knew exactly who she was. They had hooked up that summer, and it was clear she was angry that he had never spoken to her again. Instead of shoving the girl back, Whitney laughed and thought, *Screw you*. She may have walked with grace and poise, but she was hardly demure. She liked being the center of a whole new kind of attention. Love triangles were romantic: the jealous rejectee, the handsome favorite, and her, the beauty, the winner. She may have been a senior, and she may have believed she was mature, but Whitney wasn't above high school drama.

Perhaps Nick had a hunch that Whitney was about to cheat on him that night. She'd done it before. She'd do it again. But she knew Nick would take her back, because she believed she was the best he could get. Whitney's reasons for cheating never changed: Nick did drugs, went to class high, abused his body, and didn't always treat her well. He'd grown up in Charlestown, Massachusetts, with an aunt, no father, and little drive to obey rules. He spent his high school years in and out of prep schools, alternating between day student and boarding status. He was asked to leave each one for various reasons—grades, drinking, plagiarizing—and had found, by Whitney's senior year, what looked like a solid fit as a day student at a new school.

Their relationship was easier when Nick lived at home, but Whitney admitted that there was something about dating a certain kind of boarder, even one from another school. Nick's disregard for school rules and his drive to break them gave her a rush. She knew she would have been grounded for life had her parents found out she sneaked into his dorm room without permission, but his confidence fueled her belief that they would never get caught. Whitney had been following the same rigorous schedule since she was six years old—skating, school, skating, homework, and competitions on the weekends. Her early flirtations with rebellion were mere skirmishes; she had no idea how much Nick would ultimately change her.

On the night of Whitney's senior-year First Dance, for no particular reason, or perhaps for all the obvious reasons, Whitney and Tripp eventually found themselves wandering across the main quad and toward the football field. The First Dance was still going strong. As they passed the row of dorms on the main quad, they could turn around and see the backside of the student center ablaze in light, the glass walls like a crystal prism planted firmly in the ground. Whitney wasn't nervous when she asked him to go on a walk with her. It seemed like a simple request until they got to the football bleachers, sat down, and started making out. Whitney didn't need to see in the dark. She could feel Tripp's soft skin between her fingertips, first beneath his clothes and then set free in the nighttime air, just her hands and his body, no shirt, no pants, no light, instinct guiding the way.

He wanted to go down on her, but she wouldn't let him. She wasn't uncomfortable or embarrassed, like so many girls; she had supreme knowledge of her sexuality and loved having orgasms. Whitney hesitated because she wanted Nick to be the first guy to give her oral sex. She'd been doing the same to him for two years, but he'd always refused. The act, he said, was disgusting. But if he loved her, and he said he did, why didn't he want to try oral sex? Whitney was understandably confused and couldn't imagine sharing that first-time experience with anyone else.

Instead, she did what she deemed the logical next step: She reached between Tripp's legs. Giving her eyesight over to imagination, she allowed her hand to creep farther down his body, farther and farther still, until—

Whoa.

It's huge!

Enormous!

Her reaction was nothing like the first time she'd seen a penis, when she expected it to look like a water bottle, not a mushroom. This time she didn't know if she could even give Tripp head (she didn't say *oral sex* and thought *blow job* was gross), so she kept rubbing his penis with her hands. She was confident in her hand-job skills, thanks, in part, to Nick, who let her play with him like a toy whenever they lay around together, saying *Do this, do that* until she got it right.

But Whitney wanted to have sex with Tripp in the middle of all that black, concealed from the rest of the world—from Nick—indulging a momentary need. The electric blue AstroTurf track glowed in the shadows, as did the yardage markers painted on the tips of the cropped green grass. If only the night would cloak the beautiful brick back sides of the dormitories and the Old Boys' Gym, the surrounding fields spreading outward to the far ends of campus—then Whitney and Tripp would be any two teenagers about to have sex at any high school.

She knew about the locations on campus where couples had tried to have sex. The library, the snack bar after hours, dorms, random bathrooms, all of which she had tried herself. And that night, out there by the field, surrounded by the ghostly remains of football games, Whitney wanted to have sex with Tripp. She wanted him inside her, thick and encompassing, painful in that really, really good way.

She wasn't worried about getting pregnant because she was already on the pill. And she wasn't concerned about gossip because, by senior year, she didn't actually give a shit. The real problem was feeling like a slut the next day. If she and Tripp slept together, she would have to deal with Nick, and dealing with him meant either lying or facing the total number of times she had cheated on him. She knew what regret felt like (*shit*), and her go-to excuse wasn't even valid (*I was drunk!*). Whitney felt consumed by something larger than herself, something innate and overpowering: passion and all its inconveniences.

chapter four

who did you dance with?

annie **will never forget** the First Dance of her freshman year, the night her high school social life wasn't made. She wore red hot pants, a black tank top with rhinestones on the front, and chunky black loafers. She'd bought the outfit specifically for the event, the first dance of her Milton career, and when the night finally arrived, she and the other freshmen in Pryce crowded into the communal bathrooms on the fourth floor to get ready. Annie lived with over forty other girls in Pryce, and already loved the idea of being part of their family. She embraced boarding life: late nights with friends, messages left on the whiteboard outside her dorm-room door, even formal dinner, an event that occurred three times a week in the boarding community and required students to dress up and sit at tables with their dorm mates.

In the bathroom, the girls crowded in front of the mirror above the sinks, sharing advice they'd read in *Seventeen* magazine on how to do their hair and makeup. Annie spread foundation over her flushed cheeks and acne, and applied her Dr Pepper–flavored lip gloss. She'd been wearing eyeliner ever since fifth grade, but she still listened to her new friends intently. She wanted to look pretty. First impressions were important, and she hoped to attract the same level of attention at Milton that she had enjoyed at her former private school, where she was decidedly popular—desirable in all the right ways, which really meant curves and skin and sexual experience.

At the dance, Annie and her friends formed a circle, shoulder to shoulder, tight, like pearls, and when the opening beats of Britney Spears's "Baby One More Time" blasted from the speakers, they started screaming. Some girls knew the entire dance routine from Britney's video, crossing their arms and tossing their heads at just the right moments. Annie preferred Mariah Carey, her favorite singer since middle school, but she sang along with her friends, following their cues. Her blond hair went everywhere, and her starfish necklace bounced up and down above her breasts. Annie loved this sense of belonging, and this moment on display.

She instinctively understood that the First Dance was all about appearances. She took it as a sign that girls she didn't even know complimented her new tank top. They loved the rhinestones. Being part of a defined social group was also important. So were knowing the right dance moves, having the right girls in her circle, and keeping the wrong girls on the fringes. Annie may have noticed Whitney, who was dancing with her own group of girls, and she definitely noticed boys, who were everywhere. Annie looked out for the cool ones and paid attention to the girls they grinded with, shocked by the simple fact that faculty members allowed students to dance so provocatively in public. At her old school, girls and boys had to remain at least twelve inches apart.

All night long Annie waited for a boy to smile at her. Or dance with her. Or grind with her. Or ask her to go on a walk, which she would have done in a second, even had oral sex been implied. She might not have been shocked by Preston's proposal to Whitney. When would she be kissed? When would she be liked? When would she be validated? Then the first slow song came on and she was left standing there alone. Annie was appalled: She ended up in the bathroom.

Girls often flee to restrooms in droves during dances. What they do in there, and why, is just as mysterious to boys as the locker room is to girls, but it usually involves gossip, primping, and avoiding slow songs, and sometimes drinking or getting high. Annie had taken Alexa with her that night, a cheerful athlete who would later become one of the Pryce Girls. At the time, Annie was delighted she'd managed to befriend someone so cool within her first few days at Milton. Little did she know, Alexa was also on the lookout for the right clique, and was, for the moment at least, settling for friendships with girls like Annie. They were unthreatening, nice and safe, which was exactly the type of security a nervous new student might need. Of course, girls like Annie were useful only so far. Annie was antidrugs and antidrinking, which meant she could be somewhat of a dud.

Inside the bathroom, Annie and Alexa ran into a group of girls fixing their makeup as they gossiped in front of the mirror.

Ohmygod, like, so-and-so is so disgusting.

So-and-so is so hot.

Ohmygod!

On their way out, Annie saw a girl acting drunk. Upstairs at the dance, she saw another girl stumbling, surrounded by friends who tried to hold her up. Annie had also heard that there were freshmen girls sitting outside a nearby classroom sharing a bottle of alcohol they stashed in a duffel bag. *Whoa,* Annie thought to herself in big bold letters. Just a few months ago she was still in middle school, where none of her friends even thought about drinking, much less at a dance. Now it seemed like every other girl was drunk. For the moment, Annie didn't want to drink, but she wanted to be socially visible, and alcohol, she knew, was one way of getting there.

When the dance ended, Annie and her friends walked back to Pryce to check in with the dorm parent on duty. Then they flocked to the homey common room with the paintings, plants, and old lamps to relive the night.

Did you see what she was wearing?

Did you see him dancing with that junior?

They were dancing really gross.

Who did you dance with?

Annie listened in a funk, disappointed that no one had asked her to dance. She wasn't used to not having a story to share. It would've been easy to teach her friends how to give hand jobs: This is what it looks like, this is how you hold it, this is how it feels. She could have spoken calmly and deliberately, her eyes gazing upward at the dull chandelier hanging from the ceiling. Her girlfriends would have listened, because freshman year, her sexual knowledge was deemed extensive.

Annie's sexual education hadn't begun with Scott; it had begun at a party the summer after seventh grade, the moment Kenny, another older boy, asked her to go off with him in private. They found a couch and sat down, tangling their limbs until skin crushed skin. Kenny started feeling her body, her oversize breasts and stomach, under her shirt, her bra, over her pants. Annie was confused and uncomfortable. He was over six feet tall and had a muscular body, like a football player. There were expectations, she gathered, but she had no idea what she was supposed to do. Worst of all, she didn't get her first kiss.

A few days later, Annie and Kenny talked on the phone.

I think that's weird that we didn't kiss, she said quickly, as though forgetting to breathe. *I don't really want to do that. I didn't feel comfortable.*

No, I was trying to kiss you, he said.

Annie wasn't so sure.

You kept on turning away.

She listened, not knowing what to do.

Well, do you wanna go out? he asked.

I guess.

Their first kiss happened a couple of weeks later. This time Kenny was the host of the party, and everyone who was anyone in Annie's middle school was there. She looked older than her thirteen years, and her tight T-shirt accentuated that fact, calling attention to her chest, a fantasy of preteen corporeal delight. Annie loved being told she looked eighteen.

At the party, kids spiked their drinks while Kenny's parents weren't looking. Annie had never been to an alcohol party before, so she clung to her best friends, gossiping, sticking her fingers anxiously into bowls of Skittles and M&Ms.

You're gonna hook up with Kenny at this party, some of the boys said to her.

We set up a bunch of hookup spaces for you and Kenny, they went on.

There are all these different places, Kenny added, leading her to the porch.

Annie felt enormous pressure to go further than she had before, but she gave her body over to him anyway. He felt her breasts again, over and under her clothes, and she kept telling herself that what they were doing was normal.

I wanna kiss you, she finally said. *I don't want to do this without kissing.*

Kenny leaned toward her with his nacho breath and gave Annie her first kiss.

She let him take off her shirt. Then her bra. He kissed her as though engulfing her, and before she realized what was going on, he'd unzipped his pants and pulled out his penis.

What am I supposed to do? Annie wondered.

Kenny took her hand and rested it between his legs, waiting for her to begin. She stared blankly at him, then at his penis, then at Kenny again. Should she pat it? Stroke it? Squeeze it? She didn't have long to think, because a wandering classmate interrupted them. Annie was mortified. She scrambled back into her bra and shirt and followed Kenny inside, where his friends waited.

Did you guys hook up?

You definitely hooked up.

You should go hook up again.

Then one of them grabbed her butt.

Later that night, Annie hooked up with Kenny again. He unzipped her pants and tugged them down far enough so that he could jam his fingers inside her. Annie wondered if she were a different person now. Was she a woman? Did hand jobs and fingering make her older? Better? Her friends couldn't believe what she'd done. *Oh my God, you touched a guy's penis?* Their response made Annie feel good. Hooking up with Kenny was cool; now she was the one with all the experience. But it also made her feel bad; now she was the one doing the things her friends were not doing.

Sitting in the Pryce common room as a freshman after the dance, Annie could have spun these stories into an exciting tale. She could have impressed her friends and made them jealous. Until that moment, she had never known what it felt like to recede into the background, sitting with these new girls, gossiping about the First Dance where nothing, not one single thing, had happened to her.

Three years later, Annie hadn't even planned to go to the First Dance of her senior year, but Ida knocked on her door and declared that they were going to make an appearance whether Annie liked it or not. Rather than agonize over her outfit, she threw on any old pair of jeans, slipped into her sneakers, and only reapplied mascara. Outside her room, she was bombarded by younger girls trading shirts and fashion tips. Annie wasn't surprised by the provocative femininity that inspired the younger girls in the dorm that night. She read the same magazines and knew what the trends were that year: Uggs boots, short short skirts, tight tight tops, and chandelier earrings. But then she saw a usually modest and casually attired girl decked out in a low-cut tank top, heels, and glittery makeup. This, she knew, was what got a guy's attention.

Annie witnessed surreptitious sexual behavior in Pryce. If the rumors were to be believed (and she'd heard enough to know that they were), younger girls were having sex with much more frequency than when Annie was a freshman. Sneaking in, sneaking out, stifled moans from a couch in the common room when dorm parents weren't looking; it was all business as usual for some of the girls in her dorm. Annie knew her own past was promiscuous, but these girls were different. They were having sex, casually and randomly.

Where's Alexa? one once asked.

Annie shrugged her shoulders.

I need Alexa, the girl persisted. *Like, I need a condom! Where is she?*

Alexa, now one of the Pryce Girls, was one of twelve seniors in Annie's class trained to advise students on a host of issues, including drugs, alcohol, and sex. Annie shrugged her shoulders again. She tried to look nonchalant, aware that sex and sneaking out were part of some schoolmates' lives. But she couldn't believe their audacity, being so sexual at such a young age, with such careless disregard for safety, elders, or rules. How could these younger girls—these fifteen- and sixteen-year-old vixens, with their developing breasts and orthodontic retainers, their misplaced modifiers and blaring proximity to preteen life—be the ones with exciting social lives? Not necessarily the seniors. Certainly not Annie. Not ever. Or at least not at Milton.

By senior year, she was still a virgin but knew how to perform oral sex. Surely this made her a catch. Scott seemed to think so. Their relationship was still decidedly casual. Throughout the years, she gave him orgasms and he made her feel desirable—at least when it was just the two of them. In public Scott was less affectionate, but Annie assumed that most guys acted that way. Even though she and Scott had never been boyfriend-girlfriend, their relationship (if she dared call it a relationship at all) gave her the social confidence she always sought at Milton. And their occasional IM conversations made her feel like the center of someone's attention.

Scott: heyyy
Annie: hey what's up . . .

Annie: just lots of work, trying to get through senior fall

Scott: nice

Annie: umm not really

Scott: so hows your guy situation?

Annie: uhh alright

Scott: so when are we hangin out again?

Annie: not sure, maybe sometime soon

Scott: well what would you want to do?

Annie: not too sure

Scott: if i come to milton to visit, would you make it worth it?

Scott: what are the rules about guys going into your room?

Scott: what are you wearing?

Sometimes when Annie went home for vacations or weekend visits, she sneaked out of the house to see Scott at night. She'd been orchestrating the furtive meetings since the summer after sophomore year. If it was summertime, she usually wore her favorite short black skirt and low-cut black tank top—anything, really, that made her look like she was going to a dance. On nights like these her breasts were her best friends, and she strapped them into a bra that matched her thong, like the blue-and-gray leopard-print set she'd bought from Victoria's Secret.

Her primping marathon occurred in secret, after she'd brushed her teeth and put on pajamas, while her parents went to bed. Once midnight passed, Annie tiptoed down the carpeted back stairs and trekked through the kitchen. She always thought about writing a note, but what would she say? *Mom and Dad, it's 2:00 in the morning and I'm going out.* She grabbed her cell phone instead, just in case they called, examined her carefully covered acne in the mirror, and then quietly slipped outside.

Scott was usually waiting for her in his boxy, light blue car that reminded Annie of an old grandfather. Nearly every time she opened the passenger-side door and peered inside, there was Scott, unremarkable, oversexed, and unshaven, wearing cargo shorts and a ratty T-shirt. He didn't look like he belonged with a girl like Annie, and what was worse, he didn't even know how to fake it.

The moment Annie sat in Scott's car, she made herself sexually available to him without making him work hard. Sometimes he reached for her hand as he drove, but usually he just ignored her, knowing that Annie would hook up with him, bad breath or not. The premise of the late-night trysts was clearly one dimensional, but Annie always sought a connection, and, like so many girls her age, she thought that pleasing Scott was the way to make him her boyfriend.

Their most romantic hookup had taken place the summer before her senior year, when they'd tumbled in the grass between fleece blankets, groping each other's bodies.

This is fun and nice, she thought to herself.

It's the summer.

I'm sneaking out, and it's exciting.

Maybe I'll like him.

She gave Scott head, hoping to find out.

A few weeks later they were kissing in her family's living room, where she usually played Monopoly and spent time with her family.

I really want to see you naked, Scott said suddenly. *Can we turn the lights on?*

Absolutely not, Annie said.

Stand up, Scott said again. *I want to see you naked.*

No.

Turn on the lights, he said.

Absolutely not.

Stand in the light.

This was getting weird. Annie wished she'd taken more shots of Irish whiskey, as she sometimes did before her late-night visits with Scott. Eventually she did stand up, but not because she loved how she looked. Her thighs seemed enormous compared with the girls' legs she saw in magazines. Pores swelled into soft round bumps on her face, and her stomach wasn't what she wanted.

Do you want to have sex? Scott asked.

Annie contemplated the question. She'd been thinking about losing her virginity for what seemed like forever, but she never knew how—or if—she'd follow through when the opportunity presented itself. Would she lie on her back? Sit up? Would it hurt? Would she have to be in love? Would she be so casual about it, like some of the sophomores in Pryce? Would she have to fake an orgasm?

We've hooked up a lot before, Scott tried, relentless.

Do you even have a condom? Annie asked, still completely naked.

I could go get one.

No, she decided. *I don't want it to be like that.*

So they continued hooking up.

Ohmygosh! Annie suddenly thought.

There was something huge inside her. Something bigger than a finger. Then she realized: Scott had slipped his penis inside her. She thought she'd told him no. She'd definitely told him no! Was this force? Was this consent? Was this rape? What was going on?

It was just two fingers, he protested.

No it wasn't, she said.

Well, you know, I just wanted to have sex, Scott said.

Annie didn't know what to do. Could she stop the hookup? Would Scott be upset? Was it just two fingers? How could she walk away from this situation? Ultimately she didn't; she gave him a hand job instead, and then waited as he used his T-shirt to wipe himself off.

Okay. I'm going to leave, Scott said.

Yeah, that's fine, Annie said.

Can I go wash my hands?

Yeah.

She followed him to the kitchen and watched as he stood before her, shirtless, his T-shirt crumpled in a sticky ball. He washed his hands at the sink her parents used to clean the dishes, dried them quickly, and pulled his shirt over his head. And then, just as quickly as he'd come, he left.

Annie stood there alone, silent, caught somewhere between girlhood and womanhood. She didn't even know if she was a legitimate virgin anymore. *This is the last straw,* she said to herself, really believing it that time.

When Annie walked into the First Dance senior year, the student center was seething with sweaty students, all those younger girls in short skirts or low-cut tank tops, exposing various body parts, clamoring for attention. She watched girls and guys making out. Some freshmen girls were noticeably drunk, but Annie was no longer surprised. She'd quickly learned that a handful of freshmen invariably showed up wasted at school events, at least during the first semester.

Looking around, she came to the same conclusion she reached nearly every single day: She would remain eternally single. Standing with Ida, Annie was grateful she hadn't invited Scott to the dance. It would have been humiliating and pointless, but going to the First Dance alone was depressing as well. Here was the other side of Annie. That bright, hopeful young girl who looked out for her friends, adored her school, and couldn't wait to be a senior was still there, but every so often the frustrations of her social life came crashing down. The dance was as disappointing as she'd expected, and she feared she would remain exactly what she thought she'd always been to everyone else—mediocre.

The only glimmer of hope came in the form of a conversation she had with Cush, Reed's friend and fellow hockey player. Annie had heard plenty of girls talk about him before: *Oh, Cushman, he's so hot, too bad he's taken.* Yet Annie saw him as the kind of boy who was different from the hockey guys. He actually smiled at her with his dimples and said hi to her, rather than simply staring straight ahead as though she didn't exist. Annie had a tendency to mistake casual exchanges between acquaintances as something more. She'd had little experience talking with guys, and the intimacies of friendship she shared with her girlfriends never translated to her relationships with guys. The idea that they might actually admire and respect her was so alien and unimaginable that she once mistook one of her only guy friends for a crush simply because he gave her attention.

Not long before the First Dance, Annie had heard a rumor that Cush and his longtime girlfriend, Ava, had broken up. As Annie chatted with him in the student center, yelling above the music about their respective dorms, she wondered what it would be like to slow dance with him. The moment would have been the ultimate social validation, so public and yet so intimate, broadcasting her desire. She knew what dancing with a guy felt like: his arms draped around her waist, fingers stroking in small circles; their bodies so close she could feel the wet heat from his neck, his chest muscles pressing; his smell, like soap and deodorant, so potent she could almost taste it. But she knew it would have been an odd request coming from Cush. He existed on her radar in the same way that the other jocks did: They were *the* boys to know who never gave her a chance.

And so after a few minutes of casual chitchat, Annie and Cush returned to their friends. Roughly thirty minutes after she'd arrived at the First Dance, Annie was on her way home. When she and Ida got back to Pryce, they hung out until all the younger girls returned to gossip about the evening's events. As the underclassmen trickled in, they looked at Annie with shock, totally mystified as to why anyone would voluntarily leave the dance early. Annie remembered having the same reaction when she was a freshman, when she didn't yet understand what she knew now—that school events like the First Dance were really enjoyed only by underclassmen and senior guys trolling for younger girls.

This time, like that first time, she didn't have a single male prospect to report back on. Years had passed since the porch incident with Kenny, and Scott had long since replaced him in the forefront of Annie's mind. Still, her social successes in middle school with both boys informed her attitude toward guys. She learned at an early age that sexual performance, especially a good one, often brought rewards, especially attention from the boys she wanted to like her back. But at Milton, guys like Cush were the fantasy; Scott remained her reality.

chapter five

keep walkin'

Each school day, just after ten o'clock, a bell rang in the academic buildings at the end of second period, signaling the beginning of recess. Students streamed out of classrooms, heading toward the student center in one gigantic flood of teenage movement. Recess was only fifteen minutes long, a quick break between morning classes, but that was plenty of time for everything important to happen. Crushes, gossip, midmorning snacks, copying someone else's homework, the guy a girl liked who didn't like her back, the right shoes, the wrong answer to question five, the stomachache a boarder had from the caffeine pills she took, the orgasm a girl planned to have that afternoon on the third floor of the school library—it all converged at once.

For some Milton students, including Annie, recess was the most daunting moment of the day, especially after a big weekend event. Mondays were known for gossip, when everyone discussed everything that had happened, "everyone" being the DSGs and the jocks, "everything" being who hooked up with whom and how far they went. Sometimes the stories trickled down to every clique, until even random kids knew that, for example, Whitney and Tripp had hooked up at the bleachers during the First Dance. As if recess wasn't stressful enough, the student center was literally an enormous transparent fishbowl.

A couple of weeks had gone by since Senior Walk In, and already the campus looked like fall, the leaves on trees shaking in the crisp air. Outside the main entrance on Centre Street, amid the still life of shrubbery and sapling trees shooting out from between the cracks in the courtyard's patio, Annie prepared for recess. She paused to consider her outfit: khaki skirt, black, short-sleeved polo, small pearl earrings, cute flip-flops, and a pink-and-black Hervé Chapelier bag big enough to hold her flute. The nylon tote was especially crucial, because Annie thought everyone at Milton carried designer bags. Her mom said that $90 was too much to spend on a bag, but when Annie went to Europe, she did just that.

The whole point of having an Hervé was to look like a DSG. Annie spent the first three years of high school watching these teenage beauty queens. She was enamored for other reasons, too: DSGs drove cars her own father would never buy for himself, and befriended and dated the popular boys. She heard about weekends spent in various day students' basements, lips to beer cans and then lips to lips, making out, having sex, and experimenting just because they could.

The summer before senior year, Annie decided she would start dressing up for class. In an effort to distance herself from those boarders who wore sweatpants and pajamas each day, she collected brightly colored polo tops, bought a patterned Lilly Pulitzer skirt, and begged her parents for a pair of Ugg boots (the answer was no). She upgraded her pharmacy makeup to Lancôme. On those rare mornings when she had extra time, she straightened her wavy hair. Annie did everything she could to re-create a popular girl's appearance. Having the right look was one way she convinced herself that she had control over her social destiny. Time would tell, and she was hopeful.

Annie took a few steps toward the entrance to the student center, steadying herself for that chaos where everyone, even Annie, was a player in the fifteen-minute weekday social ritual. Had she followed a different path in high school, she might not have felt so homeless at recess. She couldn't undo the past, so she contemplated how to survive, which invariably involved fleeing the scene to hide out in the library until class. Still, September marked a brand-new start. She could sense possibility, the calm before the storm that was her senior year. And so she pushed open the glass doors and walked into that adolescent zoo, daring herself to be brave.

Just past the glass doors, Annie merged into the recess crowd waiting to pick up the *Milton Paper,* not to be confused with its rival, the *Milton Measure,* which came out twice a month. Annie snapped up a *Paper* and freed herself from the mob, walking into the scene she knew by heart. DSGs; jocks; the so-called Minority Corner; the soccer team; the crunchy, dorky, or artsy kids—everyone had a place, except Annie. She never felt this isolation more than when she was on the first floor of the student center, which was literally a who's who of Milton's social elite, so obvious and definable that later that year, even the *Milton Measure,* with its typical mocking humor, would print a diagram of the building, revealing which cliques hung out where.

To the left of the entrance, the DSGs sat with their thin, designer-clothing-clad legs lined up in a row, flip-flops or New Balance sneakers crossed over each other. Whitney sat in her short skirt and short-sleeved polo to match. Her hair was razor straight, and she flipped it occasionally with her hand. As one of Milton's anointed social mavens, she adored recess and loved sitting there, back straight, legs crossed, all eyes on her. Whitney wore flawless makeup and knew she looked good. Her best friend, a beachy blonde, true trophy-wife material, looked even better. The two girls huddled together on the couch, making room for a couple of friends—one a sensual beauty with dark hair and exotic features, another the quintessential WASP with a pearl necklace.

The group was busy playing one of their favorite games, watching kids enter the student center and guessing where they would go.

They're gonna to go to the right side, over to the back.

They're gonna go downstairs.

They're gonna go downstairs to the left.

Downstairs, by the—

What's it called?

The foosball table.

Whitney also watched teachers and administrators walk by. Most kept to themselves, offering the occasional hello as they passed from Warren to Wigg, but a few befriended certain students, and made a pastime of socializing with the popular kids, keeping tabs on who dated who and what had happened the weekend before. Other adults had no problem playing the disciplinarian. *Language, please!* the dean of students once barked at Whitney.

The student center was meant to be an impressive addition to campus, and it was, with its multiple lounges, computer areas, flat-screen TV, snack bar, and bookstore. As the centerpiece of Doc Robs's blue print for the future of Milton, the student center displayed affluence and prestige in new and obvious ways. The cathedral ceiling and white or windowed walls lent an appearance of openness, cleanliness, and clarity. Yet book bags, paper, and trash adulterated the space. The boxy leather couches looked as if they'd been stolen from a dentist's office, and everything felt dirty and claustrophobic, like an overused family basement run by teenage children. Before the student center opened in 2003, decades of Milton students spent recess and free periods in the academic buildings—each class to a different homeroom. One was old and cavernous, with rows of wooden desks bolted to the floor. Another was a grand semicircular space with two sets of double doors. But the student center displaced these hang-out spots, leaving them to their next lives as renovated classrooms and formal lecture halls. The way many students saw it, replacing these coveted rooms was just another on the list of traditions that Doc Robs wiped away. Beloved Senior Dog

Day and Senior Cut Day were both gone by the end of the year as well.

Every day at recess, Whitney and her friends, along with the jocks nearby and the young DSGs encroaching on the right, controlled the first floor in the student center. The senior DSGs sat at the round tables or on the couches near the computers, and knew how to behave in the spotlight. There is an innate, subconscious awareness among popular girls, and the DSGs knew that recess was the time to be seen. No matter who you were or how much attention you craved, there was always that spotlight moment when someone else was paying attention.

Whitney didn't realize that had she been at Milton a decade earlier, she might not have been called a DSG. The phrase originally referred to a group of studious, hardworking day-student girls in the mid-90s. Partying, drinking, and hooking up were antithetical to the clique's social identity. These girls excelled in academics, music, and sports, and most went off to Ivy League schools. Then the popular senior girls in the late 1990s adopted the title as their own. Like most Milton students, they were a talented bunch, with all the appropriate passions and honors one might expect. But they were also cool, so the phrase DSG took on new meaning. Over time, DSGs gained notoriety for their looks and social lives, and seemed to attend fewer Ivy League schools.

While some young DSGs flirted with the senior jocks, others sat on top of the cubbies to the right of the main entrance. It was their silver-medaled spot, where they practiced being seen until they, too, became those senior girls. Whitney was friendly with some of the young DSGs. They were nice girls. Pretty, too. Some were known for providing certain guys with the bodies they needed to create their legendary stories. Others attended Caitlin Lane's notorious basement parties with Brady, Reed, and other senior jocks. Whitney heard about their exploits.

Ohmygod, you'll never believe what I did this weekend, one of the younger girls would say to her. *I got so drunk and—*

Whitney would sit with her shoulders back, listening to this latest story about a threesome, the Dub Saw (when two boys penetrate a girl simultaneously, one in her vagina and one in her anus), or the Eiffel Tower (when a girl performs oral sex on one boy and simultaneously receives vaginal or anal sex from another boy, while the guys slap hands above her, forming the famous French point). Whitney knew all about the backstabbing and jealous rants that occasionally went on among the young DSGs, especially when Brady was involved. Come recess, the girls were usually well behaved, as though guys weren't a factor in their friendship, the point around which their public and private lives turned. Whitney, for one, prided herself on the fact that she'd never been involved in one of the hockey boys' stories. She couldn't even say *Dub Saw* and *Eiffel Tower* out loud without blushing. *I would never go out with a guy like that,* she always said. *Nick has his problems, but he isn't like, sick and dirty.*

Whitney readily admitted that being a DSG wasn't always easy. Pressure to dress well and be thin was constant, and judgments and rumors about them ran rampant. The girls were snobs, spoiled, rich, and dumb. They'd bought their way into Milton. They were mean. They were sluts. Whitney wasn't stupid or rich. There was a lot more to her and her friends than fashion, hair, and hookups, and it was a lot harder to be popular than most students believed. Besides, she insists that she and her friends didn't fit the stereotypical DSG mold. They weren't as ditzy, catty, and materialistic as DSGs in other grades, and many of their classmates agreed.

Whitney didn't have many non-DSG friends at Milton. Any unpopular or less attractive friends she had were from years of figure skating. Her coach worked with about a dozen other skaters, and not all of them were as pretty, tall, and thin as Whitney. At training camp one summer, her roommate was an unattractive girl who wore black clothes and dark makeup. They became friends despite their differences, and one night, while they lay in their beds eating chocolate, they realized just how many obstacles their friendship had overcome.

If you were at my high school, the girl said, *and we'd never met each other at practice, I would have hated you.*

You don't hate me, Whitney thought. *You love me. We get along so well.*

But she knew her roommate was right. Spending time with her skating friends stripped Whitney of her social prestige. Though figure skating was often stereotyped as a glamorous sport for thin beauties, ability was equally as important, and Whitney was just another skater trying to nail her triple lutz. She may have been one of the few girls who hadn't been homeschooled, but she, too, endured the weekly weigh-ins at her club, where her coach knew in a second if she'd been eating candy and cookies on the side.

At Milton, Whitney was known primarily for being two things: a DSG and an amazing athlete. Figure skating was going to get her into college. Few schools had clubs, and even those that did rarely recruited skaters as they did soccer, football, and tennis players. But there were a number of schools that had clubs she liked. Most important, college coaches wanted her. Whitney believed her sacrifices for skating were equally as important as those made by students who dedicated countless hours to studying for straight As. Though she was a DSG, she was also an exception, and not just because she bought designer jeans with her own money and carried a tote bag from the Gap (like Annie, her mother would never have bought her an Hervé). Whitney was known as the friend who could never hang out on the weekends; skating came first and then came Nick, leaving little time for parties. She also worked harder in school than her peers realized. Each night her routine was the same: practice, dinner, study, bed; practice, dinner, study, bed. She was proud of her work ethic, even if it wasn't her top priority.

At recess, Whitney wasn't thinking about practice and she certainly wasn't worried about college. She leaned back on the couch and wondered what would happen to her and Tripp. They hadn't hooked up since the night of the First Dance, but they hung out constantly. She didn't care what other people thought, because they would invariably draw their own conclusions. Even when Whitney didn't tell her friends all her news, they found out from each other, IMing over the weekend, saying, *Oh, we heard about the bleacher incident.* Whitney expected Tripp to blab, too. He was a boy who didn't owe her anything. She didn't mind that her social life sometimes became public knowledge. There were bigger things to think about: deciding what to do about Tripp, Nick, and college.

One of Josh's friends straightened the collar on his varsity basketball jacket and said he was going to hang out with the DSGs. Josh rolled his eyes. He would never have walked up to the popular girls in the middle of recess. Talking with one of them was intimidating enough, but having to entertain the entire clique? No thank you. Josh didn't realize that his friend usually sat there gossiping or helped them check out fancy dresses online. Josh and the rest of his buddies stood less than twenty feet away, shooting the shit to pass the time.

Who was that girl singing a cappella this morning? She looked real good.

Good luck, I already tried it and she wasn't feelin' it.

When was that?

Two weekends ago at the Hanley open house. I was chillin' with her on Joe's bed and people kept walking in and out. All of a sudden she said she had to leave. I guess all of the commotion freaked her out or something.

Was it all of the commotion or the fact that you tried to fomp the domp again without warning?

"Fomp the domp" was one of the guys' made-up expressions for fingering a girl over her pants, which was, in their world, a real sexual act. Some of them had significantly more luck and experience than Josh did, and some of them, he assumed, lied about losing their virginity. If pressed, Josh lied, too: *It was the end of last summer with a girl from home.* Josh understood what oftentimes happened. If you've done it, you talk about it, and if you haven't, you pretend you have and talk about it even more.

Josh was easy to miss at recess. He may have been 6 feet 2, with size 13 feet, but he looked like all the other guys around him who sported conventional crew cuts and warm-up jackets zipped halfway. He and the basketball guys hung out toward the back of the first floor, not far from the DSGs and hockey jocks, but there were differences between the two groups of guys. Basketball players were like tennis and soccer players: B-level guys who Whitney assumed were chill and funny, and smoked weed. Her beliefs were based mostly on hearsay (Josh rarely smoked or drank), but even he understood the differences between himself and guys like Brady. Every day at recess, Josh watched his high school fantasies unfold before his eyes, where the male leads were given not to him but to more popular jocks.

Brady, Reed, and the rest of their friends usually spent recess hanging over the railing above the stairs that led down to the lower level. There wasn't a more public location in the student center, and walking past that line of muscles and masculinity was never easy. The guys were the proverbial construction workers, watching with varying levels of amusement, criticism, or lust as girls and boys traipsed up and down the stairs. Like the DSGs, they, too, played games.

First one of the guys threw out a number: She's an eight or she's a ten.

Then someone contested the rating, because tens were reserved for the most beautiful girl they'd ever seen, and nines were rare.

That girl's an eight?

You sure?

Fuck off.

Okay, so he was sure.

The debate ended quickly, because girls walked by constantly.

Wow, one of them said.

Pig, another croaked.

She's girlfriend material.

That's a girl you'd marry.

Keep walkin'.

Get outta here.

Jillian knew about guys who rated girls with letters, as if they were tests or papers. Such blatant sexism wasn't supposed to exist at Milton. If Milton girls were truly some of the finest emerging intellectuals and leaders, how could they stand quietly by as guys reduced them to letters based solely on looks? In the past, all-school discussions had been held in the face of racism and religious hatred. But when Jillian and a few friends complained to a teacher about the guys at recess, she was shocked when the same standards didn't apply to sexism.

Walking downstairs was the most nerve-racking part of recess for Annie. Each day she would squeeze her Hervé a little harder, look down at her feet, and wait for the guys' jeans and warm-up pants to recede with every step she took downstairs. Annie wondered what they were saying about her, and actually thought about the jocks more than she liked to admit. Sometimes she wondered what it would be like to be a popular guy's "friend with benefits." She wanted an actual boyfriend, but she tried to be realistic.

Once Annie reached the bottom of the student center staircase, she breathed a sigh of relief. The lower level was always an easier place to be. Tall tables lined the perimeter, pushed up against windows that overlooked the main quad. Behind her was the foosball table, and past that was a hallway leading to various student organization offices. The seniors-only TV lounge was to her right, a dimly lit rectangular space that felt cramped even with its three semiopen walls. The *Milton Measure* dubbed the room the Cave, and referred to all its inhabitants as Cave Dwellers. At recess, the line to the snack bar snaked past the TV lounge, because ten o'clock in the morning was never too early for curly fries, a warm chocolate chip cookie, or an egg sandwich.

Annie couldn't find Ida anywhere. She saw an underclassman from her dorm and waved; it was one of her favorite parts about becoming a senior in Pryce—the friendships she could forge with younger students, stripped of intimidation, accented by admiration, someone older leading the way for someone younger. But there were the Pryce Girls, hanging out with a group of guy boarders in the Cave. Annie said hi and the girls said hi back, unaware that behind

Annie's smile was a desire for recognition. She kept walking around the lower level, wondering where Ida could be. Maybe she was in the snack bar. Or the bookstore. Or the bathroom. Annie clutched her pink-and-black Hervé bag, checked to make sure her flute was secure, and walked tall, pointing her chin up in the air, trying to look as confident as the DSGs.

Inside the Cave, Jillian had her nose in her notebook scribbling ideas for her first *Paper* article of the year. She twirled her pen in her light brown hair, which was crimped from sleeping on braids the night before, and half listened to her girlfriends' chitchat.

Phoebe, Caroline said. *Are you staring at your boyfriend again?*

He's not my boyfriend, Phoebe contested, laughing and trying to play it cool as she quickly turned her attention away from the boy sitting in a corner of the Cave and toward a strand of her hair tangled up in one of her beaded chandelier earrings. Phoebe was the bubbliest of her friends, spoke a mile a minute, and had the biggest heart.

You're totally looking at your boyfriend! another girl said.

Stop, Phoebe said, scrunching up her face as she yanked her earlobe. She was still laughing, but hoped her friends wouldn't start teasing her about her latest crush.

He's your boyfriend! You guys totally banged! Caroline squealed.

Stop, he can't hear that! Phoebe said, talking louder than she intended.

Jillian tried to block out the noise. She needed an article topic because there was a lot of work ahead of her if she wanted to take her post on the editorial board seriously. The *Paper* was a significant part of her life at school; each week she spent at least ten hours holed up in the office, shoulders hunched over one of the computers, editing articles or brainstorming new angles for the weekly editorial. Her best contributions came as smart reviews of television shows and movies, and impassioned editorials about topics like sexism and apathy.

She had a real command of language and an unconventional way of describing the most mundane observations. But writing was more than something she just happened to do well. Jillian was herself when she wrote. Reading her poetry aloud in creative writing class or writing a controversial opinion article were not daunting to her. Writing was her emotional armor. This bravery was part of her carefully crafted image, yet behind the facade, when Jillian stepped away from the computer, refastened her hair, and became a student again, this impressive, confident, opinionated young woman turned into a shy, insecure girl.

Jillian sought refuge in the *Paper* office whenever she had free time. Surrounded by old *Paper* archives, copies of the *Onion*, posters of Bob Dylan, and anti-Bush slogans, she nestled into a faded old couch and wrote. If she walked in on a couple making out, she'd go to the student center instead to take notes in her journal, using words like *mercurial* and *reductive* to indulge in her latest rant. She always carried three books with her—a light read, a serious read, and a short-term commitment, like a collection of poetry or essays—because she never knew what kind of mood she'd be in. She worshipped Joan Didion and Philip Roth, and justified her love of *The Great Gatsby* by the fact that she'd read it nearly a dozen times. She liked DeLillo, Updike, and Atwood, and made a point of disliking Vonnegut, Morrison, and Sedaris. Her father believed that if she was going to be a serious writer, she should sit down and actually do it—write a book—not just read them all the time. To him, writing was like playing sports; if she was going to play tennis, she should play to win, so that when she grew up and got a job, she could play with her bosses and get the inside track. Jillian idolized her father, but she didn't want to work for bosses and climb a corporate ladder. She wanted to write—without pressure and for herself.

If she couldn't have a boyfriend senior year—and she was convinced she'd never have one—Jillian wanted to do exceptionally well in school. She was already a star in her English classes and on the *Paper* board, and in this respect she was exactly what she'd hoped she'd become when she first got to Milton—a senior voice that students not only knew but respected. But students were recruited to college for reasons that had nothing to do with their intelligence, like hockey and family connections. So she planned to study more than she ever had before, because getting into the right college was going to make her feel so much better than any guy ever could. She told herself she would branch out and make new girlfriends. She already had Isabel, whom Jillian admired for her wry sense of humor. Isabel respected Jillian for her brutal honesty, but the two girls annoyed each other, as well. Isabel was obsessive about guys, and Jillian was flighty and changed best friends every week.

Isabel's observation was partially true; Jillian spent much of her life trying to figure out where she stood on the ladder of teenage popularity, and couldn't believe that Caroline, who sat in the Cave beaming with genuine happiness, had everything without being a DSG. Her dimples were almost permanently implanted in her cheeks and her naturally blond hair (another perfection) was pulled back in a neat low ponytail. Caroline's academic record was flawless: The SAT was in October and she had a tutor; her early decision application to her top Ivy League school was due in November and she had visited twenty-three colleges that summer; her already impressive grades were about to get even better. She marched around as though giggling to herself, unfazed that girls might have been judging her outfit (jeans and a sweater from the Gap, circa 2000) and jocks might have been rating her appearance as she walked down to the lower level. By senior year, Caroline knew that she was a rarity in her class, a girl filled with certainty, empowered in her own right. Sometimes she wondered how she'd gotten so lucky.

This was the same girl Jillian had taught how to be feminine when they were close childhood friends. Jillian loved being the expert. She showed Caroline how to lick her eyeliner, took her to Clinique to buy makeup, and instigated Caroline's first professional haircut, a layered look she wore even a year after graduation. It worked well for Caroline, but what she probably didn't know was that behind Jillian's friendly advice in middle school was a desperate cry for help. At the time, Jillian put on three coats of brown mascara, white eye shadow, pink blush, and cherry Chapstick. She wore perfume and nail polish. She starved herself. She did everything she could to look like "a pretty girl." Now, in different clothes, in a different world, Jillian vowed not to focus on what she saw in the mirror. Senior year would be about academics and extracurriculars. Tucked away in a corner of the Cave, in the lower level of the student center, Jillian wrote in her notebook and tried to shut everything else out.

Isabel scanned the boys hanging out in the Cave, sighing when she didn't find anyone worth looking at. She tucked a short strand of red hair behind her ear, dropped her shoulders, and began to pout. Recess was just another reminder that she couldn't get a guy. If her twin sister— who looked and sounded exactly like her, with the same ghostly skin and smart comebacks—had a boyfriend at Exeter, why couldn't she find one at Milton? Isabel was willing to hook up, randomly or consistently. She'd started kissing boys in sixth grade, when all she had to do was roll the sex dice and follow their instructions:

Massage lips.

Suck neck.

Lick nipples.

Okay, so she didn't let anyone lick her nipples, but later, in eighth grade, a friend dared Isabel to give a guy a hand job while they watched a movie with their boyfriends. Most of her friends had never gone that far, but Isabel reached under the blanket and rested her hand on her boyfriend's crotch, nervous yet excited, feeling slutty the entire time. She'd barely had any contact with guys since then, save for a kiss here and there with an old friend from her hometown. As a senior, she wanted to shed her uptight, girlcentric image. But she no longer had a guy outside school and wasn't invited to the parties Whitney turned down. How was she supposed to get ass—pick a guy from class? In the darkroom while making prints for the yearbook?

Actually, art history had already given her an unexpected idea. On the first day of class, as she sat at the Harkness table waiting for her teacher to begin, Reed sauntered through the door. Was he lost? Isabel didn't need to whisper a word to Jillian, who was sitting right there, because she was probably thinking the same thing. Surely this was a mistake; surely Reed wasn't actually taking their serious upper-level class. He must have been in the wrong room. But he grabbed a seat and tossed his bag on the floor, quite aware of the commotion he'd just caused.

To Isabel, Reed had been reduced to a mere caricature: the dumb hockey jock. Classes often threw the most unlikely students together, but Reed was part of the upstairs recess world to which she did not belong. He hung out with the DSGs, who Isabel thought took "stupid" English classes and cared more about straightening their hair than reading books. Aside from being unintelligent, she believed the DSGs were skanky and dirty—and she did not mean it as a generalization. Isabel assumed they passed themselves among the sports teams like water bottles at the games. Despite her overwhelming desire to be promiscuous, she looked down on the DSGs for their sexual reputations.

At recess, she and her friends dissected the young DSGs whenever they walked by the Cave.

They are so like, prepubescent and little, a friend began.

But so pretty, Jillian added.

They are pretty, the friend agreed. *They all just pile into the back of Brady's Volvo. And you can tell that they . . . think they're so cool. They're, like, hoping that people are gonna be looking at them.*

Do you remember junior year? Jillian asked. *There were actually, like, fights over Brady. People would start crying . . . They're not, like, the sharpest tools in the shed, but they're great girls. Really talented . . .*

And they could have, like, so many cuter guys in our grade, Caroline added.

But he just has some sort of aura about him, their friend said. *He is an asshole. That's the aura.*

He thinks he rules the school, Phoebe said quickly. *Everyone else does.*

And I guess that's why: 'Cause he thinks he rules the school, everyone else does, too.

The girls knew about the times when Brady showed up at parties, knocked on the door, and barged right in. Behind him stood a harem of young DSGs, fresh out of the Volvo wagon, made up, bright-eyed, smiling as if they were the lucky ones. Isabel and her friends heard about times when Brady hid empty beer cans in random places at a party so that the host's parents would stumble upon them one day in the china cabinet or microwave. Sometimes he got rowdy and made a scene. But sometimes Isabel or Annie or perhaps even Jillian looked at him and wondered what it would have been like to be his friend or girl-friend or one of his crew.

After a couple of weeks in art history class, Isabel realized that Reed was not Brady. Reed was witty and surprisingly smart. He participated in class, had intelligent ideas, and truly defied the hockey-player stereo-type. The first time they met, he extended his arm and shook her hand lightly: *Hi, nice to meet you, I'm Reed.* It was an uncommon gesture. Usually guys said hey or offered a token head nod. Handshakes were reserved for her parents' friends. Since then, their interactions had been almost nonexistent. Sometimes she wondered if Reed noticed her sitting across the table, making jokes with Jillian. Isabel knew it would be a futile effort to let herself like him, but she did like him, and be-sides, her crush was harmless precisely because she knew it wouldn't lead to anything.

This time, just for fun, she let herself think about the ungettable guy.

Upstairs, Whitney made the most of the final few minutes of re-cess by ripping on flagrant PDA (public displays of affection) violators. Whenever Whitney and Nick were together, they recognized that there was a distinct line between acceptable public and private conduct. She and Tripp behaved differently, and though a couple of weeks had passed since the First Dance, she felt like everyone at recess knew about them.

The truth (that she only gave him a hand job) didn't matter as much as what their absence from the dance suggested (that they had sex).

In some ways it didn't matter what she told Nick, because they always ended up back together. Despite their on-again, off-again status, everyone knew they were in love. In the meantime, while they were off, Whitney turned to the DSGs. There was such comfort in their shared beauty and popularity. And so she slung her tote bag over her shoulder, adjusted her skirt, and scampered with her friends toward the door, confident, blending into that pulse of crisp collars, sparkling Tiffany, and teenage semicertainty.

As the clock wound closer to 10:20 A.M., students grabbed their bags and backpacks and joined the flight to class. On the lower level, Annie headed toward the back entrance. She was still alone, and in moments like these, when everyone around her seemed to ignore her, she thought of Scott. Just the other day, completely unexpectedly, he'd told Annie that he loved her. He didn't say it in person or over the phone. Not even in an e-mail. Instead, he'd told her in an instant message. And he abbreviated it: *lyl,* for love you lots.

Scott: sup
Annie: not much, stressed, you?
Scott: nm, how was the day
Annie: stressful, just got back from like 5 meetings.
Scott: From what?
Annie: house stuff, etc.
Scott: I'm sorry.
Annie: It's ok.
Scott: lyl
Annie: ☺

He loved her. So Scott had said it, and to Annie, that counted. She never forgot that moment, when she glimpsed a different future for herself, one with a boyfriend, emotions, I love you, I can't wait to see you.

Yet deep down, she understood what he really meant: I like you because I know you already like me back. Because I know that whenever you come home you'll hook up with me. Because I know I don't have to work hard to get you. Of course she wanted him to work hard. She wanted to be courted with phone calls and visits and flowers on her birthday. She wanted to feel loved. For the moment, though, *lyl* was enough. A step in the right direction, and an exciting change from her normal routine—class, a crush from afar, flute lesson, another crush from afar, meetings, homework, and flute practice, a crush from afar.

When Annie stepped outside, the fall air was cool and refreshing, a fleeting rebirth. For once, time, identity, and popularity were suspended, her confidence rising inside her again. Annie stood there and thought of Scott, feeling, at last and momentarily, a little better.

chapter six

give me knowledge

Oh my god, Brady said, slowly, drawing out each sylla-ble, not like a girl—ohmygod!—but like a guy who had enough experience to know when a story was impressive or not. He could have been sitting in the middle of one of the long, rectangular tables in Forbes dining hall, and it could have been lunchtime during the fall semester, because Reed had just told him about a guy they both knew. The guy was having sex with a girl in his car when he got caught by the girl's father, stepped out of the car, said, Hi, nice to meet you, and shook the man's hand. With the half-used condom still dangling.

Brady chuckled to himself, this time exactly like a girl, his laugh high-pitched and delicate. He lifted his chicken patty sandwich with both hands, leaned forward, and took a monstrous bite. Reed sat at the table with him and stared down at his lunch tray, which showcased a peanut butter and jelly sandwich, that day's hot meal, and eight cups of water. He lifted a glass and threw the water back, not paying attention to the teach-ers and students walking by, making their way to their own tables.

Just steps away from Brady and Reed, the bustling lunchroom was in full gear. The scene looked much like any other high school lunch period, except for the fact that Forbes was no ordinary high school cafeteria. There was a hot-food counter, a sandwich bar, a salad bar, a panini station, a soup station, bagels, and vegan and vegetarian options. The frozen yogurt machine and dessert bar were welcomed indulgences. Located on the main quad, Forbes dining hall was more like the private dining room of an exclusive club. The room reflected Milton's tradition of understated elegance with its high ceilings, cream-colored walls, and wood paneling. Soft natural light filled the room and the tables were often decorated with fresh flowers and glass salt and pepper shakers. The best part (at least for the guys) was that food was included in tuition; they could eat as much as they wanted.

Lunch wasn't long. Sometimes students had only twenty-five minutes squeezed between classes, but there was always time for intimidation. The wood tables were like rungs on the ladder of teenage popularity; knowing where you did and did not belong was an essential component of survival. The popular kids strut in like they own the place, reminding everyone (or at least whoever's paying attention) that being cool matters. Cliques like the DSGs and the Pryce Girls traveled through the dining hall in packs, congregating, herdlike, by a food station or table. Were they discussing what to eat? What not to eat? Were they talking about class? Were they sharing secrets about the mousy girl by the exit?

A girl like Annie observed these cliques curiously, from a side table or on her way out the door, watching them whisper about something she wouldn't ever get to hear. For Annie, eating lunch was a test of strategy, luck, and fear. Descending the short staircase inside Forbes left just enough time to contemplate what she should do. Ideally she'd find her best friends, though an acquaintance would do—anyone, really, whose table she could join. If she didn't know anyone during that lunch period, she'd get something to go and bolt. It took only a few minutes to walk from Forbes to the library, and she could either eat on the way or hide in a study carrel and eat quietly.

That day, like most other days, Brady, Reed, and the rest of their friends were being exclusive. If it was a Friday, the football guys would have been wearing their orange-and-blue football jerseys. If it was any game day, the fall athletes would have been wearing some sort of uniform team attire, like shirts and ties for an away game. As if their position above the student center stairs during recess wasn't enough, Brady, Reed, and their friends created an elite lunchroom table with a prime location. Brady drafted a list of assigned seats for over a dozen guy friends, all hockey and football players. He reserved the four best seats, located in the middle, for Reed, Church, another buddy, and himself.

Reed liked being singled out at the guys' lunchroom table. He didn't know which was better, the name tags, which a friend made as a joke and one of the lunch ladies kept in a drawer day after day, or the detailed rules, which banned girls and trucker hats, and specified the group's hierarchy. "Starters" were the dozen or so hand-selected guys who always had to sit in their assigned seats. "Alternates" were specially designated replacements who could take a starter's seat if he wasn't there. "Guests" occasionally visited the table, and were often treated with mixed reactions.

Though Reed liked his role as a star starter, he also tested the boundaries. Once he showed up with two guests, who he admitted were nerdy, because he genuinely wanted to talk with them.

Hey, there's an open seat here, a starter said, probably because he assumed the guys were unaware of the rules—and were in no way connected to Reed.

What a douche bag, Reed thought, blowing his friend off to return to his guests and their conversation on biotechnology.

Brady knew that the DSGs thought the guys were being ridiculous, and even the *Milton Measure* made fun of the assigned seats. But regardless of outside opinion, Brady and the guys knew that drawing attention to their exclusivity was part of being popular.

So was telling stories. Brady, Church, Reed, and the rest of the guys loved nothing more than sharing a good story. In stories, their names were as interchangeable as the girls at the center of the anecdotes: Caitlin, Emma, Nikki, Brittney. These were the Everyguys, and the girls their Everygirls.

Adolescent guy culture is largely voyeuristic. Stories are the folklore of aspiring masculinity, and a type of currency as well. There are hookup stories. Virginity stories. Orgasm stories. Shit stories. Piss stories. Fart stories. Come stories. Masturbation stories. Period stories. Hungover stories. Drunk stories. I Can't Believe I Almost Got Caught stories. And stories so gross and embarrassing that even the storyteller blushes, and almost can't say out loud what happened.

Gratification comes in many forms. There are orgasms, of course, but satisfaction surfaces in more overt ways, too, like when Brady finagled a way to join a friend's hookup, or at least watch from the side.

Remember we went down in the basement, Brady asked Reed, *and Brittney was hooking up with, uh, uh, was it, it was Church, right?*

No, I thought it was Derrick, Reed said.

Derrick?

Derrick and Grayson were both naked in the bedroom with her.

Reed said it as though the sight of two naked guys with a girl was normal, which was actually true. Church, Derrick, and Grayson were all hockey players, and part of Brady's steady social scene.

I don't know if they actually did anything with her, Reed admitted, *or if they were just runnin' around in there.*

Brady ripped a bite from his chicken patty and continued the story with his mouth full.

We knew Conner . . . was in the basement, so we all go in there to spy. Brittney's hooking up with Derrick on the bed, and then Grayson is just standing at the end of the bed like, watching!

Reed cracks up, remembering the image.

It was hysterical, Brady says, laughing, catching his breath. He takes another bite and speaks midchew.

Finally we went back for the night. Pause. Swallow. *Jesus.*

Without question, the most popular topic of conversation at the guys' lunch table was girls. Who's hot, who's not, who has the biggest boobs and who has the best ass. Such conversations happened in their locker rooms as well, particularly the varsity hockey locker room, which Brady and Reed would soon make into their winter home. There, nothing was too vulgar, intimate, or shameful. Even a player's personal foibles were newsworthy: He farted, he couldn't get it up, etc.

Not surprising: A guy took a girl to his friend's car and had sex with her in the front seat.

Surprising: While that guy had sex with that girl, another boy listened from the backseat, where he was zipped up in a large sports bag and strategically placed, out of sight.

Reed actually believed that he and his friends were not out to degrade girls. They weren't saying, *Oh, look at that slut. Let's make her feel like a dirty slut.* They were saying, *Let's see if we can get a story from her.* So stories made the man and the man got all the stories. Brady believed that the best ones came from spur-of-the-moment decisions, not a plan conceived with a few guys the night before. Either way, it all came down to the delivery.

Being a true storyteller required the proper vocabulary. Girls can be *bitches* or *broads, smokeshows, dimes,* or *hoochie mamas.* If they're not *hot,* then they're *pigs* or *swamp donkeys.* A *cunt* is a girl and a *lady* is a classy woman. When a guy receives oral sex from a girl, she gives him *a blow job, a steam job,* or *head.* When a guy gives oral sex to a girl, he sticks his face in her *pussy, eats her out,* or goes *muff diving.* If a girl doesn't trim, shave, or wax her pubic hair, she has a *bush,* which is by definition gross.

Having sex can be described in so many ways: *I took her down, I took it to her, I killed her, I banged her, I fucked her, I knocked it out, I did her, we had sexual intercourse* (laughing). If the story involves more than two people, the girl probably got *double teamed,* which can mean oral sex, sex, or anal sex. You can get *raped by a test.* You can *suck face* with a girl on the dance floor. *Come* is also called *spooge,* and a friend who gets in the way of another guy's game is a total *cock block.*

No matter what type of guy you were or what vocabulary you used, all the guys understood that when someone said, *You gotta listen to this story,* it was time to shut up. Senior year, many of Brady's stories came from Caitlin Lane's basement parties, which made famous the tight and sexually charged relationship between these older guys and some of the young DSGs. On Friday and Saturday nights, roughly fifteen people arrived by car, making pleasantries with Caitlin's parents before heading downstairs. Brady or someone else sneaked beer in through the back door, and after playing drinking games and watching TV, people started to hook up.

If you wanted privacy you went to the bathroom, but if you didn't care, you went into the back room so everyone else could watch. Minutes after the couple disappeared, Reed got off the couch and the other guys followed, crawling on their hands and knees through a narrow hallway to spy on the hookup. A topless girl was a standard sight. So was catching someone's hand down the other person's pants.

Reed never saw anyone having sex, but he can still picture a friend lying on the pool table beneath a girl, who was wearing only a thong. There were her breasts, her stomach, her thighs, her skin sagging slightly as her head and neck rocked gently above his groin. Reed never caught one of his friends giving a girl oral sex, and never wanted to. The goal was to see a buddy get worked, not the other way around.

Brady wasn't one to brag, but Caitlin Lane's basement parties originated with one of his junior year stories. Later he recounted the evening to Reed, easing lower into his chair, remembering how the night began when he and two friends went to Caitlin's house.

So we . . . each had like, three beers each or something, so we said, let's just go in and pretend that we're absolutely shitfaced.

Reed laughed, knowing that the ploy was entirely believable; Brady was one of the few people he trusted to drive drunk.

And we all like, started cuddling with each other, Brady said, referring to Caitlin and her two friends, Nikki and Sabina.

Like that one time at Church's house, Reed interjected. *Where I slept in a bed with Hawke? Remember that picture with my arm over him, like I was spooning him?*

He looked at Brady for validation and didn't get it.

Okay, Reed said, waving his hand, *keep going.*

So we were cuddling on the couch. On the floor, on the couch, everywhere.

Yeah.

Oh, you know what we did? The couch pulls out into a bed. Brady paused. *No, we didn't even do that. 'Cause we tried to do that and the couch like, tipped over.*

Reed laughed.

So we were just on the floor. And then I remember Sabina was like—

Sabina smells like balls, Reed said.

They laughed. Brady continued.

Nikki was to the other side of me. We were just doing stupid stuff. We were like, tryin' to play spin the bottle. We were trying to get them to play stupid games . . . Nikki was next to me, and I just started like—

Silence.

You know, Brady said.

Reed knew; Brady meant he'd fingered her.

So then Nikki was like, I think we should get a blanket.

So she put like, a blanket on herself.

And I was like, doin' whatever.

Again, laughter.

And Sabina was like, lying right here. And I think she thought I wanted to hook up with her.

She's like, Oh, God, your heart's beating so fast, Brady said, giggling with his infectious, high-pitched laugh.

And I was like, If you had any idea what was going on next to you right now.

Countless other stories followed. The relationship between the young DSGs and the older guys grew over time, and not in the way that involved meeting parents and making pleasantries. The guys often had a single goal in mind: to get a story. How about we do this? they would ask. You know what would be cool? I love it when you— The girls would listen, sipping their beers.

Hanging out in Caitlin Lane's basement was much like being in the hockey locker room, only with girls and without group showers. At school on Monday mornings, the guys had stories to tell and the girls had experiences to laugh off in front of their friends. Whatever happened mattered less than when Church said hi to Nikki or Brady nodded at one of the girls.

Brady's portfolio became legendary. In addition to his own stories, he helped coordinate his friends' hookups as well. One day a buddy called on the phone.

I gotta hook up with someone like, this weekend. 'Cause . . . I gotta hook up with someone.

All right, Brady said, *you'll hook up with one of the young DSGs.*

His friend waited for a name.

Let's go with Nikki, Brady said.

That sounded just fine.

The two guys showed up at Nikki's house at night, and after winning over her mother, the threesome piled into Brady's car to pick up pizza and a movie. What they really did was park, drink, drive to the video store to grab the first film they found on the shelf, and then drink some more. Brady told Nikki and his friend to get in the backseat and hook up, which they did until they got back to Nikki's house.

Great to see you, her father said as they walked in. *Upperclassmen coming all the way out here on a Friday just to hang out with a younger girl. It's so nice of you.*

All right! Brady thought. Sometimes he couldn't believe how dense adults could be.

We're gonna go downstairs and watch the movie in the basement, Nikki said.

I'm going out to get ice cream, her dad went on. *You guys want anything?*

No, we're fine, thank you, Brady said, polite as ever.

Nikki led the boys away.

Downstairs in the basement, she and Brady's friend started hooking up.

What am I gonna do? Brady thought to himself.

First he sat and watched, but then the answer was obvious: join.

The three of them started going at it until Brady interrupted.

Nikki, you've gotta take this a little bit further.

What do you mean? she asked.

You're gonna have to give one of us head.

She picked Brady. He felt like a jerk because she was supposed to hook up with his friend, but he wasn't going to say no.

You gotta go make sure her father doesn't come down, he said to his friend.

All right, all right.

So his friend kept watch while Brady attended to Nikki's sexual needs, not because he genuinely cared, but because he hoped she would reciprocate. He went slowly because he knew she'd never performed oral sex before. Her pants were off and his hand was in her crotch, fingers twirling, when, eventually, she began to give him head. Brady lost himself to pleasure until, seconds or minutes later, while Nikki's head jerked back and forth, her neck probably throbbing, her jaw probably aching, and Brady's body twice, maybe three times larger than her own, Nikki's father appeared in the doorway holding a container of ice cream.

Brady pulled away from Nikki.

What the fuck.

What the fuck.

What the fuck.

A scowl burned on Nikki's father's face.

Guys, get over here.

Brady and his friend walked toward him.

I saw everything, Nikki's father yelled.

Again, louder: *I saw everything.*

Get out of my house.

I don't ever wanna see you here again.

The boys sprinted from the house, promising to write apology letters the very next day. In the car on the way home, Brady's friend couldn't stop shaking. Brady was petrified, and rightfully so. The consequences of his actions were unbearable. *I'm gonna get nailed for rape. I'm gonna get DCed. Or worse, expelled. What if my parents find out? What if I go to jail? We were just having fun. We weren't doing anything wrong. What in the world have we done?* Brady had had enough dumb luck not to get in any real trouble for the incident at Nikki's house. The matter eventually faded, and was replaced by new and more impressive tales.

News of the basement parties made its way through the dining hall and student center. Josh sometimes heard rumors about young DSGs sitting topless on guys' laps, their eyes glassy from beer. If only he'd made the varsity hockey team, he assumed his life would have been different. How many girls would he have had? How many Friday nights would he have spent in Caitlin Lane's basement, not at dinners with the basketball team? He was dumbfounded the day he saw pictures posted online of what seemed like the entire hockey team hanging out with young DSGs. *What was I doing that night?* he wondered, staring at the photographs.

Even before the official basketball season began, Friday team dinners began in early fall. At a long table, not so different from Reed and Brady's table in Forbes, the basketball guys talked about the season, traded stories, and assessed girls, though with a degree of decorum.

One night, Josh was the center of attention.

Speaking of crushes, Josh's got someone who's got the hots for him, a teammate said.

Yeah, who's that? Josh asked, confused, because no one had the hots for him.

Let's just say she called you the Greek god of sex.

His teammate had to be joking. Josh? God of sex? Josh's mouth spread into a crooked smile. He was flattered, and when he found out that the girl, Alicia, wasn't joking, he was also interested. Was she cute? Did she have a boyfriend? Yes, very, and no, not at the time. Alicia wasn't Diana, but Josh got her IM name and started chatting with her online. In time he learned Alicia was seeing a hockey player, but the same motivation that drove him to go after unattainable girls, time after time, rejection after rejection, took effect again.

Josh: so any fun plans for the weekend?
Alicia: hm not as of now
Alicia: u?
Josh: ehh
Josh: i play it by ear
Josh: id love to see a movie
Josh: by the way im not hinting at anything
Alicia: haha got it

So Alicia got it, but she still didn't say yes. To worsen the blow, Josh learned that she loosely threw around the phrase Greek god of sex. She probably made the comment in passing, laughing lightly afterward. He wasn't special. He wasn't admired. He wasn't even her crush. And still, he continued flirting with her online, because that's where he was at his best.

Alicia: hmm do u like anyone?
Josh: i like everyone
Alicia: haha i mean at school
Josh: only the prettiest girls
Josh: like this one girl
Alicia: who??
Josh: alicia i think her name is
Alicia: haha
Alicia: thats so sweet of u

Josh: i do what i can

Alicia: omg ur my fave basketball boy

Alicia was often vague in her responses. Sometimes she alluded to her boyfriend, but Josh didn't understand that guys weren't supposed to actively pursue other guys' girlfriends. Any girl who gave him attention appeared to him as a potential option, so he went after her wholeheartedly.

Like Josh, Reed wouldn't have participated in public hookups at Caitlin Lane's basement parties. Instead, he chose the role of bystander. Usually Reed sat on one of the couches and amused himself with the drunken antics his friends provided, all the while thinking that the young DSGs were too immature for him. Maybe it was the moral responsibility his mother had instilled in him. Maybe it was genuine disinterest in some of the girls' wiry, almost prepubescent bodies. Maybe he just preferred talking with Caitlin's mother, which he tried to do weekend after weekend. Reed believed he was so suave that he could flirt with a married woman, and was so self-confident that he thought she actually flirted back.

Reed had a thing for older women. He liked to look them in the eyes longer than he should, and ask them questions that were almost, but not quite, out of line. From time to time, it seemed these older women had a thing for him, too. Once, during roll call at his school back home, his teacher sputtered, *You look like the second love of my life, except for my husband.* And once a girlfriend's neighbor gushed relentlessly.

You didn't tell me!

What? the girlfriend asked.

He's gorgeous!

Reed agreed, especially one night in late October, as he checked himself out in the mirror in his dorm room. He wore a blue Polo, a pink oxford, and a Lilly Pulitzer tie looped loosely around his neck. He'd bought them at the Swap It sale earlier that morning, Milton's annual three-day fund-raiser that was organized by and benefited the lower school. Reed arrived Friday morning in lieu of the first half of statistics class. The school-wide flea market offered ski equipment, Rollerblades, racks of vintage clothes, lamps, and everyday odds and ends. The scene was a mixture of conspicuous consumption and Brahmin frugality, and Reed planned to make a killing. He bought sports coats and Brooks Brothers shirts, tearing off the price tags so he would have to pay only ten dollars an item.

The Swap It dance was held that night in Thatcher, a large room on the first floor of Ware Hall. As Reed walked across campus in his new duds, he battled the sharp nighttime air, walking past the fall foliage that painted Milton's landscape with shades of red, yellow, and orange. That night he was supposed to work on his early decision application. He decided to apply to an Ivy League school, just as he'd projected he would as a little boy. Numerous family members on his mother's side had graduated from Princeton, some dating back to the Depression, but his father's side was entirely unhelpful. Regardless, Reed knew that legacies weren't enough.

When Reed walked into the Swap It dance, everything was as he expected it to be. Younger girls, younger boys, a gyrating mass of students in the middle. The event was relatively boring, so he and a friend dared each other to find a girl to hook up with. Reed enjoyed such competitions; they were easy, short-lived, and, if he won, instantly gratifying. But after a concerted effort he didn't spot anyone interesting. It was only when he decided to head back to the dorm, while weaving through the crowd of kids crammed into Thatcher, that he spotted a girl who gave him the look he was searching for.

Reed had never spoken with her before, but she'd been discussed among his friends. They all thought she had this look on her face that said she wanted it—*it* being a hookup—because clearly they were experts when it came to girls' physical and emotional desires. Reed and his friends decided that someone should just grab her and do it, so he stepped up to the plate.

I'm about to go, wanna come with me? he asked.

She said yes, and then led him to the chapel.

Reed was doubly impressed. First, with the girl, for agreeing to leave with a guy she didn't even know. Second, with himself, for convincing her to hook up with him without a single conversation or casual hello. He wondered what made her so willing to hook up with someone she barely knew. He assumed she was horny. He might not have been far off, yet he wasn't right, either. Girls wanted stories, too, but theirs revolved around who the guy was and how he made her feel, not what he did to her. Reed wasn't out for commitment or feelings that evening. He wanted a story, and when she took him to the chapel he knew he was about to get a good one.

The door to Apthorp Chapel was unlocked. Reed paused on the landing, beneath the ivy climbing upward, and looked around. Up above, the chapel's Gothic-inspired stone masonry came to sharp pointed arches. Kellner, the performing arts building, loomed in the distance, across Centre Street, where some couple was probably making out in some classroom on the second floor. Cars whizzed by on Centre Street, racing past faster than the speed limit. Reed looked around him, and when he was sure no one was watching, he slowly opened the heavy door, remembering the time a hockey coach had warned him against abusing his status as a hockey player. He couldn't help himself. *This is so easy. This is too funny. This is too good. I hope I don't get caught.* He chuckled to himself, amused by the shit he could pull, and stepped inside.

Reed and the girl didn't walk down to the nave or sit in the wooden pews, where boarders slumped each Sunday evening for chapel. Instead, they turned left and ascended the carpeted red stairs to the second floor, where the massive pipe organ made for surreal company. There, overlooking the two flags that hung on either side of the altar, one for the United States and the other for Milton's class of 2005, in the very space where incoming freshmen signed the Student Government Association book and graduates returned for their weddings, the girl gave Reed a blow job.

In his world, oral sex was no longer an intimate act between two established partners. Guys expected it from girls, and many girls accepted the expectation, pleasuring the guy (oftentimes without reciprocation) and hoping for, in return, a potential increase in social status and attention. Some girls, like Whitney, enjoyed performing oral sex, honing their skills, loving the control. But even she was put off by the crass ways guys tried to get head.

Suck me off.

Give me brains.

Smoke my pipe.

Give me knowledge.

Reed never would have said *suck me off,* but from his perspective there were two types of girls. One kind he genuinely liked and therefore wanted to please; the other kind he used for a story and therefore didn't care about pleasing. Being one of the latter, the girl in the chapel received little attention from Reed. He fingered her briefly, but she was a hookup, and, by definition, didn't necessitate reciprocation. Going to the chapel was not about an emotional connection or equal sharing. It was about Reed. Getting off. And fast.

The chapel incident was Reed's best story. His friends were impressed, but still, it didn't come close to Brady's stories. Reed may not have wanted to admit it or even understand it, but he was a different kind of popular boy, a different kind of man. Reed was popular and knew how to be an asshole, but he was, despite many classmates' assumptions, reflective about what he did. What he lacked in social entitlement he had in values, morals, and emotions. Something always held him back—insecurity, vanity, perhaps even a heart.

chapter seven

he said yes

a steady chant rose from the main basketball court inside the Old Boys' Gym. The noise floated out into the lobby, past piles of backpacks and book bags, out the front entrance with its towering columns, until it reached the latecomers who scurried through the November dusk to the homecoming pep rally. The Old Boys' Gym was originally the boys' school's sole athletic facility (Milton used to be two schools, one for boys and one for girls), and still exuded the preppy aesthetic: stone stairs, old glass windows, and, high above the main entrance, surrounded by delicate twirls and dips of what looked like white icing, an orange-and-blue Milton Academy shield. Inside, Milton's athletic history hung from the walls, dusty, tea-colored photos of former Milton teams dating back to the days before World War I. The football team still had its home here, and the slightly sour odor of sweaty sports equipment still hung in the lobby from the locker room in the basement. By the entrance to the basketball court was a pack of football players in their orange-and-blue jerseys. In the middle of that pack stood Brady.

He peered through the double doors into the gym, glimpsing the last pep rally of his football career. Kids sat in clusters on the court, surrounded by exposed brick walls and grimy windows. Even in daylight the space looked dark and musty, like an overused playground from the 1920s, which it was, but the level of disdain for Nobles was paramount. The cheers grew louder. *Go Milton! Go 'stangs! No balls!,* meaning, obviously, that Nobles players had no balls. Granted, homecoming at Milton wasn't like homecoming in the movies. This was not *Friday Night Lights.* There were no cheerleaders, marching bands, or campaigns for homecoming king and queen. The quarterback may have been hot, or at least cute, but he wasn't by definition the coolest kid in school. The administration probably deemed a bonfire unsafe, and although there was a pep rally, it was irregularly attended, most often by the very athletes it was supposed to celebrate. Brady didn't care. He'd been waiting for homecoming all fall.

A mood of self-importance settled over the crowd. Attending wouldn't have been nearly as cool had the entire school turned out; being in the audience meant you were a young DSG, a boarder, or a friend of an athlete, someone with access to that world, regardless of how cursory. Students watched fall sports teams perform skits with varying degrees of preparation. The field-hockey girls did a dance routine and the soccer guys reenacted the video of Michael Jackson's "Thriller," sending one boy out to break-dance while the others mummified themselves with toilet paper. Brady didn't pay much attention to what went on inside the gym, because to him, the pep rally was about one thing: him.

Finally the screams died down. The crowd split in two, and formed a runway spanning the length of the basketball court, from the front entrance to the far end of the gym. The lights went out. The music began. The double doors flew open and a pack of football guys burst into the gym, sprinting past the crowd until they reached the far end of the court. The pack of players grew, looking more mature in that misleading way that high school guys achieve from time to time. Brady stayed behind with the seniors and starters until the rest of the team was on the court. And then, for a single moment, the entire gym came to a stop. No one moved. No one clapped. Something was about to happen.

The crowd turned toward the doorway as the emcee announced the name of the first football starter. That boy ran down the runway, and his teammates followed, each player performing a joke while flying down the court. One pretended to drink a beer, then squirted water from his mouth. Another did a dance. Finally, when it seemed as if the entire football team had assembled at the far end of the gym, the emcee leaned into the microphone and said one word: *Brady.* A head of blond curls appeared in the doorway. Brady smirked, clutching a football in one hand, and sauntered down the runway as though he'd already won the next day's game. When he reached center court, he pretended to autograph the football and then turned to a young DSG who waited near the front of the audience. He handed her the football, assuming the gesture made her night, because everyone watching knew that she was the girl he'd picked to be part of the skit. This was Brady being Brady. A moment later, he turned toward his team at the far end of the gym and threw his hand in the air. The guys barreled forward and formed a circle around Brady, jumping, shaking the floorboards, yelling, *One, two, three, 'stangs!* with the booming voices of men.

Then Brady and the rest of the team left the pep rally to meet their coaches for the annual end-of-season ceremony, on the football field behind the Old Boys' Gym. At night, Milton's fields looked like any other high school athletic grounds—flat grass marked by white lines and goalposts. They stood on the fifty-yard line with a large, empty bucket, and when all the guys arrived, the ritual began. Each senior relinquished something meaningful. Brady threw in his acceptance letter to a rival private school. Others offered their practice jerseys, an X-ray from a previous injury, a photo of the freshman football team, a cast worn earlier that season. Younger players sensed the importance of the moment, and watched the older guys with fascination, imagining themselves as seniors who had, at last, completed their Milton football careers. After everyone spoke and the bucket was filled, the players headed back up the hill, toward the gym, glancing behind them to watch their coaches set fire to their memories.

As Brady drove the Volvo home that night, he felt something inside—melancholy, and the bittersweet longing for a football career that was about to end. He'd just attended his last homecoming pep rally. He was about to play his final football game the very next morning. As he merged off the highway, he didn't notice the snowflakes dissolving on the windshield, and when he pulled into the driveway and walked into the house, he didn't think twice about the layer of snow on the ground. His mind lingered on football. Brady grasped the importance of that evening as he sank into the bed he never made, surrounded by the comforts of a bedroom that had barely changed since childhood. Sports stars still grimaced from the walls, and ticket stubs from bygone games still collected dust in the corner. The Bruins and Red Sox were still his favorite teams. And falling asleep was still a simple task for this boy whose only thought was how much longer he had to wait until it was time for the Nobles football game.

Brady looked out his window the next morning and saw over half a foot of snow. *This is awful,* he thought, heading to school anyway, because the administration couldn't possibly cancel the Milton–Nobles games. When he got to campus, he learned that a group of football and soccer guys were off shoveling a turf field at Milton High, the local public school. It was a valiant effort, but no number of guys could have cleared all that snow in time.

Brady couldn't believe the games could be canceled. Homecoming wasn't supposed to be like this. Usually students poured onto campus Saturday morning to watch their friends play in the soccer, field hockey, and football games, and watch the cross-country races. They flooded the fields with orange-and-blue Ms drawn on their cheeks, wearing Patagonia fleeces and sneakers and unseasonably adorable outfits. Fathers dressed in true New England understatement: blue jeans and sneakers, Gore-Tex windbreakers, tweed jackets, and baseball caps with their child's sports team stitched across the brim. Mothers wrapped up in smart jackets, knit hats, and gloves, talking and cheering just like their daughters. Fallen leaves framed the athletic fields, and empty tree branches reached for the sky. This was fall at a New England prep school—and it wasn't happening.

On Saturday morning, snow covered the fields and every game was postponed. Jillian couldn't have cared less, but her father was was an avid sports fan; if his daughter wasn't going to play a fall sport, he wanted to be sure that all the other athletes could play in their own games. He tried to pull some strings at a local college to move the football game to another field, but the switch didn't work. Jillian didn't know what to think. Father of Hysteric Saves Homecoming? It would have been funny, even though she hated homecoming on principle. A pep rally, games all day Saturday against Nobles, and a dance Saturday night—the entire November weekend celebrated the self-important jock culture she barely tolerated on a daily basis at school.

Jillian believed that dances were fun only if you had a boyfriend. Back when her DSG star was still on the rise, she had three prerequisites for a boyfriend. He had to play a million sports; be really, really cute; and be really, really popular. She understood preteen politics, and told herself that the ultimate satisfaction came from dumping that boyfriend when boredom took over, and dating someone else. Jillian held on to this until, seven boyfriends into sixth grade, the day finally came when Michael confessed his true and undying love for her. He was a dreamboat, so darling. She'd liked him for what felt like her entire life. Sometimes dreams did come true, at least for twelve-year-old girls whose dreams were tangible (I want the lead in the school play) or so intangible that they could still exist in young minds (I want to marry a prince); whose only hope in life was to be the girlfriend of the boy they adored.

Senior year, all Jillian had was one close guy friend and a kind of, sort of ex-boyfriend from the year before. He was a punk with an intellectual cause, and an indie-music connoisseur. Jillian felt blissfully happy for a month or two, but she nearly died in creative writing class when he read a love poem aloud on parents' day about a girl who was obviously not herself.

Most days Jillian was boy crazy, but there were a few times when she experimented with girls.

Wouldn't it be funny if we [kissed], just to see? a friend once asked.

Jillian was curious, so she let her friend kiss her.

I'm sorry, Jillian said afterward, *but I am not interested in girls.*

Over a year later, Jillian tried again. She kissed a friend in front of her friend's boyfriend, and triple-kissed two girlfriends at the same time. She saw them as natural extensions of her friendships and the results of drinking alcohol. They weren't sexual. They weren't about performing for an audience. They were about experiencing something new.

Senior year, Jillian found herself in her typical predicament: She had an overwhelming crush on a boy she assumed she could never get. Evan was an outdoorsy and artsy senior. The DSGs never would have noticed him, but Jillian was charmed that he lugged his laptop around campus, giving off a scholarly air, like a modern-day Thoreau. He was exactly what Jillian wanted. In her typical brazen manner, she decided to ask Evan to be her date to the homecoming dance. This act alone was evidence enough that she'd come a long way since freshman year, when it took a best friend and a slew of teammates to get Jillian a date to the freshman dance.

She staked out Evan in the library. Everyday he studied in the same corner on the same floor, which happened to be near the *R* section of the fiction shelves. Jillian was on a Philip Roth kick at the time, and as she perused the stacks for her next read, headphones on, her hair tied back in a braid, she turned around, saw him, and feigned surprise.

Oh, Evan! Hey, what's up?

Nothing, he said.

Chitchat.

A minute passed.

Another minute.

So, Jillian began, checking the tidiness of her braid without realizing it. *It really sucks.*

Evan looked at her.

So Carrie promised this guy she'd go to homecoming with him, and she's like, making me come. 'Cause you know, like, I'm such a good friend. And I don't really wanna go alone.

She paused, wondering if Evan saw her as she saw herself—cripplingly shy, the girl in the corner with her nose in a book. Did he know that her creative-writing teacher praised her work, and wanted to get it published? Did he read her articles? Did he think they were funny? Most guys didn't *get* Jillian. Reed, for one, couldn't believe she showed up at school in what looked like a tutu, and thought she was a feminist, which, to him, was not a good thing. Jillian recognized the limitations of teenage boys. She assumed they were intimidated by her, and she refused to flirt like a DSG. So when she wanted something badly enough, she took extreme measures.

Hey, she finally stammered to Evan. *Do you wanna come?*

She couldn't believe it when he said *yes.*

Instead of going to the pep rally, Jillian spent her Friday night at Bloomingdale's, looking for the perfect dress. She bought five of them, on sale for $40 each, and went directly to Isabel's house for moral support and an objective opinion. They decided on the black halter dress with the ruched sides, but the next night, hours before the homecoming dance, Jillian was practically hyperventilating. She couldn't believe she'd invited Evan to be her date. She changed her mind: He wasn't cute, didn't like dressing up, and barely even knew her. He hated homecoming just as much as she did, and now he had to go with her—with fat, analytical, emotional Jillian. She had no idea what she'd been thinking.

But Jillian got dressed anyway, squeezing her body into her new black number. She couldn't fathom eating a bite of dinner, but her mother's weight-loss and parenting books stared at her from every crevice in her house, with titles like *Fed Up!*, *Our Lady of Weight Loss*, *Don't Blame Mother*, and *Males with Eating Disorders* reminding her all at once that she needed to eat and had to lose weight. Jillian stared at her mother, hating her for giving her an eating disorder. Later she vented in her journal:

> i went onto my mother's computer . . . and found more e-mails . . . talking about me, how i've gained so much weight, how she thinks i'm sneaking food, how she's so worried for me, how she thinks i'm out of shape even though i run an hour every day and work out, how she's worried cuz i "wear the same thing every day," how none of my clothes fit, how she thinks i don't know how to dress flatteringly, how she thinks i don't even care about my appearance, how i have no "wiggle room," how she's talked to my father about it . . . how she wonders if it was my starving myself for so long that slowed my metabolism. and i just lay on my bed and cried until she came in my room and found me crying and i couldn't tell her what was wrong, at all. i just can't. and she was hugging me. and then i told her i was gonna go take a shower, so i sat on the shower floor for at least ten minutes, sobbing, and trying to just make myself not exist.

Jillian's mother handed her a yogurt and waited for her to eat it. Jillian stood in her tight black dress, poking at the congealed snack. She felt her mother's eyes assessing every inch of her body. She'd heard her comments a hundred times before—*Are you sure you want to wear that? It's not very flattering*—and knew exactly what her mom really meant: You look fat.

Evan pulled up to the house in his mom's minivan. Jillian smiled for a photograph in the living room, then pulled a sweatshirt over her dress and put on her sneakers. She grabbed her black patent leather heels and walked out the door, knowing she never could have foreseen this moment when she was a freshman DSG: trudging through the snow and slush to meet her date, a guy she would have purposely ignored had she still been popular.

Jillian climbed into the passenger's seat, holding her heels.

Cool shoes, Evan said.

Oh, thanks.

Are those some really like, expensive, chic shoes?

Oh no, these were like, five-dollar shoes or something.

The last thing Jillian wanted was for Evan to think she was materialistic and obsessed with shopping, even though she was. But Evan was wearing jeans and a yellow button-down shirt. It was the most formal outfit she'd ever seen him in, and that had to be a good sign. Despite her nerves, Jillian felt like her old self again, the darling social butterfly who had it all, including the guy.

On their way to school, her friend called, screaming that their favorite song from seventh grade was on the radio. Jillian flipped it on and listened to "Semi-Charmed Life," by Third Eye Blind. *Oh, I just wanted to call you and tell you I love you!* the girl said into the phone. Jillian thought she was drunk, but agreed to meet her near the Old Boys' Gym to have a drink with her in the car.

After lowering their inhibitions, she, Evan, and her friend headed to Jessups House, one of the boys' dorms. Walking into the lobby brought Jillian back to freshman year, when she and her popular girlfriends had sprinted into the dorm and waited for their guy friends to sign them in. The senior room was straight ahead and the lobby chalkboard was always filled with scribbles:

Caleb, we love you!

Jessups guys, you're all invited to our dorm tonight for movies and popcorn—the Maddens girls.

In one guy's handwriting: *Mike, call your mom.*

In another guy's handwriting: *After I call her!*

Freshman year, Jillian's presence in Jessups meant a guy wanted her there as a legitimate friend or a potential sexual conquest. Now, as a senior and no longer a DSG, Jillian was bowled over by the home-grown narcissism that wore itself everywhere. The dorm dripped with studied masculinity. Plaques and memorabilia hung from the walls, reminding the boys that they were part of a larger tradition of Jessups residents. Jillian felt naked and exposed as she stood there waiting to get parietals. Boys lounging around the entrance stared at her as though they could see through her—as though they knew she didn't really belong there. But eventually, finally, Jillian, Evan, and her friend got permission to disappear upstairs.

Most dorm rooms adopted a similar look: bunk beds or a lone twin bed pushed into the corner, piles of books, clothes everywhere, a TV, DVDs, the smell of Febreze and dirty laundry, the wardrobe pushed next to the doorway, partially blocking dorm parents from a full view of the room. Jillian looked around her friend's boyfriend's room, and when he opened his fridge, she glanced inside.

What?! she thought to herself.

You have alcohol in your dorm room?

That is ridiculous.

She'd never seen so much beer crammed into such a small space. But she remembered the days when she and her DSG friends spent all their free time in Jessups, hanging out, flirting, introducing them-selves to weed and rebels.

I used to hook up with some of them.

I used to be a permanent installment in their dorm.

I used to be one of them.

Now she was only a guest's guest. She grasped it even more now, standing in Jessups with Evan, who was awkward and drove his mom's minivan. Still, Jillian was tipsy in a dorm, breaking the rules, hanging out with a crush, and doing what she thought everyone else was doing—having a life.

When she and Evan arrived at the dance, they were closer to drunk than tipsy and trying to hide it. One of the DSGs was wearing the same dress that Jillian wore. Jillian was amused; she'd bought it because it was cheap, not because it was trendy, which, apparently, it was, since that's what she assumed DSGs liked. The theme for the dance was the Academy Awards: There were miniature Oscars on a table outside Wigg and a black-and-white dress code, all of which Jillian found atrocious and embarrassing nods to MTV's *Laguna Beach*. What could be more DSG?

She and Evan left Wigg in mock protest, and walked to the student center, hiding in an alcove on the first floor. He made fun of her heels again, and she laughed at herself right along with him, slipping them off while he wasn't looking. She felt happy drunk, and suddenly decided that Evan looked handsome. She liked knowing that anyone walking by would see her sitting with him, like a couple on a date, like a girl and a boy who genuinely liked each other. Periodically someone walked up to Jillian and asked her about Evan.

Are you together?

No! she replied.

'Cause it really seems like you are.

That's what she thought, too.

The large lecture hall in Wigg was packed with students in black-and-white outfits, grinding to the music. Glittering stars hung everywhere. In the middle of the dance floor, Reed goofed around with his friends. He looked sharp. Few people could have known his tie was Vineyard Vines, but he did, and that mattered. Reed and the guys corralled Cush, who was still getting over Ava, but Reed noticed her nearby. He recognized the fact that there was an unspoken code between guy friends: Never take a friend's girl, never go behind his back, and never lie, because a friend will always find out. But he couldn't take his eyes off Ava that night.

She had a flawless tan and long caramel-colored hair. Her blue eyes shone, and she looked just as elegant in sweats and sneakers as she did in pearls. Reed had been thinking about her since the very beginning of the school year, when, while walking with her around campus, just chatting, strolling, as though everything was normal, he caught the look that told him he could get her if he wanted. She was the ultimate conquest, but Reed sensed the need to steer a delicate course ahead, even after she complained to him that none of Cush's friends were dancing with her.

As the night wore on, Reed eyed other girls, too. He and Isabel passed like ships in the night when, after a brief appearance, she left with a few friends to catch *The Polar Express* at a nearby cinema. Perhaps she thought of him as she sat in the square movie theater seat, her legs crossed because she was still wearing her dress, remembering the last time he'd smiled at her. Over the past couple of months, Isabel had paid attention to Reed in class. He was different from his friends, and the fact that he didn't take stupid jock classes made him significantly more attractive to Isabel. His friends were the kinds of kids who took general music and opted for the easy English electives like Persuading (*designed for students who want to improve their ability to write clear, correct, energetic, and convincing expository prose*, the course catalog explained). Brady didn't even have a favorite book. And once, as a former teammate recalled, he burst into the locker room with a paper in his hand, gathered his teammates, and started reading his teacher's comment: *Brady, your paper was the worst thing I've ever read. Do you even know how to write a thesis statement? The paper's not even divided into paragraphs.* Teammates were hooting and dying. Brady wasn't embarrassed; he was cracking up because this was entertainment.

It was hard to miss Reed in art history class. *She's playing with herself in that one,* he'd said once, pointing to a painting of a nude girl lying on a bed. Isabel giggled to herself, intrigued by this boy who was so unexpected. At first her crush was just a crush. Flirtations like this one were not dangerous because they didn't actually exist in reality. Guys like Reed didn't date girls like Isabel. They didn't hang out together at recess, go to the same parties, or have opportunities outside class to hold actual conversations. Only on Mondays, during the short break in the middle of their art history double period, did they chat on the way down to the dining hall. Isabel had no idea Reed thought she was cute. She had those emerald eyes and precious features, but still, she was no Ava. Reed didn't notice Isabel at the homecoming dance, though that wasn't so surprising. To him, she was just the pale redhead in the Hysterics. A girl who seemed to know a lot about art history and spent most of her time on the lower level of the student center. And she hung out with Jillian, who, though brilliant, Reed found to be strange and certifiably incapable of being fashionable.

Jillian and Evan were still being cool and exclusive in the student center. He still hadn't kissed her yet, but they were both tipsy, and Jillian believed that alcohol was the perfect excuse to hook up. After the dance, they went to a friend's house to drink tequila and cuddle. They talked about tattoos and Jillian realized how perfect the night had been, skipping most of the dance and watching the snow and feeling like she could be herself with a boy who seemed to like her back.

Jillian's cell phone rang. It was after midnight. It was her mother. It was time to go home.

It's a special occasion! Jillian pleaded.

Can I have my curfew extended?

Please??

Her mom was resolute: *No.*

Evan parked the minivan in front of Jillian's house, and they sat there in the dark, waiting for one of them to do something. Jillian looked at him, wondering if she was going to have to do everything herself. The first time Jillian had hooked up with a guy she wore the tightest jeans she owned (faded, cargo, with holes) and a pink tube top that came to a triangular point in the front. She was in eighth grade and believed she looked sophisticated. Her boy of the evening licked her face, like a Labrador retriever, and a few days later shoved his hand up her shirt. *So this is what it feels like,* she thought to herself. *Okay, whatever.* But a first kiss should never be just a kiss. It was a magical moment when a lifetime of cootie shots, secret crushes, fear of braces, and movie scenes merged together. A girl and boy stood there, hearts racing, knees locking, because there were so many rules to remember. Tilt your head. Close your eyes. Lean in slowly. Dive in fast. Don't use your tongue. Use it, and push it deep inside. Kiss for a minute. Kiss for a second. Stop, blush, apologize, but always persevere, because at some point, whether right then or five hundred kisses later, there will be fireworks.

On the night of the homecoming dance, Evan let Jillian leave without a kiss. She closed the car door and walked back through the snow and slush in her sneakers, realizing that the entire evening had been typical. She was used to rejection. Her girlfriends thought she was strong and confident, and wondered, out loud or secretly, how she did it. But at times Jillian wondered, too.

Around Thanksgiving, fueled by frustration or boredom, perhaps both, Jillian decided to make the first move and ask Evan out again. This time she did it over voice mail.

BEEP.

Sorry I know this is really lame doing this over voice mail but I got really nervous in the car and I wanted to ask you if you wanted to see a movie this weekend.

Click.

Evan responded via e-mail.

I'm going to be even lamer than you are and respond over e-mail and say yes.

Jillian had a reason to be hopeful again.

On their date, which Jillian thought had to be a date because Evan paid for her coffee and offered her his sweatshirt, they walked around Harvard Square and then went back to Jillian's house, where the evening concluded in one gigantic awkward situation after midnight when her mother made Evan go home, and by go home she really meant she would drive him home, with the couple sitting together in the backseat. Jillian was mortified. She looked out the window and then over at Evan, who motioned toward his lap. There in his hand was a note, a scribble, something legible he'd written just for her: *hi.* She took the pen and wrote something back: *So . . . ever again? Or are you completely convinced of my dorkiness . . .* Evan: *Are you on drugs?* he wrote, *Or is my answer a yes . . .* Jillian smiled: *Big sigh of relief.* Jillian debated the moment in her journal:

> the note passing was clearly the best part of the night. so now i'm freaking out about when is appropriate to call, it's like 'swingers' with the three day rule. but even then i feel like is too soon. and cuz he's so passive i know that he's never gonna call. and here's the thing. when you have a new crush, the most frustrating thing is having to go on with normal life. because you know that the only thing you ACTUALLY should be doing is making out with said crush. so stupid things like thanksgiving . . . and like waiting until it's appropriate and not stalker-ish to call him, are soooooooo superfluous. and he's so hard to figure out. pretty much i'm just freaking out. i need help.

A few days later, Jillian got drunk enough at a party to make the first move on Evan again.

Want to go out to the car? she asked, bold and daring because of the alcohol.

No, he said. *Let's just stay here and hang out with people. It's fun.*

Okay, Jillian said.

When she finally got him out to the car, her head wobbled with alcohol. She glanced hazily at him, smiling with her hazel eyes, knowing that whatever happened in the next few minutes could change everything. For a single second she thought he might kiss her. That moment went by, and then a few more went by. She refused to miss out, so she leaned forward and made the first move again.

They kissed.

Jillian and Evan kissed.

Wekissedwekissedwekissed, she later wrote in her journal. *FINA-FUCKINLLY!*

Maybe Evan would embrace her the way men did in the movies. Maybe he would suck in her breath like it was his life source. Maybe he would become her boyfriend. Every crush, date, and hookup was a painful reminder that Michael—her first and only love, the one from sixth grade; her longest and most legitimate relationship to date—was the only one who'd ever really cared for her. Maybe Evan would change her life. Instead, he performed the perfunctory hookup behavior: He fingered her. *They all think they are such studs*, Jillian thought to herself, *but they don't know what they are doing.* Hooking up with guys was so rarely about her own pleasure. She gave him a hand job. They returned to the party.

Evan barely gave Jillian twenty-four hours of happiness before he e-mailed her that he wanted to talk. Jillian prepared herself for dreadful news.

That was a mistake, Evan said as they stood in the library during sixth period. *I just want to be friends.*

Yeah, that's fine, Jillian said.

Is that okay with you that we just stay friends?

Yeah, that's fine, Jillian said again.

Really?

Well, I don't think I need to tell you that I'd like to be more than friends, but I'm not going to force you. Obviously this is a two-person thing.

And so the relationship that hadn't quite been a relationship ended. Jillian was used to disappointment, but she didn't get it. Phoebe did, and it broke her heart. She heard rumors that Evan's friends gave him shit for hooking up with Jillian. They said she was uptight, clingy, and weird. As Phoebe saw it, Jillian was a passionate person who threw herself into everything she did. She just wasn't the type of girl to approach guys with a *yeah whatever* attitude. And that, it seemed, was what guys wanted.

i still really really like Evan, but i'm trying really hard to pretend that he doesn't matter so maybe he will see what a huge mistake he made. i want it to snow. i want to get into college NOW. i want to make out.

i'm eighteen

Whitney sat on the first floor of the student center with her back against a wall, staring into Tripp's eyes as though the two of them were invisible to the rest of the world. They occupied one of the corners by the windows overlooking Centre Street. Outside, red and yellow leaves lay shriveled on the ground. It was November and cold. Whitney wore Tripp's varsity jacket. She'd just spent the weekend hanging out at his house, meeting his mom, joining his family for dinner, and giving him head. When anyone asked, Whitney insisted that they weren't a couple; she assumed that if no one actually saw them hook up, no one could ever really know for sure. Her friends didn't get it. Tripp was so sweet. He liked her. He wanted to respect her. Whitney agreed with them, but she couldn't stop seeing Nick on the side. She spent hours and hours talking with Tripp, but her heart—more important, her body—was still with Nick.

Mom, do you think I can go to Nick's tomorrow?

No.

Why not?

Because you have to do your homework.

Mom, I'm in high school. I can make that decision. If I have homework I can bring it with me. I can do it at his house. I can do it with him.

By Whitney's senior year, her mom knew better, but Whitney was relentless.

Mom, every senior does this, she said about her grades.

I've worked my ass off.

You cannot get mad at me for this.

You don't know how lucky you are to be a parent and be mad that the worst grade your daughter has ever gotten in her high school career is a B minus. Don't even talk to me about that!

Whitney had a point. She was one of the lucky ones who knew she'd get into college. All the skating coaches said so. She'd earned medal after medal, had decent grades, and was coming from Milton Academy. Her early decision application was more of a formality than anything else—as long as she maintained her grades and didn't get DCed. With roughly seven months of senior year left, she planned to coast until graduation, which really meant slack off, party, hang out with Tripp, and have sex with Nick. She counted the days until her eighteenth birthday later that year, when she'd finally be able to scream at her mother, *Screw you! You don't have control over me anymore.* In the meantime, she settled for rebellion.

Her mom didn't recognize the girl in front of her. Whitney had the same muscular legs and long brown hair, the same angular face and energy. But now there was a hardness to Whitney. It wasn't just that she disrespected her mom; it seemed she disrespected herself and the goals she'd worked toward her entire life. Whitney's mom remembered the girl her daughter used to be—vivacious, enthusiastic, determined. Whitney had always loved skating and put her family first. She cared about succeeding. Granted, raising her had always involved rules (no subscription to *Seventeen*), limitations (no making out with boys in the backseat while her mother drove them to the movies), and prayer (as a girl, Whitney went to church and prayed for pierced ears and manicures).

But Nick's influence, her mother realized, showed itself in ways she couldn't possibly control—in ways she couldn't possibly imagine.

What was so remarkable about Whitney's life in high school was her ability to excel at skating, keep up in school, and spend at least four nights a week, at various points from sophomore through senior year, sneaking out of the house to see Nick. By junior year, he'd been kicked out of his latest boarding school and was living at home again with his aunt in Charlestown, a forty-five-minute drive from Whitney's house in Dedham. If she took a car around midnight, she had at least a couple of hours with Nick before she had to drive home, nap for thirty minutes, wake up for practice at 4:15 A.M., go to school, go back to practice, and finally head home, where she'd fall into bed and prepare to do it all over again.

It was the summer after sophomore year when Whitney first tiptoed barefoot down the stairs and sneaked out of her house. Her mom was away on business and her dad was in charge, which meant she could basically do whatever she wanted. So she grabbed her mother's keys and backed the new car out of the driveway. Whitney didn't have her license yet, but she was armed with a teammate's sporadic driving lessons and sex tips, which she and Nick had already put to good use. That night she took him to the beach. In her sixteen years she'd never known such perfection—stars and water, a blanket, incense, weed and alcohol. She took a swig from the bottle and waited for Nick to light his blunt. Then police lights came on.

Shit! Whitney thought.

I don't have a license!

I stole my mom's car!

We have alcohol and weed!

Like, this could not be more illegal!

She sprinted down the beach and ducked behind a rock. This was the moment when all her mother's warnings were about to come true. She looked back at Nick, who was still frantically gathering their illegal paraphernalia. And then suddenly, luckily, the flashing lights faded and the police car disappeared.

In time, Whitney just got used to being lucky. Nick made her feel like nothing would ever happen to them. They were untouchable as long as they were together. And so when they got back to her house, they went upstairs, past her parents' bedroom, and into her room next door, where they had sex against the wall she shared with her parents.

Whitney's immersion in this rebellious teenage world rarely triggered consequences—until the night she took her dad's SUV. She was driving on the highway just before dawn, miles from Dedham, when her brake pedal froze. The car coughed, shook, and died as she pulled off the road.

Ohmygod, what am I going to do? she thought. *I am so screwed.*

For the first time in a long time, Whitney panicked. Nick wasn't there. She was alone in the middle of nowhere. Where was her cell phone? She had to be at the rink in a couple of hours. It was raining. And she didn't have any shoes. The tears started falling.

Ohmygod!

She was sure she was dead.

She got out of the car and ran as fast as she could in a random direction, her bare feet slapping against the wet pavement. Up ahead she spotted a house with lights on. Her tireless thighs got her there, and she crept up to a window to peer inside. There, sitting side by side, was an elderly couple.

Ohmygod, there is a God, she thought as she knocked on the front door and prepared to play the innocent. The door opened.

My car just broke down, she sputtered, pushing hair out of her face.
Like, I don't know what's going on.
I need your phone.

The elderly couple looked at this barefoot young girl with soaking wet clothes and overplucked eyebrows, who said *like* too much, and, despite her predicament, seemed somehow forceful and brave.

I need your phone, Whitney said again.

The couple let her inside.

She dialed furiously and waited for her mother to pick up.

Mom?

I am at these people's house.

I think I was sleepwalking.

And I took Dad's car.

And it broke down.

And I don't know where I am.

And I'm really confused and scared.

Her mom picked her up right away. The next morning at school, Whitney told her friends what had happened. They couldn't believe it. Her father didn't believe it. She almost didn't either, but there invariably came points in her life when, while trying to scare her mother, she really scared herself.

There was a point in high school when Whitney's mom still believed her daughter was a good girl. She knew nothing about the time, sophomore year, when Whitney got drunk at a Dave Matthews concert and kissed seven guys, some of them from Milton, some from skating, and some she'd never met before. Or the time, after Whitney and Nick started dating, that Whitney and a girlfriend hooked up together in front of their boyfriends. *You have no pride in yourself,* her mother would have screeched. But on a scale of 1 to 10, 1 being entirely asexual and 10 being obsessed with sex, Whitney considered herself a 9.5. When she and Nick first started sleeping together (she called it *fucking* or *having sex,* rarely *making love*), she'd slipped into his dorm room whenever she visited him at school. Once she got her license, she swung by his dorm even when she had to be at the rink less than an hour later. She'd park the car in the first spot she found, run to Nick's room, have sex, sprint back to her car, and barely make it to practice on time.

Her first orgasm—in Nick's bed, his aunt's bedroom nearby, at some odd hour of the night—was delicious.

Wow! Whitney thought. *Wow! I'm really in love with this guy.*

Whitney thought she was going to be with Nick forever. They were going to go off to their respective colleges, visit on the weekends, travel over vacations, graduate, and get married. To Whitney, an orgasm meant love. The idea that she might have to go through high school without sex or a boyfriend was as foreign to her as the idea that a boyfriend might actually want to give his girlfriend oral sex. Nick still refused to go down on Whitney, and she didn't get it. She'd given him head a million times. If he truly loved her, he'd want to make her feel good. She had supreme knowledge of her sexual self, but, like her friends, she always turned to the DSGs with questions. What are dick ties? Is that a queef? No question was left unasked.

What is wrong with him?

Does he have ED?

No??

Is he gay??

Whitney thought she knew what she was doing with the "pulling-out" birth control method. She and Nick relied on it for over a year, but after three pregnancy scares she ultimately had to tell her mother—her traditional and devoutly religious mother—that she'd been playing sexual roulette with her life. Despite safe-sex talks, national campaigns, health class, and friends' close calls, Whitney, like many girls and boys her age, assumed she'd always be safe. Later in senior year, Jillian would become so desperate to lose her virginity that she'd get drunk and ask everyone at a party for a condom. Brady often "forgot" to use condoms in the first place. Teens like them—privileged, intelligent, going somewhere—didn't get HPV, herpes, chlamydia, or HIV. Whitney could never have asked Nick if he'd had unprotected sex with anyone else. Condoms were annoying. Whitney's mother got her the birth control pill just in time, because Whitney had already started cheating on Nick.

Why am I with him? she'd ask the DSGs from time to time. *He's so fat. He doesn't do sports. He's not good looking. He's not right for me.* They listened, shaking their pretty heads and wondering if this time Whitney might actually leave Nick for good. *We'll see what happens,* the girls said to one another. And so off Whitney went to find another guy. Each one was slightly different, but they represented her ideal equation: preppy and hot—the type of boys that, ironically, Whitney's mom would have liked, not because they were good-looking but because they were kind and clean-cut. As long as the guy knew what to do during sex, Whitney was satisfied.

Grayson, for example, fit the mold because he played hockey and was a year older. She used to walk around campus with him and Church, listening to them talk nonchalantly about having a threesome and doing the Dub Saw.

You should definitely let us do this to you, guys like them said to Whitney.

Okay, she replied. *Ha ha. Real funny.*

Sometimes she stayed right there, letting them indulge their fantasy and believe she might actually let them treat her like a young DSG (which, at the time, she was). But she prided herself on the fact that she'd never been one of the girls they used for a story. It was a particular badge of honor, but when she finally slept with Grayson, she regretted it right away. How could someone who was so cool and had had so much experience be so bad in bed? Whitney couldn't have cared less that she had sex with another person. She regretted wasting a sexual experience on someone who made it so unsatisfying. This was regret. This was guilt. This was cheating on her boyfriend.

After Grayson, Whitney turned to an ex-boyfriend and then a one-night stand with a hot guy she met on vacation in the Caribbean. Each time, though, Whitney eventually went back to Nick.

I feel so comfortable with him, she rationalized to herself.

He knows my body inside and out.

He's gonna protect me.

He's my best friend.

He's seen me at my worst.

I can show up without makeup on.

I'm the best thing he's ever gonna get.

No girl wants to be with him.

Not even an ugly girl wants to be with him.

Even for a confident and self-assured girl like Whitney, being vulnerable was worse than settling. Safety was precious, and she loved knowing that if she ever needed him, all she would have to say was, *Nicholas, I need you,* and he'd be on the next plane, train, or bus ride to her, no matter where she was.

November passed. Fall turned to winter. Whitney's family celebrated her eighteenth birthday, wondering what could possibly happen next, because all she talked about was how everything was going to change. Now she was an adult. She skipped a few skating practices. She slacked off in school. She expected her early decision acceptance letter in the mail any day, making her that much closer to leaving home for good. Fights with her mother grew from frustration to hatred and disgust. Whitney disappeared for weekends at a time, telling her mom she'd come home on Saturday and then not showing up until late on Sunday night. Entire weekends were consumed by the void that was Nick's bedroom. The two of them would have sex, smoke, eat, and have sex again. Her mother had no idea where Whitney was; all she knew was that she was in the process of losing her daughter.

Whenever Whitney asked her mom if she and Nick could hang out in her bedroom, the answer was always the same.

I really want you guys down here, her mom said. *You don't have to be talking to us, but—*

Mom, that's ridiculous. What if we just want to go like, sit upstairs and look at pictures?

Her mother wasn't stupid, and, eventually, Whitney lost it.

I want to be with him, Mom.

I'm a senior in high school.

I'm eighteen.

No, her mother said.

Screw you! I can leave and you can't do anything about it because I'm technically an adult!

Whitney was furious. She stared at her mother, fuming. Why did she always have to ruin everything? Why did she always say no? Whitney was so angry she threw a water bottle at the floor. That's when her father came storming in. He was a quiet, gentle man. But when he got angry, Whitney knew she'd really done something wrong. This time he didn't walk in patiently or calmly. He didn't try to explain himself. He assumed the reason for his anger was obvious, considering Whitney had just thrown a bottle at her mother—or so he thought. So he burst through the door and lunged at Whitney and pushed her up against the bed. She screamed and flailed beneath her father's grasp, his hands grabbing her by the neck as though she were a dead chicken.

Afterward, Whitney packed a small bag, called Nick, and left home for good. Her mother sent her father to their summer home and asked Whitney to come home, but she didn't want to. She saw a psychiatrist and cried abuse, but even she knew better: Her father was the scapegoat. The real problem was her mother.

Whitney walked through Nick's front door with the intention of never leaving. Life in his house was a million times better. His aunt spoiled her rotten, taking her out to dinner, lending her the luxury SUV, proofreading her papers, and paying for everything. She and Nick had sex whenever they wanted. He had dealer contacts near home, so they got high almost every night, drove to Pizzeria Uno and White Hen for late-night food, and sometimes smoked in the morning before Whitney left for school. She was in heaven. Her mother was beside herself.

Whitney's mom called Nick's house begging Whitney to come home.

Please understand, I need my daughter back, she told his aunt.

Meanwhile, her mother's friends were outraged.

Just get rid of your daughter, they said.

She's moving out on you.

You know, she can't do that to you.

Stop paying for her, stop giving her things, and end it, they concluded.

In some ways Whitney's mom believed her friends were right. Nick turned Whitney against her family. He made her lazy. He convinced her to try marijuana. He disrespected her parents. Years later, Whitney would learn that the only person who kept her mother sane was Whitney's grandmother. *You need to stand by your daughter,* she instructed, and that's exactly what her mom did. She had faith that Whitney would someday snap out of it. For the time being she had to be patient, and that meant doing things her daughter's way.

Around the time Whitney left home, she also quit skating. After she missed a couple of practices, she skipped a few more. And then one day her coach made Whitney and her best friend walk in front of him so he could inspect their bodies. Whitney spent her entire life fitting into tight clothes and, lately, comparing herself to the other DSGs, who had skinny sticklike legs with thighs that seemed half the size of her own. All around her, girlfriends and teammates seemed to starve themselves or binge and purge. On training trips, some skaters ate only desserts and other times they ate next to nothing. Her coach was dissatisfied. Whitney needed to eat less. She needed to train more. Nationals were coming up in a couple of months. She had to perfect her long program. Practice her spread eagle. Nail her jumps. Actually, she needed to stop skating, and that's exactly what she did.

For the first time in her life, Whitney felt as if she was making her own decisions. Her new life with Nick seemed normal, as though lots of teenage girls moved in with their boyfriends, ignored their parents, disregarded responsibilities, and did whatever they wanted whenever they chose. Whitney thought that living with Nick was the mature choice. She felt like an adult. Finally she was a woman.

congratulations!

Over six weeks had passed since roughly two-thirds of the senior class submitted their early decision applications to schools across the country. It was now the second week of December, and futures were about to be decided as decisions arrived in students' mailboxes or appeared on Internet sites. Isabel, Caroline, and a few other girls in the Hysterics were all waiting to hear back from Ivy League schools. Jillian and Whitney vied for small liberal arts colleges in New England, as did Brady. Reed and Josh aimed straight for the top of the Ivy League. At recess, students traded notes on who got in where and who (voices lowered) got rejected. The differences were obvious. A girl bursting through the doors from Centre Street, frantic and wild, crying and racing to her friends—she was accepted. Another girl sitting quietly nearby, leaning into a hug, about to cry very different tears—she was deferred.

For Annie, walking through the hallways in Pryce was an exercise in compartmentalizing regret. Friends wrote *CONGRATULATIONS!* with markers across the whiteboards hanging outside seniors' dorm rooms, so that everyone knew when another girl had gotten into school.

Congrats! You did it! Senior spring, here you come! When Annie got to her tiny bedroom, she tied back her hair and felt remorse. Why hadn't she just picked a school and applied early? She slumped back in her desk chair and closed her eyes.

They're done with the process . . . ohmygosh, I haven't even started yet.

I have to do almost all my applications.

I really need to keep on working.

She didn't want to think about what lay ahead over winter break: writing essays, filling out applications, explaining to her parents why she was so behind, and then, once she got back to Milton in January, keeping her grades up all the way until April, when she would finally hear back from her colleges. She couldn't start any of the work at school, either, because she always had another test to study for or three chapters to read. She had to prepare for the annual winter concert. And then there was always a younger girl in Pryce who knocked on the door at an odd hour of the evening to commiserate about how much work she had, how much she missed her parents, how much she hated so-and-so, and how much a certain boy was ruining her life. By the time Annie crawled into bed at night, she felt as if she'd diffused at least fifty stress stories, given in to at least two distractions (a TV show, dressing up for fun), and not accomplished a single productive task.

When she finally went home to Lenox for winter break, she turned her bedroom into a makeshift college application prison, and wrote essays to an obscene number of schools about why she, out of tens of thousands of applicants, should be accepted. Her parents couldn't believe Annie had waited until the last minute to write her essays. They didn't get it: School was *so* stressful; she had *no* time; there was *too* much to do. But they helped in any way they could, reading drafts and offering advice she rarely ever took.

Her mom spent the days fretting about fixations that seemed infinitesimally insignificant to Annie, like creating the perfect table setting for the family's Christmas dinner. Annie sometimes confided in her mom about stress and school, though never about guys and friends.

Yet she realized something of great importance during her fall semester: She was lucky to have the mom she had. When her parents came to school for Parents' Day in October, they joined all the other moms and dads who descended upon the grassy quads to follow their children from class to class, meeting friends and teachers, and generally assessing the Milton experience. For a single day, families were suddenly on display in front of a demanding audience of peers.

Mom, you're wearing that?

Dad, please don't bring the camera.

No, you cannot introduce yourself to Doc Robs.

Annie's mom fell asleep in biology class, but she wasn't as bad as the woman in Annie's ethics class during sophomore year who said, *If I'm in an elevator and I see a black man, I am going to be more scared.* The whole class turned toward the mother and then at her daughter, who cried, *Mom! You can't say that!* No, Annie's mom wasn't nearly that bad.

Throughout Parents' Day senior year, Annie sat uncomfortably in each class, wearing a pink dress shirt and a black cardigan, trying to be noticed. Friends told her how much she resembled her mom, and as Annie walked around campus that day, she surveyed all the other mothers. One overly tan woman wore a Burberry coat and carried a big Chanel bag; another showed up in a fur coat and flashy duds. The DSGs' moms dripped in gold, but none were as provocative as their daughters. Annie regarded her own mom, her wonderful, simple, loving mother who wore an understated sweater and scarf on Parents' Day. Annie realized how much she loved this woman, and how lucky she was to have her.

The only reason I'm coming home is to see if I got into college or not, Whitney reminded her mother as they drove around her neighborhood looking for the mailman. She sat erect in the passenger seat, as if preparing to take to the ice, and ran her fingers through the ends of her hair, pulling out knots while she frantically scanned side streets. It was December 15, and Whitney had been living with Nick for almost three weeks. His aunt continued to treat Whitney like her angel, and Whitney's mother was still beside herself. She didn't raise a prima donna or a quitter. She didn't know this girl who'd left home and made demands. But she would have given anything to see her daughter—to watch her, touch her, or just listen to her silence.

Whitney shrieked.

The mailman!

Her mom jumped out of the car and, minutes later, ran back waving something in the air. Everyone knew that deferrals and rejections came in thin envelopes, while acceptances arrived in packages with pamphlets, catalogs, and paperwork. Whitney squinted her eyes through the car window, trying to guess the size of the letter in her mom's hand. Between her fingers was a small white envelope. It was paper thin.

I didn't get in, Whitney thought. *Ohmygod, I didn't get in.*

She was supposed to have been accepted. The skating coach had recruited her. He'd promised her. Getting into college was supposed to be easy. Her mom got back into the car and handed the envelope to Whitney, suddenly recognizing the daughter she used to know—alive, nervous, full of feeling. Whitney tore open the letter, looked at her mom, and cried. There, on the left side of the page, toward the top, beneath her name was the word *Congratulations!*

The past seventeen years had always pointed toward this moment, and all Whitney's mom wanted to do was take her out, celebrate over dinner, and treat her like an adult. Instead, Whitney made her mom take her back to Nick's house, where she commemorated her acceptance by getting high. Later that night she wrote an abomination of a history paper with lazy sentences like *It actually it was* and *The Civil War was a great.*

A couple of weeks later, Whitney finally went home, but only because her mom offered to take her to the Caribbean. The trip was a bribe, though hardly a novel idea, as their family had been vacationing on the same island for Whitney's entire life. Her mom thought that spending a week with family might remind Whitney of who she was and where she came from. But all Whitney planned to do was wear skimpy outfits, flit around in a bathing suit, cheat on Nick, and go clubbing with her older cousins, the confidence of a twenty-one-year-old plastered across her adorable baby face.

Whitney heard a rumor that Jillian had created the Stupid People Who Got Into College List, and put Whitney's name in the number one spot. Whitney thought the whole thing was typical. She understood that people hated her for getting into a top college because she was an athlete, but she'd worked just as hard at figure skating as Jillian had in school. Besides, girls like Jillian weren't supposed to have to make such lists. Jillian wasn't someone anyone expected to be turned down by a college. Even Whitney knew she was a brilliant writer and exceptional student. If anyone was going to get into college, it was Jillian, and Jillian thought so, too.

That summer, she'd spent two weeks in the car with her parents, which was hell in and of itself, but the whole purpose of the trip was to look at colleges, and that made everything worse. Jillian didn't sleep. She dreaded rest stops. She realized she had to organize a writing portfolio and make a tennis video. Yale was amazing, but she didn't think she could get in. Swarthmore was *frightening*. Haverford was *inbred* and Bryn Mawr was like *some weird cult*. The only good part about Johns Hopkins was that she got to visit John Waters's house. NYU was depressing because it made her realize graduate school would be so much better than college. And every so often, Jillian contemplated rolling down the car window, leaping outside, and getting run over by oncoming traffic.

The college office gave her a list of reach and safety schools; Vassar was the perfect choice, and she had a near-guaranteed acceptance. Jillian decided to apply early, but the process was an unfathomable challenge. The SATs came like weight gain, uninvited and entirely dreaded. And her essays and writing samples were like sending out pieces of her heart for the entire world to read, judge, and reject. Jillian turned to her journal:

> i started thinking about [everything I have to do for my application] on the
> drive home and i started hyperventilating and we pulled over at a rest stop
> in framingham so i could use the bathroom and i threw up and then i just
> started bawling. luckily my dad took the train home so he wasn't there. it
> was just me and my mom. so she gave me a big hug and we stood there for
> a while so i could catch my breath. when you actually have to record on a
> few pieces of paper everything you've done with your life up until now, it
> makes you feel like a failure. i would never want to be anyone else but
> myself, but, at this time, i can't help but wax about how unfair it all seems.
> and i'm fat.

As college decisions arrived in mid-December, Jillian watched many of her classmates get into schools early. The *Paper* joked that it was easier to get into the Oval Office than to get into college, but Isabel and Caroline were both accepted by their Ivy League schools. Some classmates might have wondered how a student like Isabel, who didn't seem to excel at anything in particular, made it into the Ivy League. They underestimated the breadth of her intelligence; she didn't get A pluses because she didn't try very hard, yet she actually was quite brilliant. Once she got into college, her extracurricular activities had served their purpose. She dropped photography, tutoring, and the public issues board, though she'd never stop analyzing films and culture. When Phoebe was deferred by Yale, she laughed it off even though she was devastated, joking that she would become a rock groupie.

One day Jillian came home shouting all sorts of good news, only to find her mother standing at the kitchen counter, holding a skinny envelope with Jillian's name written on the front. This was it, her moment of revenge, the proof that she was successful and desirable—that all her hard work over the past few months had paid off. Jillian was waiting for more than a decision from a college; she was waiting for a decision on the rest of her life. She opened the letter. She unfolded the paper. She'd been rejected by Vassar—not deferred, but rejected. The letter was proof of what Jillian believed all along: popular girls like Whitney got everything.

basically there is no justice in the college process and it's so corrupt. it's sooooo ass backwards. (except for a few exceptions) . . . i'm bitter. but i wake up and there's snow and i make tea and i listen to my awesome wintry music and i think about the OC and chrismukkah and i think about [my English teacher] and . . . everything's a little better. and then i remember teh TEN BILLION [college essays] i have to do.

Reed was deferred from the Ivy League. It was a mortal blow, straight to the gut, because James Bond wasn't supposed to get turned down. But Reed refused to get upset. Instead, he focused on his list of schools for regular applications, comforting himself with the fact that he didn't plan to apply to a single safety, unless he counted Trinity College as a safety, which he didn't. His life generally continued in its typical fashion. He and Cush dressed up like ninjas. He watched cute girls at recess and ogled Ava from afar. Hanley guys spied on dorm mates who brought girls up to their rooms. Once a guy videotaped himself having sex with his girlfriend. And once two guys hid under the bed while another hid under the sheets, all in an effort to watch a friend hook up with a girl and persuade her to perform strange sex acts. She wasn't convinced.

One evening, just before winter break, Reed ran into Isabel in the Hanley hallways. She stood there with a girlfriend, looking awkward and surprised.

I'm going to get some food, Reed said, uncertain as to whether he'd just made an announcement or an invitation.

The girls followed. He took them to the dining hall and then upstairs to his dorm room, having no idea that he was, quite literally, making Isabel's life. So this was how girls and guys got together, she realized: by total chance, by random run-ins around campus—or while hanging out in the dorms. The imposing brick was so familiar and representative, a private school uniform that was just as recognizable and meaningful as the Coach bags and the designer jeans worn by the DSGs. And now Isabel walked around it with a popular hockey guy, passing other Hanley boys milling around the doorways and staring at her as though they could see through her.

Isabel and her friend had been in Reed's room for only ten minutes when parietals ended, but before she left she took one final glance around. There was his bed. There were his pillows. That was his desk and those were the drawers where he might keep his underwear. Were those floral sheets? Just being there was surreal, like glimpsing the inner sanctum of someone she desperately wanted to know. She could have stayed there all night. She liked knowing that she'd finally ended up in a guy's dorm room, as though hanging out with a hockey jock was something that happened every day.

Later that night, Reed's friends badgered him.

Do you ever hang out with her?

No, Reed said.

Fat ass, fat titties, his friend croaked.

Mmm, okay, Reed said.

He paused to consider Isabel, because he'd never really done it before. When he learned she got into the Ivy League, he realized she was just as smart as he thought she was. He sensed there was something more to her that he hadn't uncovered. And Reed always liked mystery. Isabel was intriguing precisely for this reason—and because she wasn't a DSG.

I bet you can't [get together with her], a friend dared.

Watch, Reed said.

Winter break meant many things to Reed. No more teachers. No more papers. No more grades. No more cafeteria meals or rigid school rules. For a couple of weeks, he would be free. Some of his friends were off to mountains, beaches, or their living room couches. Like many boarders, he went home to see his family and finish his college applications. He decided that the school he applied to early was not the right place for him. He wanted a college with an old boys' mentality and girls who had a reputation for being hot. He wrote his essays diligently, completely confident that at least one of his schools would want him.

Brady went through the process with a similarly blasé attitude but with less to back it up, and Josh, poor Josh, got deferred from his Ivy choice and struggled to finish his regular applications.

Isabel was one of the lucky ones. She spent winter break in the Caribbean celebrating her early acceptance with her family and a friend. Surely this was what high school was supposed to be like: free time, boys, going to bars. On the first night of the trip, Isabel, her cousins, and her friend picked up some American guys at a local club. The guys were in their twenties and taught the girls how to walk like a member of the Crips, the infamous street gang. Isabel wasn't terribly impressed. One boy didn't attend college, another said he'd traveled the world (which she learned meant two months in Ibiza), and none of them was tough. Still, the girls were smitten, if not by the guys themselves, then certainly by the attention. Eventually someone mentioned getting high.

Oh, we know the bartender, one of the guys said.

He's who we always get weed from, the other added.

Why don't you guys just come back with us, to our beach?

The girls excused themselves to consider the invitation.

This is kind of stupid, they whispered.

But whatever.

We'll just go back to our place pretty soon.

The girls went to the guys' hotel, which had private villas and beach property. Isabel's cousin made joints by emptying the tobacco from cigarettes while Isabel and her friend stood by the guys' truck trying to figure out which one was cutest. The girls were drunk, and forgot about the promise they'd made to each other earlier that night: These guys may be good enough to talk to, but they were *no-gos*, which meant unworthy of a hookup.

Later, when everyone went swimming, Isabel had a lot of firsts. She got fingered (she was indifferent to the experience: *It was just like, okay, I'm being fingered*), swapped guys with her girlfriend, and then kissed her girlfriend. This final act was not a sexual thing. It was a vacation thing. It was risqué. It was also something she knew she never could have done at Milton, at least not around guys like Reed. Here, guys noticed her. They wanted her despite her status as a Hysteric and her recess locale in the Cave. She probably wouldn't have kissed her girlfriend had the guys not pushed their heads together. But they did, giving the girls an audience. Isabel was going to college. She was starting a new life. She was having a random hookup.

The next morning Isabel's mother's cheeriness jerked the girls from their hangovers.

Did you have a good time? she asked.

In response: *Yeah, it was okay.*

To each other: *Let's not do that again.*

But then they did do it again.

Isabel and her friend spent another evening with the Crips-walking older guys. Isabel went swimming with one of them. Behind a rock, half submerged in the water, she kissed and straddled him, whispered, *I'm a virgin,* then let him lead her down the beach. When they got there, there being away from her friend and the other boys, she leaned over his body and dug her knees into the sand. Brushing wet hair from her face, she hunched over him, dropped her neck, and put her mouth around his penis. Salt mixed with sand. It was revolting, but she persisted, up and down, up and down, until she couldn't take the taste any longer. She stopped, sand grinding between her teeth, rinsed her mouth and began again, all too aware of his age (twenty-one), unsure if she should be embarrassed or empowered that she had to take a break at all.

Later that night, back in the girls' hotel room, Isabel reported the details to her friend and her cousin.

Ohmygod, the girls squealed.

That's so exciting.

Your first time!

Then her friend said she'd thought there was a sixty/forty chance Isabel had gone off to lose her virginity that night.

I was absolutely not going to have sex with him, she insisted, annoyed that her friend thought she was that dirty.

The next morning Isabel was miserable. She thought she'd been ready for oral sex. She didn't actively want to go down on that particular boy, in that particular setting, but she didn't *not* want to either. Regret stings hard when you realize the consequences of what you've done. Isabel had never pictured her first time giving head, but if she had, it never would have been like that.

With guys who thought they were gangsters, she thought, *in the middle of the water. Like, gross.*

It felt kind of dirty.

I didn't feel taken advantage of.

But it was just kind of like, eww.

Isabel started to cry.

When she returned to Lexington, back to quiet streets and a quiet home in her small New England town, Isabel's tears turned to laughter. She redefined the trip as one big joke and e-mailed all of her friends: *Man, I have a crazy story.*

chapter ten

lift the jaws

for Brady and Reed, December was about something more awesome and possibly more meaningful than the outcome of early decision applications. It was hockey season. Practice began in late fall, but December marked the true beginning of the season, and with the annual Flood-Marr Tournament just before Christmas, the Tabor Tournament over New Year's, and games twice a week starting in January, there was a lot of bonding time ahead, which was, of course, part of the reason the guys loved hockey so much. Walk through the main entrance of the ACC and go down a central corridor dividing the basketball courts and the hockey rink. Punch the security code into the last door on the right, push it open, walk past a pile of hockey sticks, and enter the boys' varsity hockey locker room, a world where rules don't exist.

Brady lingered in the locker room showers after practice. Water streamed down his body, splashing the beige tiles beyond the edge of the stall. There were no shower curtains (the guys had ripped them off themselves), and the air was thick with steam. Water swirled into soapy bubbles before disappearing down the drains. Sometimes thin rivers of yellow urine trickled into the foam. Sometimes the guys had pissing fights and sometimes they covered the entire floor with water and soap to make a shower slide. Brady arched his back and tilted his head into the water, letting it flatten his curls. The hum of his teammates' conversations went something like this.

Dude, did you hook up with Mary? I heard you did, man, nice work.

Nah, whatever, I don't really talk about that shit.

Whatever, just tell us!

Come on.

We're not gonna fuckin' go up to her and be like, Oh, so I heard you gave head. Just tell us.

Guys, let it go, he wants to be a pussy about it, let him, his call.

Of course we hooked up, dude. She gave me a fuckin' blow job.

You finger her?

Yup.

You eat that shit out, man?

No response.

Don't dodge it, dude, did you? You bang that chick?

I mean, you know her, you know how she is. That's all I'm saying. Fuck you guys if that's not enough. You're like a buncha chicks; all you want is gossip.

Yeeeaahhh, you totally fucked her. Good shit, bro!

Brady would have chuckled, but he was exhausted from a hard practice in preparation for Flood Marr. When he and the guys got back to the locker room that day, they devoured a rack of subs that Brady's mom had brought in to celebrate his birthday. She'd brought a cake, too, which just sat there amid the sweaty equipment.

Hey, Brady, someone said.

Brady closed his eyes in the shower, feeling full and warm all over.

Turn around.

He did, and Church threw the entire cake in his face. Green and white frosting slid down his body to the shower floor. Water turned the chocolate cake soggy. Everyone was hysterical. This was life inside the varsity hockey locker room.

Dude, you see this? a teammate once asked as Reed strolled in. The boy was completely naked, with one leg perched, and pointed to where his pubic hair should have been. Behind him were white walls and rows of individual wooden cubbies that were about three feet wide, three feet deep, and seven feet tall. The smallest guys on the team could stuff themselves inside their cubbies if they brought their knees up to their chests. The biggest players had enough room to sit comfortably, even among the jerseys, underwear, elbow pads, shin pads, pants, and gloves hanging from the metal hooks like lifeless skeletons of protective padding.

I just fuckin' waxed this shit, the boy said. *Try it.*

Reed looked at his friend's hairless groin, contemplated the suggestion, and laughed. He didn't take the advice, but another time he and Brady stood in front of the mirror together, also completely naked, discussing the pros and cons of shaving their pubic hair.

I tried going up once, Reed said, admiring his abs. *Let me tell you, it was deadly.*

All right, Brady began, *what you do is, you go down and then to the side this way and this way.*

They stood in the main locker room. Helmets rested on top of the deep, yawning cubbies, and bags were stuffed underneath. The stench was thick. Boys were usually naked or only half clothed, and loved behaving badly. Sometimes they peed or hocked a lugey into a teammate's mouth. One guy performed "dick tricks," like making it look as though he could inflate his balls.

In popular culture, the male hockey player is thick and powerful. He sweats, grunts, and slams opponents into walls. He oozes testosterone as he slices up the ice and whacks the puck into the goal. The cheering crowd feeds his adrenaline, and this adoration, even at a school like Milton, whose team wasn't particularly talented, persisted in the locker room and on a now-defunct hockey website which offered a comprehensive hockey-culture education. There were pictures of guys packing a dip and *puck bunnies* scantily clad, seductively staring out from the computer screen. A glossary of terms offered sexual moves and names for girls. Reed's personal favorite was *shit tickets,* meaning toilet paper. The website was not simply a guide to the hockey player's life. It was a nod to a sports culture that promoted the use and abuse of girls, and was accessible to all.

A photograph of Milton's hockey team in 1912 boasts eight varsity players wearing simple uniforms, protective knee padding, and narrow black skates. Their bodies are lanky, and their coach, who stands dead center, wears a suit, the only true sign of masculinity. The image hung virtually unseen in the Old Boys' Gym, but walk across the driveway, into the monolithic ACC, and Milton hockey takes on a new identity. In a photograph of the 2004–2005 hockey team, the guys look like a formidable force. With twenty-two players and a handful of coaches, the guys are omnipotent with their grid-caged helmets, shoulder pads, and thickly laced skates. The padding accentuates their chests. The boys look like high school heroes on steroids, though their mothers and fathers and teachers know they are just teenage boys playing a part.

Brady, Reed, and the rest of the guys were convinced they could do anything together. Their friendships were unbreakable. Their behavior was shameless. They'd seen each other naked, probably more often than their girlfriends (when they had girlfriends), and their shared status as Milton hockey players fed their burgeoning egos and taught them that girls, parties, and hookups were part of their reward.

What went on inside the locker room tantalized girls who had a thing for boys' secrets. Did the guys actually run around naked? Did they really measure their penises and make younger players do embarrassing things? Curiosity stemmed from crushes, hookups, and sexual experiences: What if he told his friends I gave him head? What if he said I wasn't good? What if he told them how loud I screamed? For a girl, the idea that a player might talk about her in the locker room can be intriguing—I have his attention; he wants to brag. But it can also be threatening—he thinks I'm a slut. Whatever was said, the girls' interest made the boys believe that their own behavior mattered.

Reed wasn't surprised by the locker room antics when he first got to Milton. Like most boys who grew up playing hockey, he hung out with older guys in locker rooms, listening to them swap stories, brag, and make heads turn. Reed paid particular attention. One guy said he'd had sex with Tara Reid. Another swore a famous singer had fucked his entire junior hockey team. The stories could all have been lies, but their authenticity mattered less than the fact that they were possible. Soon, what were once surprising locker room conversations became fairly unremarkable.

Hey, Justin, how big are your sister's boobs?

Hey, hey, Coach said.

Everyone went silent.

How big are they? Coach asked.

Reed quickly learned that such exchanges were normal. They were expected. They were his future, too.

In Milton's hockey locker room, players respected the tacit hierarchy: Seniors stood above juniors, who stood above sophomores, who stood above freshmen. Newcomers almost always got shit, but older guys liked taking an interest in a younger boy or two, giving them the kind of embarrassing attention that would help them rise in the ranks, putting them on the track to becoming a leader.

You have a girlfriend who's like, incredible, an older guy would begin, talking to an underclassmen.

You gotta speed things up with her.

She's too cute.

You're moving like a turtle on this one.

The younger boy looked at his high school idol, petrified because he knew what was coming next.

I'll talk to her. Don't worry about it. I'll hook it up for you, the older guy would say.

No, don't, the boy would chirp, horrified at the idea that this hockey god, this total man, would tell his adorable girlfriend she should try anal sex. *Don't do that!* he would yell.

Reed and Brady thought Coach Cannata heard hundreds of these conversations during his first two years at Milton. Banter was part of the hockey tradition, but the guys knew that Coach took the sport seriously. He was there to win and assumed his players were there to train. He was an attractive man with slick, dark brown hair and an extensive hockey resumé. He'd come from a major hockey program at Northeastern University, had over a dozen years of collegiate and prep coaching experience, and helped lead various United States Select Teams to gold medals. The 2004–2005 season was his second at Milton, and it was clear to Brady and Reed that he planned to boost the program. He brought a respectable work ethic to the ice and didn't put up with crap from anyone. Practices were intense. Total dedication was expected. Drinking and misbehaving were forbidden.

Reed resented Coach Cannata's tough tactics. Though Reed peaked at the end of the season his junior year, scoring twelve points in the last four games, Coach gave him a hard time about his weight. That summer, Reed went on a diet and trained like a professional. He arrived at preseason fitter and leaner than ever before, but he never felt Coach acknowledged the change. And then, for what seemed like no reason at all, Coach dropped him from the second line down to the third. Reed was a senior. He was a good player. He wasn't supposed to be dropped.

Guys old enough to remember Milton's former coach had experienced a very different leadership style. He was the living, breathing Boston stereotype of a homegrown hockey talent, and generally believed that if the guys played well and tried hard, they were doing enough. While his coaching style seemed largely at odds with the elite prep school, he'd graduated from Milton and understood who his players were. They remember him not for teaching hockey skills or refining skating technique. He taught them a way of life.

You guys are playing like hell.

Don't be sissies.

Saturday night, do your thing.

Go nuts.

That beloved way of life, however, did not translate into a successful record. The Milton guys kept losing. Potential star players chose other private schools over Milton. Or they were lured to different parts of the United States or Canada to play junior hockey, a competitive program for men ages twenty and under. The former coach's days were numbered when the administration found out his players drank at their hotel while playing at a tournament. He may not have known what the guys were up to, but he left the next year, which was when Coach Cannata had come on board.

With a veteran coach at the helm and a new crop of stellar players—eight in total, all personally recruited by Cannata—Reed and Brady had high hopes for their senior year season. At first they were apprehensive about team dynamics, because integrating so many new guys into an already cohesive brotherhood was risky. But the new guys fit in seamlessly. The team had already defeated Buckingham, Browne, & Nichols (BB&N) and tied Thayer, and they claimed second place in their division at the Flood-Marr Tournament, which brought together eight of the top hockey teams, as well as division I and II coaches who were on the lookout for new recruits. It was a solid showing, and the guys were ready for their next challenge, the Tabor Tournament over New Year's Eve held at Tabor Academy, an ISL school on Cape Cod.

Brady bemoaned the conflict for two whole months. He couldn't remember a time he'd gone to bed before midnight on New Year's Eve. The team spent the holiday in a shabby motel near Tabor Academy. With hours to go until midnight, they crammed into one of their rooms and turned on the TV. Guys sprawled on the floor and beds and listened to each other crack jokes and share their best sex stories. One by one the boys spoke, the older guys watching the younger players squirm, dreading their spotlight moment. The site was oddly reminiscent of a slumber party, where girls cuddle in blankets, sit on pillows, and play truth or dare. At the same time, friendship reigned inside the hotel room. If the guys couldn't drink and party with their buddies, this was the time to make teammates into brothers.

In early January, students returned to campus from winter break. Milton was a snowy idyll. Stalwart brick buildings and acres of grassy quads were shrouded in white. Misshapen snowmen appeared outside dorms or on the main quad, and students wrapped themselves in scarves, hats, and mittens. Plows barreled through campus, clearing pathways and sidewalks for students. Exams loomed at the end of the month, but hockey season was in full swing. The guys went to practice each day, sometimes on the ice, sometimes in the weight room, sometimes until as late as eight thirty P.M. They played games most Wednesdays and Saturdays, but there was plenty of time to dick around.

One Saturday afternoon in mid-January, Brady, Church, Quinn, and Taylor, another teammate, started drinking when the hockey game ended. They headed over to Nikki's house, and by nine P.M. they were exhausted, almost comatose. The night was going nowhere, so they concocted a plan. All four players accompanied Nikki to the bedroom, where they started hooking up with her. Clothes came off. Everything was public.

I think I'm just gonna get out of here for a minute, Taylor said.

Brady chuckled.

I really can't do this, Church said, because he supposedly had a girlfriend.

Instead of leaving, Church walked around the room watching Nikki, Brady, and Quinn hook up. As the threesome kissed, made out, and got naked, Church grabbed a bottle of body lotion and squirted it all over them. Then he gave instructions. Brady, you go there. No, Nikki, stay here. Brady was surprised she even agreed to have sex with him.

Brady thought she would have done it right there, while Church and Quinn watched, but he didn't let it happen. To this day, he still isn't sure why. Maybe other guys walked in. Maybe he felt satisfied with the story as it was. Maybe, just maybe, he sensed ambivalence in Nikki's voice. Still, the moment was, without a doubt, the best story of Brady's Milton experience.

One or two guys like him became seniors on the hockey team each year. They drove beat-up cars or giant SUVs. They had girls and stories for miles. And whether they had money or were on scholarship, they walked into the locker room with silly grins on their faces, food in hand, saying they'd just had sex in the Milton Hospital parking lot. The other older players would look at them, thinking, *Of course they're pulling that,* and the younger players would look at them, thinking, *How are they pulling that?* The answer, these boys like Brady would say to the younger player staring at them in awe, was to practice: *Lift the jaws, you guys can do it.*

While Brady was off making legendary stories, Reed was busy plotting his next conquest. He decided to go after the impossible—his good friend's ex-girlfriend. Ava was the kind of girl he wanted to treat like a young woman. She was a DSG, but she was better than the DSGs. She had natural beauty and elegance, and she looked better in sweats than some of her friends did in their preppy outfits. At first the challenge was purely intellectual. Reed wanted to see if he could make Ava like him. He wanted to see how far he could go. In the process, though, Reed fell for her, and he thought she was falling right along with him.

Around mid-January, Reed went to Ava's house to watch the New England Patriots game. Cush was out of town that weekend, and Ava said a couple of friends were going to stop by, too. Reed signed out of his dorm for the night, showed up at her house, and found that he was her only guest. At first he told himself it was just a friend thing, but as he sat next to her on the couch, watching television in the dark, he remembered that look she'd given him in the beginning of the school year, and how adorable she'd been at the homecoming dance. Something more exciting was in store.

Reed wasn't entirely aware of what he was doing until he realized he'd been kissing Ava for a solid ten minutes. He felt drunk, as though he were having the first kiss of his entire life all over again. But he didn't do anything more, and as he fell asleep in the guest bedroom, he was pleased with himself, sure that something else was going to happen. The next morning, Reed found Ava in the kitchen, cooking eggs over easy. He watched this giddy, amazing girl, realizing that she was the one who'd taken the first step—she'd invited him over when she knew it was forbidden. Of course there was regret: *Oh shit, what about Cush?* But desire trumped deference, because kissing Ava was like nothing he'd ever felt before. Reed wanted her, but he also cared about Cush, his own reputation, and public opinion. He didn't know what to do.

While Reed jockeyed for Cush's ex-girlfriend, Josh persisted to flirt with girls online who did not like him back. He thought about Diana, his crush from freshman year. Four times a week he sat in her proximity in the class they took together. Once she wrote *I ♥ Josh* on her binder. Once she leaned over and he saw down her shirt. And once, when they met to do homework, she changed out of her gym shirt right there in front of him, as though standing in a sports bra in front of a guy was an everyday occurrence. Josh looked for any excuse to ask Diana about their homework, but usually she replied with disinterest. So he continued pursuing other girls.

Alicia was still in the picture. Correction: Josh thought Alicia was still in the picture. He kept thinking she'd break up with her boyfriend, and she kept talking with him online, so he was relentless, because part of not being *the man* meant not knowing when to quit.

Josh: do you play a winter sport?
Alicia: used to play hockey, then last yr i tried squash and didnt like it . . .
Alicia: i dont know what to play
Josh: you should play the new sport they are offering
Josh: i think they call it hanging out with josh
Alicia: hahah i dont know if thatll fill my PE requirement . . .

Josh: while we're on the subject of being cute
Josh: shit
Josh: nevermind
Alicia: what?
Alicia: im confused
Josh: i was about to say something that i shouldnt
Alicia: oh
Alicia: i think i catch ur drift
Alicia: thats cool
Josh: in a way i think you do

Josh had the ability to hope beyond all barriers and disappointments. No matter how many times he got shot down, rejected, ignored, or taken for granted, he signed back online, IMed Alicia, and tried to flirt. Earlier that year, she'd told him that *The Lion King* was her favorite movie. Being smart and smooth, Josh asked his parents for two tickets to the Broadway show, which was coming to Boston in January. The idea was brilliant, he thought. He was being sensitive and thoughtful; every girl wanted to be taken to see a show in the city; Alicia would definitely say yes.

Alicia: whyyyy josh whhhyyy . . .
Josh: would it be too weird?
Josh: what your boyfriend doesnt know cant hurt him
Alicia: so now u want me to lie??
Josh: you lie?
Josh: of course not . . .
Alicia: eek i dont know
Alicia: id love to but id feel bad . . .
Josh: like i said i dont want to hassle you but it would be fun
Josh: its not like were going away to some romantic island for the
    weekend . . .
Alicia: i know, what about thqat girl u like tho?
Josh: she was the girl i took to jerry seinfeld

Josh: im not taking her to the lion king a year later after nothing
    happened

Alicia: lol well i thought u still liked her . . .

Josh: well she doesnt like me

Josh: hard to believe huh?

Alicia: yes

Josh: touche

Josh: well what will it be . . . this ISNT a HUGE decision . . . one
    night . . .

Alicia: well should i ask my boyfriend?

No, Josh did not want Alicia to ask her boyfriend. They could have sat together sharing a box of Peanut M&M's, enjoying such on inventive show. He could have whispered in her ear. He could have complimented her outfit and made her feel beautiful. He could have made her happy, he was sure of it. Nothing made sense. Wasn't a date what every girl wanted? Prince Charming? Someone to whisk her off her feet and treat her like a princess?

Josh waited until the day of the show to ask a friend to join him. *The Lion King* was amazing, but he looked at his friend sitting next to him, knowing the evening wasn't supposed to be this way. It wasn't until years later that Josh realized how inappropriate his request had been. Alicia had a boyfriend. Not just a hookup, but a serious, long-term boyfriend. If Josh had been Alicia's boyfriend, and someone else had asked her out, he would have been furious.

Just when Josh's latest efforts with Alicia failed, he found himself on a couch at a party, flirting with a girl who was actually flirting back. Her name was Erica and she liked making fun of the drunk kids around them. She was pretty—nondescript, but decently pretty—and then she confessed that she lived in New York City. Of course Josh would meet a girl who seemed to like him and just so happened to live in another state. Later that night, Erica left the party. Josh went home alone. A few days passed until he chatted online with one of her friends.

Josh: shes cool . . . you have to let me know when shes back in town

Erica's Friend: yeah u liiiiike her

Josh: man . . . i like everyone . . .

Erica's Friend: she thought u were really cool

Josh: thats cuz i was with dylan and rj

Josh: no much competition when their taking off their shirts

Erica's Friend: hahaha shutup

Josh: but ill take the compliment . . .

Erica's Friend: u wanna chill next time she comes to town?

Erica's Friend: yeaaaa u do

Josh: clearly

Erica's Friend: cleeearrrly

Josh was psyched. Maybe Erica was sitting in her room at that very moment, chatting online, telling a friend about this cute guy she'd met in Boston who was really tall and had unkempt brown hair. Maybe she would call him and then visit him. Maybe they'd go on a date and then, later, after dinner and a movie, they'd go to another party, talk on a couch, walk up to a bedroom and kiss, make out, and then maybe, just maybe, she would kiss his neck and chest, working her way down until she gave him oral sex. Suddenly, without any warning, Josh was back, ready to try again. He may have been the "nice guy" who turned to romance to get the girls. Brady may have been the stud and Reed may have been the smooth talker, but they were all teenage boys lusting after the same rewards: hooking up and feeling like men.

chapter eleven

wear your lucky underwear

Over the past week, began an editorial in the *Milton Measure*, just days before exams began during the last week of January, *some drastic transformations have overtaken the Milton campus. Hockey players are in the library. The once-overflowing coffee supply in Forbes Dining Hall often mysteriously disappears by midday. Students find themselves having trouble spelling their own names. Yes, it's that time again: exam week.*

Annie stood in Forbes during lunch, clutching the *Measure* and skimming selections from *How to Survive Exams*:

Do not take any advice from a senior who has been admitted to college.

Wear your lucky underwear. Federal law requires this to be a thong.

Get parietals. A lot. This is great if you take anatomy.

See if you can bribe your teachers. "Special" favors are an option.

If [that] fails, and you are not expelled, research your teachers. Find out dirt about them, and blackmail them for good grades.

Study (optional).

Annie couldn't have disagreed with this last item more. The whole week leading up to exams, she passed late nights in the crowded Pryce common rooms, where nearly all the girls studied and stressed, some subsisting on Easy Mac and chocolate, others on Red Bull, caffeine pills, or Ritalin. Annie never relied on prescription drugs to help her study, but she'd tried caffeine pills a few times. She would have given anything to know she'd do well on the exams. Her entire life seemed to be compressed into biology, calculus, and the rest of her classes, as though their outcomes would determine her happiness forever. But she spent half her nights listening to Pryce girls whine about their own work. You have a ten-page paper due tomorrow? I have a math exam *and* a French exam, and I haven't even started studying. Well, I have honors physics in the morning. Annie listened dutifully, silently screaming to herself: I have to get into Barnard!

While Annie burrowed into her textbooks, praying that the information on the page would somehow leap into her brain, other (especially younger) Pryce girls hooked up. Some students thought that doing well in school precluded romance. There were too many assignments to complete, too many places to be, and too little time to find a girlfriend, boyfriend, or steady hookup. Boarders, though, had that added advantage of being around each other every single day of the week. Regardless of rules and dorm parents, they lived within steps of each other in a little community of overworked, overpressured teenagers with raging hormones and acres of fields to disappear into with that special boy or girl.

Annie heard things. She may have missed the sophomore girl who had sex with a guy on the common room couch hours after check-in, but she heard a story about a girl she knew from childhood—a tomboy with curls who now straightened her hair and covered her eyes with designer sunglasses—who gave Reed a blow job in the chapel.

Be careful, Annie heard older girls had explained to the younger girl. *Things like that get around.*

Oh, well, I always do that when I hook up with a guy, the girl had said.

You don't have to do that! older girls had said. *It's not expected!*

Annie wished she'd received the same advice when she was younger. She would never forget that time outside with Kenny. That time in her living room with Scott. That time when Scott asked, *Can I come on you?* as she gave him a hand job. He ignored her, saying, *Oh, sorry,* after doing it all over her favorite starfish necklace. Annie was just a scared little girl at the time. She couldn't go back in time to remove the prints that boys had left on her, but these younger girls still had a chance, if only they would listen.

Just a couple of weeks before exams, she and a friend had gone shopping in downtown Boston. Annie liked escaping from Milton on the weekends. City life suited her. She'd walk the mile or so from campus to the gritty stop for the T (Boston's mass transit system) and catch an inbound train. The trip was at least forty-five minutes, but she didn't mind. While other boarders grew stir crazy in the dorms, she wandered around Newbury Street after her flute lessons, visited the Museum of Fine Arts, or studied at a long wooden table with green lamps at the Boston Public Library. That afternoon Annie's cell phone rang.

Hello?

What are you up to? a boy asked.

It was Scott. She couldn't believe it was Scott.

Going to Copley Place, Annie said, referring to the high-end shopping mall.

Oh, I'm heading over there right now with a friend. Do you want to meet up?

I guess so, she muttered, wishing she'd worn something better than sneakers and a pink Gap hoodie. She and her friend went to Sephora, the upscale makeup store, to enhance themselves.

Earlier that year, Scott had asked Annie for a picture of herself. She'd settled on a photo taken on the night her dorm went bowling and all the girls dressed up in provocative outfits. She was wearing a short skirt and her face looked decent (she zoomed in to make sure), so she sent it with a disclaimer: *It's not a good picture.* His response was typical: *Oh. Yeah. It's okay.* She hoped this time would be different. Maybe hanging out with Scott during the day would lead to something more. Maybe they'd talk and listen to each other. Maybe they'd find something in common.

As she picked through Sephora's makeup testers, Annie couldn't help but feel annoyed. Why did Scott have to call her? Why did she agree to meet him? Worst of all was her realization, at the very moment he walked into the store, that despite everything (unfulfilling hookups, almost having sex, his rare phone calls), she still cared what he thought.

He looks a little chubbier, she whispered to her girlfriend when Scott and his buddy showed up.

Annie let Scott hug her, pushing his soft body into her. He was familiar and repulsive all at once. And definitely bigger, too, though not in a muscular way.

I like your hair, he said.

Oh, thanks, Annie muttered, impressed that he'd noticed her new highlights.

It looks good, he added.

She thought so, too.

The foursome headed down Copley's passageways, the two girls in front and the two boys trailing behind. As they walked past stores like Express, French Connection, and Neiman Marcus, Annie whispered to her friend.

I don't know what to do, she said. *He's annoying me and he's not attractive.*

No, no, her friend said. *He's cute!*

Annie knew she was just trying to be nice. Ida would have given her an earful.

What's the deal with him? she always asked.

You need to decide: Are you going to date him or are you going to cut him off?

Ida didn't like Scott. Most times Annie didn't either. When she was with him, though, or when he talked with her online, she remembered that he was all she had.

You should come to Northeastern sometime, Scott said outside J. Crew.

Annie looked up at him. Didn't he realize they'd just spent possibly the most awkward afternoon together? How could they hang out at Northeastern if they couldn't even hang out at a mall? Had he asked her the same question sophomore or junior year, she knew she would have accepted. But her expectations had changed; she no longer expected anything from Scott—or, for that matter, from most guys. And what if she went to visit Scott? Getting permission from her dorm parent would be hard enough, but she didn't even want to think about the assumptions his friends and roommates would make if she showed up and slept over.

Okay, this is the end, she said to herself. *We are not going to see each other. This is so awful for me.*

Scott, being his relentlessly charming self, tried again.

Like, you should stay over anytime.

Annie didn't know what to say, so she gave him a hug and said good-bye, turning away for what she thought might actually be the last time.

A snowstorm hit campus the weekend before exams, starting on Saturday, January 22, dumping over a foot and a half of white powder on the Milton campus. The administration postponed the first day of finals from Monday to Tuesday, giving students more time to study or slack off. Jillian stressed. She absolutely adored snow, but she wanted to take her tests, do amazingly well, and get to the following weekend. Now she had twenty-four extra hours to obsess over not getting As, not getting into college, and becoming an overall failure.

Her rejection from Vassar still stung. It was embarrassing. A total defeat. Jillian didn't get it: She was a vital editor for the *Paper,* an all-around talent, an amazing writer, but even the college counselors at school expressed their customary skepticism.

> i had a really depressing college meeting where i was like "hey, i got nomi-
> nated to be a presidential scholar!" and the college office is like "oooh but
> you still suck and you're not gonna get in anywhere you want to go" and i'm
> like "but look i found the cure for cancer!" and they're like "but you didn't
> take chemistry!" and i'm like ". . . and aids!" and they're like "DIE, YOU
> FAILURE!" and they get their little application gnomes to come and slowly
> disembowel me with . . . plastic forks. and then there was this thing called
> making out that didn't happen. . . .

When Tuesday finally arrived, Milton's annual exam routine began. Campus turned quiet. The student center emptied. Students spread out on the library floors. Tests took place twice a day in the ACC, marking another change in school tradition. Exams had always been held in the large-class homerooms that the student center replaced. Instead, in 2005 students trekked down to the basketball courts in the ACC, where fold-up tables and chairs were set up for the entire week. At lunch each day, students showed up in sweatpants and glasses, trading answers and guessing how many questions they got wrong. Jillian discovered what it felt like to get all As, even in French. Annie did moderately well. Whitney coasted through Spanish, bombed math after smoking weed instead of studying, and walked into her English exam an hour late, after she and Nick parked to hookup and the car got stuck in the snow. (At graduation, one of Whitney's best friends committed this infraction to memory: *Some advice: don't show up to exams late in college because you were desperate for a quicky.*) Isabel made to-do lists and rewrote all of her notes. Reed fared just as well as he always did. Brady kind of, sort of studied. Josh survived his three-hour biology lab.

Exams ended the following Saturday afternoon, and the Hysterics could not have been more excited. Phoebe, Caroline, and a few other friends watched the movie *Anchorman* and prepared for a friend's party later that night. Jillian planned to go, too. The party promised to be a debaucherous celebration: no more work, no parents, all alcohol and friends. Jillian needed a plan, because Evan would be there. She'd cried for two straight days when he dumped her in November. Mascara bled onto her cheeks. She ate. She didn't eat. She vowed to be a nun. Jillian understood why she should hate him; he'd used her, dumped her, wasn't cute, and wasn't cool. She was better than him. She deserved more than him. But what would have happened had their flirtation continued? Maybe they would have continued hooking up. Maybe they would have exchanged goofy presents over the holidays. Maybe they would have made out in the *Paper* office and then kissed on New Year's Eve. She might have let him into her life, given a part of herself over to him, vulnerable and in love. Yet nothing had come of it. Though the spiral of emotions from earlier that year was still raw, the real truth, the embarrassing, honest-to-God truth, was that she wanted to win him back.

She told her mom and dad she'd be out for the night: I'm sleeping at a friend's house and there won't be parents there. Grow up. Get over it. I'm a senior. I want to do what I want. Then a friend made her promise to be good.

Now, you're not gonna hook up with Evan tonight, her friend said on their way to the party.

I'm not, Jillian firmly repeated. *And you have to try and stop me if I do.*

At the party there were boys, beer, and plenty of opportunities to be a fool. Someone broke out Twister. Kids mixed vodka with juice and snacked on chips and pretzels. Jillian walked around thinking, *I'm not gonna hook up with Evan, I'm not gonna hook up with Evan,* but the moment he grabbed her hand and pulled her onto his lap, she paused. *Okay, I guess maybe I will hook up with Evan.*

They went upstairs, hazy and drunk. Jillian walked behind him, remembering a conversation they'd had the day before, when he told her how much he loved a girl who went to another school.

If he loves this other girl, Jillian thought to herself, *why are we doing this?*

He doesn't like me.

He's rejected me before.

This is so stupid.

But she followed him anyway. The alcohol erased their history. Lust took over. Jillian forgot that while hooking up may have gotten her attention, it wasn't going to get her a boyfriend.

Downstairs, Phoebe was in the bathroom helping a friend who was throwing up. The girl was blackout wasted, and Phoebe held her hair back, making sure her own chandelier earrings didn't fall in, too. She wondered what the girl would do in college when she got drunk and didn't have her best friends to take care of her.

Phoebe wobbled into the living room.

No, Jillian, don't do it, she suddenly heard a boy say.

Jillian was alone, and drunk, asking everyone for condoms.

Do NOT give it to her, Phoebe told the boy, fairly drunk herself. *What are you doing?* she asked Jillian. *What are you doing?*

Don't worry about it, Jillian said, red with alcohol and the embarrassment she wouldn't properly feel until the following day. *Don't worry about it.*

There are no condoms here, Phoebe said. *You are not gonna have sex. Please, Jillian, don't.*

Okay, Jillian slurred. *I won't.*

Phoebe thought that was that. If Jillian didn't have a condom, she wouldn't have sex. She couldn't; not randomly, not drunk. But Jillian wanted to lose her virginity. When she was in middle school, she'd dreamed it would happen on prom night. She never imagined her high school sex life would be braided together with alcohol, parties, and random hookups. Her mother had always taught her that oral sex was sacred, not to be given out casually and randomly. Jillian listened. Sex, however, was different. She wasn't the only girl in her group of friends who was still a virgin, but she hadn't had a serious relationship; she didn't know which was worse, losing her virginity to Evan or not losing it at all.

No one gave Jillian a condom that night. She broke the news to Evan, who said *Fine* and hooked up with her anyway. Eventually they returned to the party, and then later, after Jillian fell asleep in a bed alone, Evan returned, pulled back the covers, and snuggled in. His arms and hands pressed into her skin, his entire shape curving around her, knees into knees, back against chest, his body loving in its detached sincerity. It was weird. It was nice. It didn't matter, because they both passed out.

The next morning Jillian woke up early. Evan was curled up on the other side of the bed—*far away* on the other side of the bed. There was a pillow between them. Jillian arose in a haze of regret. There was nothing quite like the morning after. Her head pounded. Last night's behavior rushed back, making her head pound even more. She remembered begging for the condom, seducing Evan, and making a scene. He should have earned her body. He should have worked for her trust. But she let him have her and envelope her, and now, in the aftermath of a drunken night, with tangled light brown hair and bad breath, Jillian was relieved she was still a virgin.

Getting up was better than lying in bed, grasping for a forced intimacy with Evan, so Jillian headed downstairs. Bodies lay all over the house, the lucky ones snoring on beds, the unlucky ones awkwardly positioned on sofas or chairs. The sun streamed through the windows. Jillian went into the kitchen and started cleaning up. Phoebe woke up on the living room couch around eight A.M., too early to be awake but too late to fall back to sleep. She got up brightly, put on her earrings, and found Jillian. An hour later Evan appeared.

Can we just talk about this now, Jillian asked, *so we don't have to talk about it later?*

I have nothing to say to you, he said.

She couldn't speak.

She couldn't move.

She'd seen him almost naked.

He'd seen her almost naked.

Surely this was grounds for verbal communication.

But all Evan did was turn toward the door, walk out, and slam it hard behind him.

Jillian cried. Everything was just like the fall again, only this time she should have known better. She assumed everyone would think she was desperate, because that was what she would have thought about a girl throwing herself at a boy who had absolutely no genuine interest. Phoebe was sympathetic (it wasn't in her nature not to be), but Isabel's attitude was clear: *You brought this on yourself.*

Jillian already criticized herself enough. She understood the irony of her actions, and told herself she didn't deserve her friends' support. She'd behaved like a young DSG, contributing to the very social culture she despised. Still, Isabel's apathy hurt. It wasn't until months later that Jillian learned what Isabel had really said about the Evan situation: *It's as if Jillian was holding a needle up to her eye and saying, Should I do it? Should I do it? and we all said no. And she [almost] did, and wanted us to feel sorry for her.*

Jillian left the party on Saturday morning and, later that afternoon, while visiting a friend, worried about it all over again. She gorged on chocolate. She watched *Romeo and Juliet.* She showered three times. At home Jillian couldn't unload the truth to her mother: *And then we hooked up! And then we almost had sex! But we couldn't find a condom. And then the next morning he said he had nothing to say to me and slammed the door.* No, Jillian could not utter a word. Her mom probably would have flipped out and lectured her on the dangers of sex. All Jillian wanted was comfort. A time machine, a boyfriend, revenge. She imagined a surge of glory. An apotheosis. Anything to justify the scene she couldn't erase from her mind: disheveled, drunk, running through a house looking for a condom.

no one has ever ever ever treated me more disrespectfully i have so many things i could say but i've already spent the whole morning hyperventilating and chewing the ears off all my friends. i really don't think i will ever speak to him again. my stomach is one huge bedsheet knot and the thought of seeing him in class makes me want to puke. maybe after graduation i will just walk up to him, tap him on the shoulder and say "fuck you" and then i will never see him again.

Like all other weekend stories, Jillian's behavior fizzled into an embarrassing memory to her friends—*Like, ohmygod, I can't believe you almost had sex with Evan*. After a while, she and Evan talked cordially again at school. Life returned to normal, because that was what usually happened. Jillian still hated the DSGs, studied hard, had best friends and enemies, and fretted over boys who did not give her the time of day.

Just as quickly as exams took campus by storm, they were over. To many seniors, the most difficult part of the year was behind them. They didn't have to take finals in June, and with college applications already completed, seniors could coast until graduation. After February would come spring break in March, and April meant the start of senior spring. There would be parties, warm weather, time to slack off, and the prom. Girls would wear skirts to school and tan themselves on the quad. Boys would play ultimate Frisbee and drive with the windows rolled down.

It wouldn't be until weeks later that students would be thrown into something more difficult and confusing than any exam had ever been—until they would begin to put together the pieces and figure out exactly where they were and what they were doing when everything went down on that cold Monday night in January. Heavy snow quieted the campus as five varsity hockey players made another story, this one a sexual act that would shake everyone—those directly involved and those still unaware of it.

abigail jones and marissa miley

On that evening, the night before exams began, nearly a week before Jillian hooked up with Evan, students studied. Annie pulled all-nighters. Whitney slacked off with Nick. Isabel made to-do lists. Reed studied with Ava. They hadn't kissed since that night at her house, but they hung out under the radar, just trying to be friends. Ava pestered Reed about the status of their relationship, and then, when he didn't offer a definitive reply, she asked him about a rumor she'd heard. Something involving a hookup among a group of hockey guys and a girl. Something involving oral sex. Reed knew exactly what she was talking about. Earlier that evening, on his way to meet Ava, he had run into a sophomore friend on the hockey team.

It's going to happen, the boy said. *Do you want me to keep you posted?*

Yeah, sure, Reed said. *Give me a call next time it happens.*

Ava asked about the rumor again. Reed didn't respond, because what he knew was so audacious, so outrageous, he didn't dare say a word.

Miles away from campus, removed from the Milton Academy bubble, Brady was snowed in at home. For once he wasn't part of the stories his teammates were spinning. Brady didn't know that the one time he was left out of the loop was the luckiest moment of his life.

chapter twelve

that's such a rumor

five of Reed and Brady's hockey teammates were on their way to the ACC from Forbes dining hall on the night before exams. It was the Monday after the snowstorm and the air outside was freezing. The five boys—three juniors and two sophomores—looked like they were smoking oxygen as they strolled down crude pathways shoveled through the snow like mazes. On a winter night, Milton took on a quiet elegance. Buildings receded into the blackness, only their outlines and rooftops detectable against acres of white powder. The five players had just finished eating dinner after an afternoon of practice. Not everyone trekked to school through the snow to skate and lift, not even Brady, but these five boys, four boarders and one local day student, had a short walk to the rink. Besides, this was hockey season. They loved their team, and many players would have lived in the locker room if given the chance.

The boys headed to the ACC, making their way to the varsity hockey locker room. They walked down the central corridor that separated the basketball courts and the hockey rink, paused at the door, punched in the security code, and slipped inside. At some point Zoe, a sophomore boarder, sneaked inside. Only those involved know exactly what happened next. Two other boys stumbled upon the group and promptly left. The original five boys eventually sat down in five hockey cubbies, leaned back into the open wooden stalls where hockey gear hung, and waited.

Someone made the first move. Perhaps one of the boys motioned to Zoe, or another told her to begin, or someone else unbuttoned his jeans, if he was wearing jeans. Perhaps the boys grew calm. Perhaps they realized they were about to make the biggest mistake of their lives. Perhaps she paused in that altered reality, no longer hidden and private but suddenly visible, her act so defining, a force snapping her alive. She knew exactly what to do. She kneeled and began; one boy, then the next, oral sex performed on all five in turn.

Reed believed this was the kind of story that truly made *the man*. He closed his eyes and imagined the whole setup: his buddies lined up in the cubbies with their pants unzipped, Zoe crouching below them, moving down the line, giving head while the guys made comments like *How's that blow job going?* and *Is she sucking it good?* Reed could have been one of them. That Monday night, while he studied for exams with Ava, he waited for his five teammates to call his cell phone and invite him to join. They never did, and later he would see this as a very fortunate moment. At the time, though, he wanted to be included. He already knew what was going to happen, because that night's event was actually round three. Zoe had spent part of Saturday night giving head to three guys in a dorm room, and part of Sunday night doing the same to three guys in the same locker room. Monday night was not novel, but it would become infamous.

While dodging Ava's questions, Reed remembered how he'd learned about the first two stories from the weekend. Two nights before, on

Saturday, a junior on the hockey team showed up in Hanley with news: He and two friends had just received blow jobs from a girl in someone's dorm room.

When?

Just then.

From who?

Zoe, that sophomore boarder.

Reed wasn't surprised to learn that she was the girl involved. He'd heard rumors about her sexual promiscuity, but he wasn't familiar with Stoneface, a game the group supposedly played, in which guys sit around a table while a girl crawls underneath, performing oral sex on each of them in a random order. The winner is the last boy to show an expression of pleasure, the one with the stone face. Reed didn't know which was more shocking, the game itself or the fact that Zoe agreed to give the guys head the very next night, on Sunday evening, in the hockey locker room. Each boy had his turn leaning up against the sinks, back to the mirrors, legs spread apart. Zoe, wearing a rugby shirt, crouched beneath them and performed. Reed knew all this as fact, because he saw the pictures a buddy took on a cell phone. This night paved the way for an even bigger event the next day, on Monday.

Reed wasn't sure he would have participated had his friends called on Monday, the night of the third and most notorious story, but he still wanted to be included so he could have declined the offer himself. He wasn't looking for physical pleasure or an easy orgasm, but hearing secondhand was hardly the same as being there.

Even Brady was impressed. *Who on earth is this girl?* he thought. *Wow. WOW.* Aside from his initial shock, he thought the stories were almost too premeditated. To him, part of what made a story a story was spontaneity, creativity, and a guy's ability to think on his feet. He thought his teammates' acts were too planned and clinical. It was hard to be impressed by a group of guys who got a girl to do something that she did voluntarily, over and over again.

Regardless of his opinion, Brady knew that all the guys had to keep their mouths shut. Locker room confidentiality was a loose agreement, and most guys knew that stories leaked to players' friends. But once in a while something so fantastic took place that everyone respected the need for secrecy. Still, Brady feared a disaster in the making. What if Coach Cannata found out? What if the school found out? What if Zoe told her friends what had happened? He'd handled tense situations among his friends before. That time a friend had sex with a girl in a car while another guy listened from the backseat, Brady was there to assuage the tension when the girl freaked out and the backseat witness got upset.

Brady was relieved when exam week passed without any mention of the stories. Besides, most rumors eventually faded, and Brady had no doubt that the same would happen with this latest great story. But the first day back to school, on a Tuesday in early February, a girl walked up to him during recess.

Tell me about what happened in the locker room, she said.

I don't know what you're talking about, he lied.

You have to.

Brady waited.

I know you were there, she said.

No, I really wasn't.

Which locker room story was the girl talking about—Sunday or Monday? What exactly did she know? Regardless, the oral sex stories were out. Brady couldn't believe it and, at the same time, totally expected it.

A couple of weeks passed. By mid-February, rumors about what had happened, particularly the third story involving the most boys in the hockey locker room, simmered below the surface.

It's so ridiculous, students whispered.

Wow, that girl's a whore.

If she wants to like, jack off five guys, that's her deal.

Two days after Valentine's Day, on a Wednesday, Brady finished class around noon and headed to Forbes for lunch. He floated between the tables and students like he did every day, a hot meal steaming on his plate, a grin plastered on his face. He sat down with the guys at their long table to dig in.

Do you have a minute? a woman said to him.

Brady turned and saw it was one of his favorite teachers. She was one of those faculty members who devote themselves to students' lives, both academically and socially, and remain favorite teachers year after year. Brady stepped away from the table, feeling his friends watching from behind.

The [administration] is running around, she said. *They know about it.*

Jesus Christ, Brady thought, the school knows about one of the oral sex stories. But how? From who? Which one?

You have to make sure, the teacher continued, pausing, looking at him closely. *You have to promise me you weren't there.*

Yeah, Brady said before divulging what he knew.

He wasn't surprised that this particular teacher confided in him. Brady liked to think of himself as the go-to guy both inside and outside his social circle. He may not have been one of Milton's shining academic stars, but he had a talent for leadership and knew how to gather the troops. Friends listened, and that was a gift, not something he'd learned in a classroom. Brady cleared his lunch tray and left Forbes in a daze. The extent of the consequences seemed endless: DCs and expulsions, public embarrassment, legal action. Brady was sure his last Milton hockey season would be canceled.

The boys' hockey locker room was packed later that afternoon. Guys tossed their clothes into their cubbies and put on their game armor and orange-and-blue uniforms. Brady was so used to the routine that he forgot about the conversation he'd had earlier in the day with his teacher. Because in the locker room, someone invariably flipped on the stereo or pissed into a bottle or told a story or spit out a game plan, and they stood there listening, being Milton Academy varsity hockey players.

Their game against Belmont Hill was huge. Brady knew that Milton hadn't beaten the all-boys school in years. But with the eight new players, the Mustangs were a competitive team. They won that afternoon, five to three, and after the game, Coach Cannata rallied the team together and said he wanted to go undefeated for the rest of the season. There were only a few more games left.

Brady was walking on a cloud. It wasn't until he got home that he remembered his conversation with the teacher at lunch. Usually he sank into the couch to watch an episode of *The O.C.* or whatever Boston sports team was playing that night. He'd do a little homework, catch up with his family, talk online, and then go to bed. Instead, a friend who lived in Hanley asked him questions over IM.

What's going on?

What on earth's happening to the hockey team?

Brady felt a sinking feeling consume him.

The next day, on Thursday, Brady and Church talked at school.

Shit's about to hit the fan, Brady said.

What are you talking about?

The school knows, Brady said.

Church went silent.

Wow. They're gonna get kicked out probably, Brady said.

No, no, no they won't.

No one could be sure.

Brady had to warn his teammates, because what had started as just another story spiraled into something so much bigger and uncontainable. He called one of the five boys involved and told him to get ready.

Talk to the guys and get your story straight, he said.

You guys gotta figure it out.

What followed over the next day and a half would blur together for

Brady, Reed, and the rest of the hockey team. But other Milton students as far removed from the hockey scene as Jillian and Annie would remember these cold February days more clearly than they remembered their own graduation. Rumors spread that Zoe had spent Wednesday night in the health center. Paranoia grew for those boys who were either involved in the two previous incidents or present during the third locker room incident and had yet to be identified (like the one taking pictures on a cell phone). They'd evaded detection so far, but no one knew exactly what the school knew. Even witnessing the behavior was an offense that could get them suspended, because the students had sneaked a girl into a boys' locker room.

Some students said the five boys were definitely getting expelled, and soon there was talk of criminal charges, because Zoe was only fifteen years old. In Massachusetts, it's illegal to engage in sexual intercourse or "unnatural sexual intercourse," which includes oral sex, with a minor, a child under sixteen, regardless of whether or not that minor consents. To commit such a crime is to commit statutory rape. Three of the five hockey boys were seventeen years of age or older and could therefore be tried as adults, while two were under the age of seventeen and could therefore be treated as juveniles. Soon kids heard that Zoe's family was going to sue the school. Bad news seemed unavoidable.

I'm really scared, one of the five guys told Brady.

Of course he was scared. He and the four other guys were, at that very moment, the subjects of a school-wide investigation into an incident of unusual proportions. On Thursday, the administration ordered all five players involved in the third incident out of class and escorted them to separate rooms. School administrators sat with each boy, and instructed him to write down exactly what had taken place in the locker room that Monday night in January. Without calling their parents, they complied. What none of them could have known was that Zoe had already written her own statement earlier that week, when she and her parents met with administrators and had had time to contemplate what to say.

At practice that afternoon, Brady learned that the five guys weren't allowed on the ice or in the locker room. Nothing made sense. Coach Cannata had no pull? This new hockey leader, who'd come to Milton with the express purpose of expanding the school's program and creating a better team, faced the loss of five of his top players.

Unbelievable, Brady thought as Coach explained the situation. *They could get kicked out.*

Brady recalled all the nights he'd spent with the guys, dicking around, cruising across town, drinking and making memories. The time one of the five guys dumped a girl because Brady broke up with her friend. The time Brady pulled over to let him throw up after his friend tried to prove he could pack chewing tobacco inside his lower lip. The time, ten minutes later, Brady pulled over because his friend tried yet again. The times they convinced some girl to hook up with them at the same time. All the evenings in the locker room talking about girls, showering without curtains, unself-conscious, naked, and content because they didn't want to be anywhere else.

On Friday morning in the student center, Brady and the hockey guys attracted an unfamiliar kind of attention. Their presence was unmistakable, partly because of their blue warm-up suits, which they wore on game days, but mostly because everyone knew it was decision day. Five of their teammates were in danger of being suspended or expelled. At that very moment, select faculty members and administrators met to determine how to handle the boys involved in the third incident. Anyone looking close enough (and most students were) saw that those five players weren't dressed in their blue warm-up suits. Stripping them of their uniforms—the very status symbols that proved they were Milton Academy varsity hockey players—was a result of the boys' temporary suspensions from the team. Their street clothes were their scarlet letters, and everyone knew it.

Brady tried to forget the fact that this might be the last time he and his teammates hung out together. Usually he had a story to tell or something to say about someone, but this time, the unflappable alpha boy was speechless. A couple of friends started snapping pictures. Brady tried to smile. The tension was palpable. The five guys must have been scared shitless. So was Brady. Reality hit: These might be our last pictures together as a team. He smiled harder, looking past the camera at the crowd of students who stared back at him with looks of pity, amusement, and disgust. This was Milton Academy; everyone had an opinion, and few were shy enough to hide it. Watching these boys was like witnessing a train wreck in slow motion, only the crash had already occurred and now, here in the middle of the student center, the aftershocks began to rattle.

The scene in the student center looked much like any other morning except, of course, for one discernible difference: Everyone was talking about the exact same story—Zoe, the boys, and the locker room. Questions came from all around.

Was it her idea?

Was it their idea?

She was just fine with it?

How did people find out?

How did the school find out?

Was it someone's parents?

What kind of retard tells their parents?

Student opinion splintered: Some sided with the girl and some sided with the boys. Some thought the hockey players were disgusting and despicable, and deserved every possible punishment. Others couldn't believe the school sent Zoe home on nondisciplinary administrative leave, as though she was a victim forced to participate in the stories not once, but three separate times. If the guys were going to get suspended or expelled, she should too. Regardless of which side students took, everyone understood that this was no ordinary disciplinary case. Usually student leaders were involved in DCs, and the infractions were more apparent. Plagiarism, class cuts, and drug use didn't compare to this situation, which was hazy at best.

Whitney sat in her corner on the first floor, glaring at the obnoxious hockey guys. She'd first learned about the stories from Tripp a couple of weeks before, and even she, the girl with all the sexual experience, the nights spent sneaking out and disobeying her mother, was shocked.

There's no way that that happened.

That's too ridiculous.

That's such a rumor.

Whitney accepted that the guys' involvement was typical. She was sick of hearing about the gross things they did with girls, like Eiffel Towers, orgies, and now this game called Stoneface. She also knew about Zoe's sexual past, and who *didn't* notice the scandalous outfits she wore to school? But she couldn't reconcile a young girl voluntarily giving head to multiple boys at once. How twisted and pornographic. How *Playboy* and Skinemax. Didn't her jaw hurt? Her neck? Her knees after pushing against the floor? Where was her self-respect? Whitney understood the irony of her position; as her friends said, *You do this stuff, too.* Yet she believed the oral sex incident was different.

Whitney took it for granted that she knew how to tell a guy *no.* She'd learned what regret felt like; having sex or giving head might feel right in the moment, but later, the consequences would always come roaring back. Had the guys asked Whitney instead, she never would have said *Yes!* or *Only if I'm drunk!,* which was exactly what she heard Zoe had said.

So what made her do it? Perhaps it was the thrill of being chosen, or the assumption that the guys might come back for more. There was the *hey, what's up?* Zoe might receive in the student center at the right time and in precisely the right place so that all the right girls—the popular and older ones—would be standing nearby and watching. It occurred to Whitney that Zoe may have wanted to participate—that she liked the idea of being with several guys at once, pleasuring them as though she was the only one receiving their attention. Pleasing these guys meant befriending them, which might one day lead to a relationship. Or perhaps it just showed she could be as casual as the guys about hooking up.

Josh observed the scene in the student center from his usual perch in the back of the first floor. He'd heard about the oral sex stories just as he heard most pieces of gossip—while listening to his friends talk about girls. One of the five hockey players interrupted their banter.

Yeah, well, that story doesn't come close to the story I have in the locker room, with a girl.

Josh listened to the tale in disbelief.

The kid had to be joking.

He couldn't possibly—

He couldn't seriously—

He and four friends got head from a girl in the hockey locker room?

This was one of those crazy stories Josh could imagine happening only to guys like hockey players.

Jillian walked into the student center and passed the hockey team. As she headed downstairs, she was disgusted by the sight of the young DSGs crying and fawning over the guys. In their cute little outfits, the girls attached themselves to the huddle of players, mourning the potential loss of five guys they adored. Jillian thought the scene was absolutely absurd. What in the world had possessed these girls to even want to touch those boys after everything that had happened?

Jillian, being Jillian, recognized that Zoe's behavior was part of a larger high school culture in which sex and girls' deference to boys reigned. Milton was just another cog in the male-driven machine that encouraged young girls to perform oral sex liberally and casually. She hated to admit it, but there came a point in high school when she accepted the fact that a boy could slap a girl's ass and laugh it off as though it was a casual handshake. Or he could hook up with a girl, ignore her the next week, and then try to hook up with her at the very next party. But Jillian also sympathized with Zoe. The girl had been the subject of sexual rumors all year, and now, at least, she had a way out of Milton, even if it did involve administrative leave.

In the Cave, Jillian and the Hysterics confessed their shock to each other.

Wow, that's like, so disgusting.

Those guys are sleazeballs!

She's so misguided.

Eww, something else Zoe did.

Isabel sat there wondering what was going on upstairs. When she asked Reed if he knew any details about the situation, he rolled his eyes, which she interpreted as a *yes*, but he didn't say any more. Isabel was the only one of her group who thought the oral sex stories were totally consensual. She sided with the boys, and Jillian was appalled. Lately Isabel had been spending more time with Reed. Jillian thought she was acting like a Stepford Wife, tiptoeing around Reed while he brainwashed her with his hockey jock mentality.

Yet Annie knew of girls in Pryce who shared Isabel's opinion. She watched them rally around the hockey guys while she quietly identified with Zoe, understanding all too well the unique pressures of being a younger girl involved with attractive, athletic, older guys. Even Caroline understood, though not out of personal experience. This academic star, teacher's pet, best friend, and girlfriend, understood, on some level, where Zoe was coming from. I could have been her, she kept thinking over and over. Caroline realized that each of her friends had compromised herself in similar ways that year, all in an effort to get a guy. Just because Caroline hadn't done the same didn't make her any better or more sexually moral; she'd simply gotten lucky.

Every boy and girl, at some point in his or her life, is a restless virgin. And every girl may have her own "oral sex incident." Oral sex may not always be involved, but the behavior (a hookup, a blackout, a one-night stand) pushes her over a threshold into a new arena of experience. For Isabel it was giving head to a guy she didn't know over winter break. For Jillian, it was almost losing her virginity to Evan. For

Whitney, it was having anal sex with Nick, which she ultimately did the summer after she graduated. For Annie, it was going back to Scott again and again. The details of Zoe's actions may have been anomalies (oral sex on several guys, a boys' locker room), but her behavior—at least according to rumor—was not anomalous. Zoe is the only one who truly knows whether what she did in the locker room was her over-the-edge act.

At first Zoe may have thought the idea was ridiculous. Oral sex in a public place? It could be risky. She could get caught. She could get an STD. Still, the act held such potential, because these were varsity hockey players. If Zoe was hesitant, something must have changed her mind. Maybe she thought they would kiss her, touch her, and say, *You are beautiful*. Or please her in return. Maybe she wanted to witness the guys in their most private moments. All because of her. Maybe she believed she was selected, the girl singled out from the entire school. Or maybe she didn't view the third incident any differently than she viewed the first two, or any of her previous sexual experiences—or those of her classmates. After all, Nikki and some of the girls in Caitlin Lane's basement hooked up with more than one guy, too.

If Zoe had second thoughts, she probably didn't let on. Almost every teenage girl assumes, at some point, that guys talk about her behind her back—this is what she looked like, this is how she did it, this is how she smelled, this is how loud she screamed. For some of the hockey guys, the assumption was quite likely true. And for a girl like Zoe, the questions might have been: What if the guys told their friends I backed out? What if they spread rumors about me? What if they said I didn't know how to give head? What if they ruined my life?

On Friday morning, Reed was stuck in English class. His cell phone was on, and he sat there staring at it, willing it to ring. The guys were supposed to call if they heard any news. He was ready to march out of class and have his life change—not because he'd participated in the incidents (thank God he'd never gotten that call), but because the five guys involved were like brothers. The night before, Reed had cried.

Just relax, a friend said. *It's going to be okay.*

You really don't know who's in the administration and how they're going to take this, Reed said.

He'd heard that the 2004–2005 school year marked the first time Milton had permitted Coach Cannata to recruit players who did not meet standard academic requirements. It was a big moment for the team as well as the school, and now, six months later, a group of hockey players had landed the academy in this controversy. And so Reed understood that the fate of his friends was about to be determined by administrators he didn't know or trust—by people who didn't get what the hockey world was like and didn't understand that what the guys had done was almost expected behavior.

The three juniors involved were the kind of kids Reed expected to get involved in this behavior, but the two sophomores were younger and more impressionable. Reed couldn't fathom what was possible— that his friends could be expelled and Zoe could suffer nothing. There was no way that the guys forced her into that situation. First, he thought she was a slut. Second, he knew she'd done it before. Third, she had three chances to say *no*—on Saturday, Sunday, and Monday. And the idea itself was so excessive and outrageous that the only way his friends could have posed it was as a joke. He saw no sense of moral ambiguity here; oral sex had nothing to do with feelings, responsibility, or emotional age. The acts were part of an implied social exchange: oral sex for social clout. Everyone involved must have been in agreement without even having to agree, because getting head from a girl was not a moral issue. For hockey players, it was something they deserved and expected.

Reed coveted the privileges that he and his teammates enjoyed, and now their world was crumbling. Where was the respect for hockey players? What happened to the prestige? Why wasn't anyone turning a blind eye? At other prep schools, Reed thought, hockey guys were adored. At Milton, their power no longer counted. Reed's friends suddenly faced public shame, punishments, expulsions, possibly even criminal records. This was a real world filled with consequences that Reed and his friends had never considered. There was a higher order above hockey star and social leader. Stories, girls, and sex may have meant something in the locker room, but these boys were learning that some laws trumped their fairy-tale world. Nothing mattered in the face of rules and Milton's disciplinary board. Later, Reed would realize that hockey players didn't hold sway with the courts or police, either.

The early hours of the day went by without any news. While Reed sat in English, Brady skipped class. So did other players on the team. At some point Brady headed across Centre Street to Ware Hall to talk with his favorite teacher and see if she had any news.

Go back [to the student center], he remembered she said, *and tell me as soon as you hear of anything.*

But Brady couldn't move. He couldn't go back to the student center, where his friends waited in mourning, the girls weeping on their shoulders, everyone else—the entire school, all those kids he didn't know—staring at them and making assumptions. No, Brady couldn't go back. And so in the privacy of a small office, across the street from a scene only the newspapers could love, he hugged his favorite teacher and cried.

When English ended, Reed bolted to the student center for recess. The first floor was packed, and as he walked in, he called one of the five boys to find out what had happened.

Well, we're gone, the boy said.

What? Reed asked.

We're gone.

What? he asked, louder.

We're gone.

This was impossible. Reed stormed up the ramp between the student center and Wigg and stopped short in the hallway. Photographs of retired Milton faculty members hung from the walls, and in their presence, in utter silence, Reed's head dropped. He pushed his hands through his hair, eyebrows bunched together. What the hell was going on? These guys were his friends, and now they were expelled, and he knew he could have been one of them. He'd tempted fate that night; *Yeah, sure,* he'd said, *give me a call next time it happens.* Was he stupid? What if he'd gone? Reed stood alone in the hallway, pacing, charged with fear, relief, and guilt. He couldn't believe it could have been him.

Church and a few other guys found Brady in the teacher's office in Ware and told him the news. No one said anything. They all sat down and stared. Brady wished he'd been there that night. He wasn't necessarily interested in getting head from Zoe, but he would have made sure the incident occurred elsewhere. His friends should have gone to someone's car. Or someone's dorm room. Or five feet outside the locker room. Anywhere but inside. Brady was a senior and a leader. He was supposed to set an example. He could have prevented everything and saved his friends. At the same time, he believed that if you did something knowing that getting kicked out was a possibility, you had to accept the consequences. Did the guys really expect any other outcome?

It didn't occur to Brady that some of his own sexual experiences had been risky as well. He'd had the orgy with Nikki at her house just a week before the oral sex stories took place. Sure, they were off campus. And sure, they were all friends, so the guys assumed Nikki would be okay with whatever they did. But the overall behavior was similar, and so were the guys' motivations: to hook up, get some ass, and make a story.

The incident prompted only one fear in Brady: that the administration might find out about a birthday party he and some friends had attended earlier in February at a hotel in downtown Boston. There were two rooms, one for the kids and one for the parents. When Brady arrived, Zoe and a friend opened the door to the kids' room in their bras. Alcohol was everywhere. One girl danced seductively on his lap. Zoe took a shower with her bra on, and then a guy threw cake on her. When the parents knocked on the door, Brady hid in the bathroom with a bunch of other kids. Then someone pulled back the shower curtain to reveal a girl and a guy having sex in the bathtub. Brady had seen a lot in his high school career, but never anything like this.

The hotel party would later become just another infamous detail of the oral sex incidents, but back in Brady's favorite teacher's office, he worried he might get in trouble for simply attending the party. When the teacher had to go to a faculty meeting, she told the boys to go back to the student center.

Just compose yourselves, she instructed, *and go back over with everyone else.*

The hockey gods, who always seemed so unbreakable, listened.

As Brady left Ware Hall, the row of buildings on the other side of Centre Street looked just as it did every other morning. Wigg's thick white columns, Warren's flat brick facade, the student center's ostentation. Everything looked normal, yet nothing was as it should have been. Brady pushed open both sets of glass doors and set foot on the first floor.

Reed walked back down the ramp from Wigg to the student center. It was clear that most people knew about the expulsions. He kept looking around for someone—no one in particular, but just someone who would know how he felt. There was Brady. Standing in the doorway. Both guys stood a few feet inside the student center. They looked shell-shocked and lost, and when they spotted each other, it was as if an invisible force was drawing them together.

Reed and Brady lurched for each other and embraced. Brady started bawling, burying his head in Reed's shoulder. Reed squeezed him back. They held each other for a long minute. Neither could remember the last time he'd cried so hard. Brady opened his eyes and peered out from underneath his curly blond hair. He watched students gawking. He knew what they saw—two big boys in their blue jumpsuits hugging and crying. And he recognized what was in their eyes—disbelief and a new understanding. They knew what he and Reed now knew. No one was untouchable.

chapter thirteen

is it possible?

it was as if death slithered onto campus that Friday when
the five boys were expelled. Watching the hockey players embrace
was like seeing your father cry for the very first time; their chests heaved
and their faces scrunched up, the grief both potent and audible, yet entirely unbelievable, because these were the kinds of boys who were not
supposed to cry. The expulsions were so profound that many teachers let
their students talk about what had happened during classes. Once the
school day ended, the administration held assemblies for each class,
where the dean of students was going to formally announce the DCs.

Usually seniors walked through Straus's narrow white doors to visit
the college office, but that afternoon they dropped their bags and backpacks, shed their winter coats, and gathered in the large, open library.
Sitting on brown leather couches and sprawled across the frayed rug,
they waited to see what the dean of students had to say. Jillian sat with
her hair piled on top of her head, contemplating how the *Paper* should
cover the expulsions. When the dean stood up in front of the senior
class, she spoke somberly and carefully, revealing nothing more than

what most students already knew—that five boys from the hockey team (three juniors and two sophomores) had been expelled for their involvement in the third incident. So the academy still knew only about the last oral sex story from that weekend in January. At least that was their official stance; rumors about other incidents had made their way around campus. Suppressing the name of the girl involved was a pointless gesture, Phoebe thought, as most seniors knew exactly who Zoe was.

When the dean left, administrators opened the floor to questions. This was a very Milton tradition. As Jillian listened, she realized that the bent of the student inquiries represented a widely held opinion that Zoe was just as responsible for what had happened as the boys.

Why wasn't Zoe expelled?

What was going to happen to her?

This was her fault, too.

Damn straight, Reed thought, sitting near Jillian.

Jillian believed the boys were at fault, but before she could write anything for the *Paper*, there was so much more to understand beyond the cursory details that the dean provided. The DC process itself had been controversial, since the decision came straight from Doc Robs and the administration, without any student input. There was Milton's reputation to uphold. And then there was the emotional intensity that seemed to have gripped everyone. As an independent student publication, the *Paper* didn't need permission from the school to print its articles, but teachers and administrators cautioned editors that their coverage could have a major impact on the school and its image.

The *Paper* was, at least theoretically, the voice of the students, but Jillian saw that choosing a side reflected one's social identity at school. There were girls versus boys, jocks versus nonathletes, boarders versus day students, and so on. Jillian sensed the factions now, and would see them more clearly later, when, after writing an editorial on behalf of the *Paper* staff, at the request of the editor in chief, she found that some coeditors disagreed with her argument. She wrote:

Let's not kid ourselves: the recent sexual scandal may be more pronounced or more horrifying than what else goes on at Milton, but it did not come out of nowhere. . . . If any good can come from these sad events, it will come when we have the courage not only to treat the symptoms, but also to cure the disease. . . . We need to stop judging women based on their sexual history. This means two things: not exploiting women based on their reputations, and not using their sexual histories to blame them for another's actions.

Later that afternoon, Brady dragged himself to the locker room to get ready for the game against BB&N, located on the Charles River, near Harvard Square. He'd skipped the assembly to hang out with friends at Emma's house, and then went back to school to say good-bye to four of the five boys who now had to move out of their dorms, meet their parents, who'd driven from faraway states, and go home. There was only one boy left, the day student who was exiled to a life that remained within a mile of the school, near friends, a team, and an entire world that he was no longer permitted to be part of. Now, while standing with a puffy face in the exact place where the incidents occurred, Brady looked around the locker room, unsure of how to grasp what he was seeing—his favorite place, his home for the past few years, suddenly missing its whole crew. The locker room spoiled in the presence of absence.

Now that Milton had lost five players, including a master defenseman and a goal scorer, beating BB&N would be a challenge. Before the guys boarded the bus, Coach Cannata gave a pep talk, and then the father of one of the five boys stepped into the locker room. To this day, Brady remembers only two points from his entire speech: *Being on a team is a very special thing*, and *My son will be all right*. Here stood a man, just an ordinary man with a wife and children, a house and a career, whose son had been expelled for his sexual behavior. The boy was either ridiculed or supported, depending on who was asked. He was appalling, coercive, and vulgar, some said. Or he was seventeen and just being a boy. And he was this man's son.

How does a parent react? There is a period of despair and disappointment, but then it has to end. One figures out how to make life go on, even though what has just happened is shattering—it appears in the movies or on TV, but not in real life. There is embarrassment and shame. Claiming this boy as one's own in front of family members, friends, and teachers? Knowing there were others—and knowing how many? But this father connected with his son's previous life by reaching out to the team. He probably stared at the guys in front of him, realizing his son could have been one of them. How easily the situation might have been reversed. The father looked at the players and spoke. Look ahead. Stay together. Love each other. Play hard. *Being on a team is a very special thing. My son will be all right.*

When the bus rolled onto the BB&N campus, the Milton guys hit the guest locker room fast and then rushed onto the ice. Proper hockey etiquette said that visiting teams warmed up after the home team, but that afternoon, the Milton players couldn't stand another minute enclosed in another locker room, staring blankly at each other and the spaces where their friends belonged. The guys passed pucks to each other just as they did every day at practice. Yet the absence of their teammates was palpable. This wasn't like losing a game, when egos were momentarily deflated. This loss was deeper, and as the guys sliced up the ice, their parents and friends filled the stands, watching these stout rectangles of blue, white, and orange, knowing how painful the game was going to be.

The buzzer sounded. Milton took the lead in the first period. BB&N pushed back hard and was up by the third period. Fueled by adrenaline and distress, by pure hatred for a school they had once adored, the Milton guys endured, and when the game ended, Brady looked up at the scoreboard; Milton had won with a score of 6–4. *We just did something pretty amazing,* he said to himself, knowing that the team played with more emotion and unity than it had in a long time.

The guys huddled together at one end of the rink while their parents waited by the exit. Coach Cannata was the last person to step off the ice, and when he did, a reporter from the *Boston Globe* approached. *A school matter . . . Not an athletic issue,* Coach said as he motored past, holding a clipboard, giving nothing away. Less than twenty-four hours had passed since the expulsions, and already the media clamored for the story. In the guest locker room, Doc Robs showed up and said how proud she was of the way the team had played. When she left, Coach explained that no one was to speak with reporters. Later that night, after the team went to Wendy's for dinner, while Brady gave a ride to two young DSGs, his mom called to say that a reporter from the *Globe* had already phoned their house. That's when it really hit him: The story was going to be huge.

When Brady woke up on Saturday morning, his mom handed him the front page of the *Globe* and pointed out a headline: "5 Students Expelled at Milton Academy." Holy shit, Brady thought. He assumed the story would make the newspaper, but not the front page. At least not so fast. He started reading.

Milton Academy expelled five students on the boys' hockey team yesterday for allegedly engaging in sex acts with a 15-year-old female student in a boys' locker room last month, according to a school spokeswoman.

That much was true.

Cathleen Everett, the school spokeswoman . . . said she did not believe the case involved "a rape of any kind."

Definitely true.

"The boys participated in a situation that involved a 5-to-1 ratio of boys to the single girl. Regardless of any other circumstances, that ratio by definition represents a pressurized situation, and the boys should have known that," [Everett] said. "It was a situation where coercion, either implicit or explicit, was an element of the interaction."

Bullshit.

David Traub, the spokesman [for the Norfolk district attorney's office], said that statutory rape laws generally cover all sex acts. "A 15-year-old cannot legally consent to sex; that's the way the law is written," Traub said.

Bullshit!

Milton Academy, founded in 1798, has 680 students, kindergarten through 12th grade, both day students and boarders. Those who live at the school, in grades 9 through 12, represent 34 states and 16 countries, living in eight, single-sex "houses."

Brady knew this wasn't just about five kids getting booted out of school for misbehaving. This was a story about hockey players getting expelled from a New England prep school. Money, privilege, and famous alumni helped to turn the story into a scandal.

Reed sat in his brown leather chair, cell phone to his ear, ranting to his mother, Carol. The team was a disaster, he said; the school didn't have the whole story; he wanted to join a protest group.

Mom, can the hockey season just be over?

This is miserable.

Carol had never heard Reed sound so negative. He was a different boy from the one she'd first sent to Milton, who called home asking how to do his laundry and adored the school precisely because of its hockey team and opportunities. Now he was disillusioned. He resented a sport and a team he'd always loved. Carol was worried, but she never doubted Reed's innocence. She assumed he had enough sense to say no in situations like this one.

Reed did anything he could to keep his mind off the obvious—*guys I lived with in the dorm, teammates, really good friends, all thrown out.* A love triangle was the perfect distraction. Ava, he decided, would be his escape from the incidents, and Isabel would be his escape from Ava. Earlier that week, Reed had done the unthinkable: He'd asked Isabel out on a date. A real date, with dinner and conversation and butterflies in the stomach. They had planned to get together that Friday night after the BB&N game, but with the expulsions and the hockey drama, Reed canceled. All he wanted to do was hang out with Ava. He doesn't remember where Cush was that night, but as he and Ava lay on her bed watching *The Notebook,* they leaned into each other, almost kissed, laughed, and kissed for real even though they'd made a pact not to.

Is it possible to like two people? he remembers Ava musing.

Reed wondered. He wanted Ava. He was also intrigued by Isabel. And he sensed that Ava wanted Cush, too, who had been trying to win her back. Reed was a good, moral guy. He'd spent his high school career protecting his social image and trying to collect stories without inciting controversy. But now, in the wake of the oral sex incidents, Reed couldn't help himself. He wanted Ava regardless of Cush.

Never let a girl come between two guys, his father said, trying to be Reed's conscience.

You're playing with fire, his mother added. *Which is more important to you, your relationship with a friend, someone you might know your entire life, or something that might be fleeting?*

Reed didn't want to answer her question, so on Saturday night, a day after his friends had been expelled and his kiss with Ava, he devoted himself to his buddies. He stood in front of his closet debating what to wear, and finally chose his Italian-style blazer, a yellow button-down oxford, put a Polo underneath and popped the collar. The final ensemble was more posing-in-front-of-the-mantel-at-a-country-club than Reed had expected, but he looked himself over in the mirror, running his hand over an inch of black hair.

Cush stopped by to shoot the shit. He layered his pin-striped blazer over a dress shirt and waited for Reed to finish primping. The guys were reverse versions of each other, Reed with his preppy style and chiseled features, Cush with his vintage chic and smooth model face. The boys acted like friends because they still were, and when Reed was ready they headed down the Hanley stairs, met a day-student friend, and set off to the night's S & S meeting.

S & S was short for Steaks and Stogies, the secret club Reed, Cush, and a dozen or so other guys created senior year. At first the express purpose was to eat lavish meals, but Reed helped to transform the club into a full-fledged men's society devoted to dressing up, drinking wine, smoking cigars, discussing business, and being exclusive. S & S emulated Skull and Bones at Yale, with a touch of Princeton's eating clubs. The word *steaks* referred to filet mignon, and the members' collective image, Reed believed, was antithetical to the stereotype attached to the hockey team.

Over the past few weeks, Reed's vision of what it meant to be a Milton Academy varsity hockey player had been reduced to a mark of shame, a disappointing affiliation that was now impressive only to certain kids at other schools, who, when they learned he played hockey at Milton, looked at him with awe and respect, as though being part of the infamously oversexed team still retained a pinch of dignity. Reed saw discrepancies between the privileges of being a guy like Brady (girls, hookups, parties) and the privileges of being an S & S guy (culture, refinement, sex appeal). S & S members were smart and good-looking. They transcended social cliques and respected each other. The prestige was what Reed had been dreaming of before he even got to Milton.

Josh felt the same way. He couldn't believe the guys asked him to be part of a secret club. Reed reminded Josh of his older brother, the sophisticated young man with an infectious, we-can-do-anything attitude. Though Josh later saw Reed as an overzealous dreamer, aligning himself with these kinds of guys brought him one step closer to becoming any sort of *man*.

That Saturday night's meeting was held, as usual, at a member's house. The guys showed up in jackets and ties, and dined on squash soup, steak, and chicken kindly prepared by the host's parents. They talked like boys pretending to be men, discussing topics such as the club name, the design of its S & S crest, and whether or not they would buy expensive watches for graduation. Reed argued for a TAG or a Breitling, though at a few thousand dollars apiece, the watches demanded a financial plan. He threw out crafty ideas on how to raise money, and then at some point during the evening, someone shouted for everyone to come into another room. The TV was on, and there on the screen was coverage of Milton's hockey expulsions. Josh watched the news summary and felt cool. He was dressed up with a dozen other guys, each one handpicked from his class. They'd just eaten an extravagant meal and were now watching news coverage about their school. For once, he was on the inside.

After dinner, Reed and Cush went to a classmate's party and tried to forget about everything. Reed was in his element. He drank, flirted, and felt as though he could do anything. The evening had been the perfect temporary fix for the incidents and the Ava-Isabel dilemma—until Brady arrived with one of the guys who'd been expelled.

The weight of the room shifted when they walked through the door, as if someone's parent had just died. No one could stop staring and no one knew what to say. Reed walked up to the boy and gave him a hug. Some of the girls were still crying about the expulsions. The boy himself was as unmoved as ever, just like he'd been the day before, when Brady visited him in the health center after the disciplinary decisions were announced, and saw him trying to be strong, saying he just wanted to move on, so obviously in denial. Reed felt bad for the kid. Maybe it was being at a party with former classmates or missing last night's game, but this boy now looked completely different to Reed, as though he finally had an understanding of what had just happened to him.

I used to make fun of losers at school, he told Reed that night.

But the fact of the matter is that they still go to high school.

Like, I don't do anything.

Now I'm kinda the fuckin' loser.

Reed wouldn't have put it quite like that, though the statement was true; the boy no longer went to high school.

Reed looked around the party for distractions. A buddy rushed inside with a beer in his hand, raving about how it was the same one he'd hidden in a snowbank a couple of months before. Another friend had sex with a girl upstairs, didn't use a condom, and later learned that the girl supposedly had an STD. When the party ended, Reed left with a friend to go to an afterparty at Ava's house.

It was late at night. Kids hung out in her kitchen and then dispersed. Reed grabbed a seat on the couch between Ava and Cush, wondering if anyone else had a clue as to what was going on. When most friends migrated upstairs, Reed offered to help Ava clean up the kitchen. It was just the two of them in there, and before Cush returned, Reed and Ava kissed for the second time since they'd promised they wouldn't.

Later that night, Reed lay awake in a guest room while Cush talked with Ava. He wondered who she would pick, him or Cush. Clarification came with a surprise visitor. Reed heard the door creak open. Footsteps. Shhhh. Ava crawled into the bed. He looked at her. She was beautiful. She was right next to him. He felt as if he was having an affair. Reed ran his hands all over Ava's body, on top of her pajamas and her underwear—everywhere but underneath. He wanted to touch her and make her feel good, but he was suddenly aware of the possible consequences. What if she woke up and thought, *Ohmygod I just did this in my house . . . Cushman will freak out?* What if she regretted it the next day? What if Reed lost Ava and Cush? Reed stopped himself, because Ava wasn't like the other girls who were there to serve a single sexual purpose. He actually cared about her. And Cush. And now, in the moment he'd been waiting for, he couldn't make the next move.

The clock read six A.M. when Ava woke up and tiptoed back to her own bed. Reed watched her leave, thinking he'd been such a good kid, imagining the harassment he'd get from his friends if he decided to tell them what had happened: *You could have gotten away with whatever, they'd say. Why didn't you do it? Why?*

Isabel spent Friday and Saturday thinking about Reed. After months of flirting, she thought she might actually snag the ungettable guy. But then the expulsions happened and Isabel worried he might postpone their date. She told herself that he would be overwhelmed by the incidents. He couldn't possibly think about taking her out when he was exhausted from the stress and needed to be with his friends. On Friday at school, she watched him hug Brady in the middle of the student center, sobbing for everyone to see. Isabel wanted to be sensitive. She tried to understand. But at the seniors' meeting that afternoon, when she randomly landed a seat near Reed, all she could think about was going on their date.

Every girl knows what it's like to sit next to the boy she adores: There he is, the crush, the most coveted boy in the room. He is so close, a few inches away. There are his legs. They look so strong. There are his jeans, gathered perfectly around his sneakers. How does he do that? She thinks she hears him breathe. Was it a sigh? God, what if he's sighing because he's sitting next to her? What if she smells? She thinks she might smell. She wonders if he notices how fat her thighs look when she sits. Maybe she should say something. She could whisper it in his ear. She wouldn't have to get too close.

Eventually, after much deliberation, Isabel mustered the courage to speak.

We can take a rain check if you want, she said, leaning toward Reed. *Like, I guess this must be a hard weekend for you.*

Oh, I'll let you know, Reed said in his typical casual manner. *Let's keep it on the schedule. It will be a nice break.*

Isabel beamed.

The moment a girl realizes she has a chance—not just a 1 percent chance but an actual chance—with the guy she adores, expectations emerge. Ohmygod, he's taking her out on a date. Her crush is taking her out on a date and she has to entertain him for who knows how many hours, be totally endearing, alluring, and funny. What should she wear? Maybe she should buy a new shirt. Would he notice? (Reed would.) She wonders where he'll take her. Maybe it will be fancy. Maybe she should wear her push-up bra. She decides to make a list of topics for conversation. Like the menu and his favorite movies and whether he likes his meal. She thinks of a couple of jokes. And something witty and charming, because she *is* witty and charming.

Whatever Isabel thought about at that moment, she had no idea Reed's mind wasn't entirely preoccupied with the oral sex incidents. He wasn't actually thinking about their date either, which he postponed. Isabel was only a distraction from his real distraction, Ava.

Without even knowing about Reed's other love interest, Jillian tried to warn Isabel.

If he tries to move it to Sunday night, don't go, she instructed.

A, it's your friend's birthday, and that's more important.

B, it says that you're independent and have a life if you don't go.

It doesn't say that you don't like him, she said. *But if you do go, it says that you're letting him control your life.*

Yeah, yeah, you're right, Isabel said.

But when Reed asked her to go out on Sunday night, Isabel agreed. She planned to see her friend before and after the birthday party, and besides, didn't everyone understand how important this date was to Isabel? Jillian didn't. To her, best friends came before boyfriends, and definitely before non-boyfriends. She felt as though Isabel's obsessive tendencies, which she'd previously directed at fleeting crushes, film, or funny stories, were now focused entirely on one person, and that one person was Reed, a hockey jock, a player, one of the kids who rated girls as they walked down the student center stairs.

Less than twelve hours after Reed made out with Ava, he met Isabel for dinner at the Cheesecake Factory. They ate avocado appetizers, chicken marsala, and angel hair pasta, and Reed decided that she was pretty. Not Ava pretty, but he liked the fact that she didn't wear makeup. And those eyes, her deep, delicate green eyes that popped against her cashmere sweater. Isabel captivated him in a way no other girl ever had before. She was feisty and acted as though she had him wrapped around her finger. She called him out for wearing a yellow shirt with a popped collar—for the very image and mystique he worked so hard to cultivate. *Oh, you are a brat,* he thought, meaning it in only the best way, because Isabel was more confidant than he'd thought.

After dinner they went back to Reed's dorm room to hang out. He put on *Cruel Intentions* and cuddled up to her on the couch, wondering if he'd kiss her before parietals ended. She snuggled in and held his hand. He had no idea what to do. Isabel wasn't like the DSGs, who would have looked good on his arm and in his bed, but what did he really have to say to them besides *What are you wearing* and *Who is your dad?* The problem with Isabel was that after their witty banter ended, Reed realized that he was the one who actually had her wrapped around his finger. She didn't make the chase exciting.

He must have sensed his own hesitation, because he only pecked Isabel on the lips before she left to go home that night. Reed spewed out bullshit justifications—I'm tired, it's been a long weekend—but the truth was worse: He didn't want to ruin his chances with Ava. Still, regret loomed everywhere. Cush was his friend. Isabel was a fascinating girl. Ava deserved to be more than a prize.

The next evening, Reed and Ava talked online.

This isn't going to happen, they decided. They tried to be optimistic:

Maybe sometime . . .

If we were to bump into each other . . .

Sometime in the future . . .

But later that night, before Reed fell asleep, his cell phone beeped. He had a text message from Ava. *I've been lying in bed and you're all I can think about,* he remembers she wrote. *I wish you were here with me. Can't stop thinking about you.* So she had second thoughts about letting Reed go. He did, too. But the next morning Cush barked at him for no reason—and for every reason. Apparently, somehow, he knew something. Reed's fling with Ava—and his dreams of living like James Bond—were over.

While Reed was pursuing his love triangle, families across Massachusetts sat down to breakfast on Sunday morning, looked at the front page of the *Boston Globe,* and read the headline: "Milton Academy Rocked by Expulsions." Within days, the story of the expulsions had become a real scandal. Local news sources released new information: Zoe may have performed oral sex on the boys as a birthday present; police were investigating statutory rape; no one had yet been charged. Milton emerged as a character unto itself, described as a *picturesque private campus . . . the 200-year-old alma mater of poet T. S. Eliot and Senator Edward M. Kennedy.* Soon the story made it to the *New York Post* and the *Washington Post.* The public posted comments on Internet blogs. Everyone, it seemed, had an opinion.

Whitney loved seeing her school in the newspapers and on TV. Despite the school's embargo on the media, she spoke with a reporter, as did a handful of other students. Jillian answered questions once, but only to deflect what she felt was sensational coverage of a very tragic incident. *Why don't you just leave the school alone?* she asked. As one Milton junior said, *It's a really bad thing to have on your college application.*

Expelled from Milton Academy. Weeks went by, and the media's presence on campus became overbearing. Everywhere students looked there was another reporter going after another student, hounding someone walking on Centre Street or using IM screen names to get more information. Students threw snowballs at reporters and campus security tightened. Milton restricted access to school events, particularly hockey games, but the media's attention only grew.

The police continued to investigate the locker room incident, and whether it constituted statutory rape. The Department of Social Services assessed the adequacy of Milton's supervision and school policies. The *Boston Globe* reported that Zoe's father said *She'll be fine* as he unloaded her bags from the car outside their New Hampshire home. But no one knew for sure.

Jillian felt bad for Zoe, and contacted her by e-mail. *You don't know me,* Jillian began. *But if you ever want to talk . . .* Zoe wrote back soon after; she appreciated Jillian's note and insisted that she was fine. Almost too fine, Jillian thought.

Amid the hype and criticism, Milton staunchly and publicly defended its position. Cathleen Everett, the school's spokeswoman, reiterated that the boys' actions had been atypical of Milton students. *It's outside common norms. Unfortunately, adolescents make big mistakes,* she said, revealing how remarkably out of touch the school really was with the lives of some of its students. Doc Robs wrote e-mails and sent letters home to the parents of all Milton students.

In the first letter, dated just days after the expulsions, Doc Robs stated that the five boys had failed to meet Milton's standards of conduct. Their behavior, she said, *violate[d] community norms* and *[impinged] on the rights and well-being of others.* Any situation involving a ratio of five boys to one girl was, by the school's definition, *pressurized. The boys,* she maintained, *should have known. It was a situation where coercion, either implicit or explicit, was an element of the interaction.* Milton, therefore, had to expel the five boys. The girl, a victim by legal definition, was placed on administrative leave.

Doc Robs invoked sympathy when she admitted that Milton was *struggling* against what she called the *cultural tide* of *adolescents'* social and sexual behavior. She characterized her students as adolescents even though two of the boys involved in the incident were seventeen years old, and one was eighteen. Adolescents? Adults? The lines were murky. And so Doc Robs went out of her way to describe the school's *comprehensive and structured* supervision. Her point, of course, was that those students involved in the incidents had found a way to circumvent the system.

Then, in a second letter dated March 3, Doc Robs made public what Brady, Reed, and many other students had known for weeks: There had been not one but three oral sex incidents over that weekend in January, what she called *a short and unfortunate pattern of behavior by a small group of students.* She used the same arguments: The school has rules, these students broke them; teenagers face difficult decisions, parents face a cultural gap on sexual behavior. Ever the educator, she closed her letter by directing parents to readings on the culture of teenagers today.

For some parents, Doc Robs's letters ripped open a vein of communication that had rarely taken place at home. Not all parents openly discussed sex with their children.

Josh's mom, for one, was shocked.

Do you know anything about five kids being expelled? she asked at the dinner table. *What would you have done in this situation?*

Obviously I would never find myself in that situation, Mom. I have a lot more respect for women than those kids.

What else was he supposed to say? That he'd always wanted to be one of those kids?

As February turned into March, questions continued. Were there more incidents involving sex? Was anyone else involved? Was group oral sex a prep school thing? A teenage thing? A hockey thing? How prevalent was this behavior? There were few answers, only more developments inciting even more complications. A senior was suspended for a week, and a fifteen-year-old boy was placed on leave. Both of them had been involved in the incidents, though their participation and disciplinary action were not directly mentioned in Doc Robs's letters. Some students knew of another boy involved in the incidents who had, so far, remained under the radar. And so the saga continued. With rumors of more disciplinary actions and oral sex stories on campus, Doc Robs's letters seemed an ineffective bridge across the vast generational divide that she acknowledged but could not cross.

a meaningful relationship

reed arrived at the W hotel with his bag of preppy clothes and a strip of ribbed Trojan condoms, ready to take on New York City. As he rode the elevator up to his floor, he thought about how incredible his weekend would be. That year in early March, just before spring break, Milton sponsored a cultural trip for students that seemed to defy its rigid rules. A weekend with little parent or faculty supervision, days spent in museums and nights without structure, sleeping in accommodations students could organize for themselves— the trip was exactly what Reed had been looking for. He thought the irony was perfect: An administration that fretted over parietals and other boarding rules, that had just waded through a very public scandal, was going to let a bunch of students run around Manhattan unsupervised? He signed up immediately, and so did Isabel.

Neither of them knew exactly what they were doing, but over the last few weeks they'd passed the initial steps in a Milton "relationship." Reed took Isabel to Bertucci's, leaned toward her, said, *I think I owe you this,* and kissed her hard. They watched a movie and hooked up, which meant she gave him head and he gave her oral sex (for twenty seconds).

He realized that the rumors guys spread about girls smelling like cheese, tasting like fish, and having bushes weren't entirely true. In fact, he found the experience fairly pleasant.

Skills aside, Reed must have done something right, because at the hockey team's last game, when Milton played Nobles and reporters swarmed the rink, Brady teased Reed about Isabel, whom he'd caught staring down at the ice with big eyes.

She was looking at you the entire time, he said.

What the hell did you do to her? the guys joked.

Teach me your ways!

Reed loved it. But those who knew him best saw an unhappy boy. After only a couple of phone calls, his mother sensed the big picture. Hockey, the sport that had constituted Reed's afternoons and evenings, vacations and summers, best friends and girlfriends, had betrayed him that year. He'd lost five teammates. He resented his school. He was apathetic, broken, and tired. And heartbroken, too, after Ava chose Cush and Cush learned the truth about Reed.

Reed needed distractions, so he decided to make a list of girls he thought would be hard to get, and then planned to go after them. He excluded DSGs on principle, and considered only girls he'd noticed before but didn't know—the kinds of girls his friends might say are hot, though never in front of a group, for fear that a buddy would look at the girl, then back at him, and say, *Are you serious?* Isabel landed on the top of the list. With her Reed felt like himself again, the impressive hockey jock. For whatever reason—genuine interest, convenience, or boredom—Reed focused on her first.

As he opened the door to his suite in the W, he walked into a living room where opulence seemed to go on for miles. There were reds, whites, and blacks, a bedroom with a king-size bed, a huge couch, a minibar, and, for whatever reason, a basket filled with condoms and personal lubricant, among other things. Reed's two friends were already there. Trevor was a stout senior athlete who had a Boston accent. Josh, whom Reed knew from S & S, was the kind of guy with whom he could have actual conversations that had nothing to do with girls, hockey, or partying. Reed's father was staying at the W, too, but his room was on another floor, and Reed didn't plan to see him.

Reed dropped his bags and the guys opened a bottle of tequila Josh had brought back from a vacation in Mexico. Three boys who looked nothing alike—Reed with his dark hair, Trevor built like a rectangle, and Josh towering above them both—threw back a shot to celebrate the start of what they hoped would be the first great weekend of senior spring. In the corner stood a girl Josh had invited over for the night. Reed thought what's-her-name (Erica) was unattractive and annoying, but then, she'd made fun of his pink sweater. The color was salmon, actually, and Reed had bought it for precisely this reason. But he was in New York City. Staying in a fancy hotel. There were no parents and no rules. He was far away from Milton. It was time to call Isabel.

Uptown, Isabel, Jillian, and Phoebe tried on outfits before they went out. They were staying in an apartment that belonged to one of the girls' family members, and their latest triumph involved pacifying Jillian's parents, who believed their daughter had gone off to roam the streets of New York without adult supervision, free to go to parties, get drunk, do drugs, meet the wrong kinds of guys, and come home to Boston in a body bag. Isabel held shirts up against her chest, her soft arms bent, and assessed herself in the mirror. She smiled and watched the green in her eyes disappear as she squinted. Then she made an announcement: She planned to lose her virginity that night with Reed.

Just as long as you know like, it could be awkward afterward, Phoebe began, with the care and concern of a true friend.

It's not gonna be like, perfect.

I really don't want you to be drunk when you do it.

'Cause like, then you're less likely to use a condom. Just make sure that you're in the right frame of mind.

Isabel got it. Her friends didn't want her to sleep with Reed and then regret it later, like Jillian had almost done with Evan in January. They wanted her to be 100 percent sure, and she was. She wanted to have sex with Reed. She couldn't imagine being a virgin when she graduated from high school. College was supposed to be about crazy drunken nights, random hookups, and walks of shame. She didn't want to lose her virginity to some random guy, but she didn't want to pass up that random guy in college just because she was still waiting for her first time to be special. Reed, however, wasn't random.

That night, Isabel made Jillian and Phoebe promise to come with her to meet Reed. The girls agreed, and when the threesome walked into the W on Friday night, they found him and Trevor waiting for them in the lobby. Isabel was relieved that Reed wasn't staying with hockey guys like Brady and Church, but Jillian took one look at Trevor and thought, *Ewwww, gross!* because he had yet to live down his performance at a dance freshman year, when he grinded into her body, touching her in inappropriate ways.

The boys asked the girls to sit, explaining that they had to hang out downstairs while Josh did whatever he was doing with a girl upstairs. Phoebe was disgusted. How gross and how guy. Very quickly, this classy hotel, this mature evening, had become seedy. Isabel realized that her friends had been right; the situation was weird. Three boys rotating girls in and out of one bedroom? Where would she and Reed go? Where would they have sex? Oh God, what if the others heard? Phoebe listened to Isabel think out loud.

I don't think I'm gonna do it, Isabel said.

I don't think it's the right time, especially like, where he's staying.

I'm not gonna feel comfortable.

The awkward social clash wasn't lost on any of them: two hockey jocks ushering three of the Hysterics through the gates of luxury and intoxication. Never in their lives had Jillian and Phoebe expected to be in a hotel room in New York City getting drunk with Reed and Trevor. They had nothing in common with these boys except, of course, Isabel. But once the group got upstairs and drank a little tequila, the tension eased. Trevor got wasted. Phoebe got drunk and even bubblier. Jillian made nice with Erica until Josh led Erica back into the bedroom and closed the door.

Hours went by. Jillian and Phoebe were bored. They looked over at Isabel, who was snuggled up against Reed on the couch while he watched a basketball game. Their features clashed, his black hair against her pale face and red hair, but they looked oddly adorable together.

Are you sure you want to stay here? Jillian and Phoebe asked Isabel when they wanted to leave.

Yes! Isabel said.

Are you sure?

I'm fine, I'm fine, she insisted.

If you're going to stay, don't come back. Just stay.

I'm fine, Isabel said again.

Jillian and Phoebe weren't so sure. The rule between best friends was to leave no one behind. But this time they were in New York City and they were seniors about to be in college. They were old enough to make their own decisions. Jillian understood that sex was not the way to begin a relationship or even a casual fling, but Isabel kept insisting she was okay with whatever happened.

Phoebe pulled Reed aside.

Don't let her leave tonight, she said, leaning in, tipsy and serious. *Like, if she's gonna leave, just have her leave at seven, when it's light out.*

Reed promised.

Phoebe and Jillian left to meet their friends.

Isabel stayed behind, ready to let whatever was going to happen, happen.

Josh had been anticipating the trip to New York ever since he'd met Erica at that party a few months before, when they sat on a couch and made fun of their drunk friends. They'd joked about meeting in the city, and now here they were, in a suite at a nice hotel, in the master bedroom that Josh had somehow miraculously claimed for himself. As he closed the door, he blocked out Reed and Trevor, the girls, and his past. A CD mix of slow Dave Matthews songs played. Josh lay down on the enormous king-size bed and talked with Erica.

They got to know each other. She was pretty. Kind of. Not as cute as he remembered, but she had dirty blond hair and flushed cheeks. Regardless, it was cool to be in a hotel bedroom with a girl, especially after they'd joked about it over IM.

> Josh: how many people do you think can comfortably sleep on a king bed
> Erica: what gender
> Josh: mixed
> Erica: sounds like an orgy
> Josh: more or less

Josh could hardly believe they were there, just the two of them, lying on a bed together. Things like that didn't happen to him, at least they hadn't since eighth grade, when his friend had orchestrated Josh's very first hookup. Now, as he inched closer to Erica, a girl he barely knew, he realized that he'd gotten there on his own. He got her IM name, he got her number, and he asked her to come over to the hotel to hang out. But years of sheepish behavior and lame hugs on doorsteps hung over him. Josh was on the brink of becoming a new man, a more experienced man, and so he kissed Erica.

There was nothing special about it. Erica was not Diana, or any other girl he'd had a crush on. But they persisted, kissing, talking, kissing, talking, until Josh asked if she'd ever had sex before.

Would you want to have sex with me? Erica replied.

No, Josh said, blushing.

You're a good kid, she replied.

He supposed so. But he didn't really want to be a good kid. Good kids ended up like him: a senior, a virgin—an *oral sex virgin*. And still, the question had leaped from his mouth before he even knew what he was saying. Josh didn't actually want to lose his virginity to a girl he barely knew; he wanted to share that moment with a girlfriend, with someone he wanted to see again and again. As he kissed Erica, he realized there was one thing he did want from a girl he barely knew—a blow job.

I don't feel comfortable having oral sex with someone I don't know well, she said.

Great, Josh thought.

If we're gonna have oral sex, she said, *I want to have a meaningful relationship with you.*

Did she really say what he thought she'd just said? *If we're gonna have oral sex?* What was he supposed to say? What would his friends have done? Did she actually want to give him head? Everything had been so easy: Meet a girl at a party, like her, call her, invite her over, get her into a bedroom. The hard work was supposed to be over. Josh searched for the right words, but in the end he did what came naturally to him. He acted like a good guy.

Well, this is the first night, he said warmly.

Erica must have liked his answer, because she kissed him again.

They grasped each other's bodies, and as he peeled off her clothes he discovered she had a belly that hung over her underwear. Her skin wasn't soft. She had weird moles. She wasn't delicate, and she wasn't even built in the sexy way that Josh liked. This girl was ugly. So he did what he thought he was supposed to do: He reached for her vagina. Josh thought he knew what he was doing. There was a hole and a clitoris, and like those of most other teenage boys, his fingers started flapping. Erica said he was good at it and then grabbed his penis, slamming him all the way back to eighth grade and that horrible Play-Doh-like hand job.

This isn't going anywhere, she eventually said.

Obviously, Josh thought.

She finally stopped.

This is gonna hurt for a while if I don't do this, Josh said, touching himself.

Okay, she said.

Isabel kept slipping between the cracks of the pullout couch and rolling over the springs in the mattress. She dug herself out and kissed Reed, who would later learn that Trevor had woken up on the floor in a mostly drunken stupor and caught Isabel without a shirt on. Trevor silently grabbed a blanket and lugged himself toward the bathroom. Isabel fell between the cracks again. When she reemerged, she traveled down Reed's torso, pushing her red hair out of her face. His body was like an artwork, tanned and defined, and he worked on it as devoutly as she avoided the gym. Isabel's head moved farther down Reed's body, and he leaned back as she started giving him head, glancing at the basketball game, watching the players hustle around the court. Reed felt like *the man.* This was how it was supposed to be. New York City, a suite at the W, a girl he liked giving him head. He forgot about hockey, Ava, Cush, and college, and, for the first time in his life, he let himself not care.

Sometime between the blow job and the end of the basketball game, sex came up.

Is this gonna be one of those things that like, you're not gonna talk to me the next day? Reed remembered Isabel asked.

Oh no, he said.

I don't believe you.

No, no, of course not.

I don't believe you.

Trust me, he said, thinking to himself, *I'm probably not going to talk to you again.*

Isabel thought Reed seemed genuine. Granted, Trevor was nearby, she was lying on possibly the most uncomfortable mattress ever created and her breath smelled of tequila. But she was ready to have sex. And Reed had brought condoms.

I'm overthinking it, she decided.

I like Reed as much as the next guy.

I like Reed a lot.

I'm going to do it.

A girl imagines losing her virginity under perfect circumstances. She knows where she will be, what she will wear, and who she will be with because she's been planning the moment forever. The mood is just right. There is nervous chatter and loving kisses because she adores this boy, the one who's about to make her his. Clothes come off. She sees his chest. His belly button. His hip bones. He unfastens her bra. He says she looks sexy and she blushes, knowing this is love, because in her fantasy, she is in love. She wonders if she will be good at sex. She hopes his penis isn't too small. Or worse, too big. What if she has to pee? What if he goes in the wrong hole? He wants to spread her legs and she lets him, opening herself, surprised by how intense the feeling of wanting can be. She closes her eyes and waits for it to happen, knowing she will replay the moment for the rest of her life.

For Isabel and Reed, the task for the first fifteen minutes was penetration. Isabel was in pain. Reed was frustrated. He'd heard stories from his friends about having sex with virgins. Sometimes there was blood. Sometimes it pooled on the sheets, dried in the guy's pubic hair, or left streaks between the girl's legs. But they'd gotten this far. Reed was almost inside. *We gotta figure this out, we gotta go through with it,* was all he thought. Until—

Penetration. Finally. They were actually having sex. They were both losing their virginity. Then it was over. After Reed finished, all he wanted to do was sleep. He lay back, amazed by how easy it was to have sex. He imagined endless positions and orgasms. He wondered, for a split second at least, whether Isabel had had fun. Did she like it when he threw her up against the couch and then the windowsill, pumping himself into her from various directions? Probably not. But she seemed willing. Very willing. *Wow,* he thought. *That didn't take too much work.* He wondered which girl on his list he could get next.

Isabel tried to wake Reed up early the next morning. He smelled like sleep. His head pressed into the pillow.

Okay, she said. *I'm gonna go.*

Do you want me to walk you down? he mumbled.

She looked at him. He was wearing only boxers.

Don't worry about it, she said.

Reed wondered if she'd be able to hail a taxi and get home safely. But he was comfortable in bed, so he let her leave alone, just another high school boy pretending to be a gentleman.

As Isabel walked through the lobby, she wished she'd brought a change of clothes. She tried to flatten the red knots protruding from the back of her head. So this was what a walk of shame was like. Could people tell she still had sex on her—smelled like bed and heat and bodies, like a virgin who'd just given herself to a boy she barely knew, in a hotel room that had seemed a lot nicer the night before, a couple of hours after having a shot of tequila, with the TV on and someone else sleeping nearby?

She hailed a taxi, tears in her eyes. It was only seven A.M. She wanted to be back home, safe and untouched. Or she wanted to feel like a woman in love, because losing her virginity was supposed to have changed her. It was supposed to make her feel grown up and experienced—liberated to have the one-night stands and random hookups she anticipated in college. What was left of her former self? Who was this girl crying in the back of the taxi, suddenly aware of her body in ways she'd never been before? On the outside she looked the same. Her skin was still pale. Her face was still freckled. Her soft tummy still stuck out when she sat. But inside, she didn't know herself anymore.

As the taxi sped uptown, she clutched the condom wrapper from the night before. She'd spotted it on the floor when she left the suite that morning and had grabbed it, her only tangible evidence of losing her virginity. She clutched the foil and, later, slid it between the pages of her diary.

When Isabel got back to the apartment, she slept on the couch until Jillian and Phoebe woke her up. The two girls remember what came next.

We had sex, Isabel confessed.

It was just so awkward.

It's okay. I'm fine with it, she insisted. *It had to happen.*

But Jillian and Phoebe were prepared for the worst, and hardly surprised when Reed ignored Isabel at the museums.

First she tried to talk to him.

Then she ran to Jillian: *What should I do?*

Back to Reed.

Back to Jillian: *What should I do?*

She cried and then said she was fine. Cried and then said she was fine.

If you want something, Jillian instructed, *you have to ask for it. He's not gonna bring up the relationship question. He's not gonna know what you want.*

Whatever, Isabel replied. *I don't want to force him into something that won't last.*

But of course she did. No matter how many times she denied it, she wanted Reed to want a relationship. And Reed had no idea what he wanted.

I don't know what to do, he confessed to Jillian at one of the museums.

The answer was obvious to her: Talk with Isabel and ask her how she feels. Yet Jillian advised lightly.

Don't make her upset, she said to Reed. *Just realize that like, what happened between you guys is a big deal and like, I think you need to realize that. Don't make her upset.*

It's okay that we had sex, right? It's okay that we're not going to be girlfriend-boyfriend, right?

Jillian couldn't even respond.

All afternoon, after the students dispersed from the museums, Isabel waited for Reed to call. The hours ticked by.

It's fine, he'll call later, Jillian and Phoebe said.

You can come out with us; we'll have a good time.

Let's get like, really dressed up!

Oh, I have nothing to wear! Isabel moaned.

What about what you wore last night? That was so pretty!

No, if I see Reed I can't wear what I wore last night.

Jillian and Phoebe agreed.

Wanna borrow something? Jillian asked.

Oh I have nothing to wear. I feel so gross.

It's fine, Jillian tried. *You looked so pretty in that thing you wore last night. You'll look gorgeous.*

Isabel was adamant, so Jillian took her shopping. It was already eight P.M. but they found a shop down the street and descended upon the dressing room with handfuls of clothes. Isabel wanted something she loved, because if she saw Reed that night she had to look amazing. Nothing fit. Nothing looked right. And so after rejecting all the options, Jillian took her back to the apartment. Isabel really lost it.

Ohmygod! she wailed. *I'm so ugly! I'm so fat! I can't believe I let him see me naked!*

Jillian and Phoebe stood there watching the uncontrollable grief take hold, seeping into Isabel's bones, rattling fantasies of intimacy and love that she'd convinced herself she truly understood. Isabel's eyes reddened. Her soft little body shook as she threw everything in sight. And somewhere in that apartment, on a wall or on the living room table, a clock ticked on. Early evening turned into nighttime. Reed was not going to call.

Reed cut into his filet mignon at 21, amazed that Bob Kraft, owner of the New England Patriots, had just walked through the door. He,

Josh, Trevor, a couple of other friends, and one of their fathers sat around a table at the famous New York restaurant, living life as Reed always thought it should be lived—replete with luxury, money, beautiful clothes, and food. Next the group hit the Oak Bar at the Plaza, where Reed kicked back a glass of champagne. Josh had a Grey Goose martini, and a couple rounds later, after the other guys ordered drinks, the bill came to roughly $200. Josh offered to pay, fighting through his shock, hoping someone else would slap down a credit card. One of his friends eventually did, and on the way out Reed tipped the maître d' $50.

Later the group split up. Reed and a friend headed to Marquee, one of the most exclusive clubs in the city. The boys were able to cut in line because Reed's friend knew the bouncer, and when they got inside, Reed was overcome by the drinks, the gorgeous people, and oh the girls, the girls, the girls. He walked around looking older than his seventeen years, probably the only guy there wearing a blue-collared shirt, a pink Polo sweater, and a blazer. He drank Coronas and something with Red Bull, danced with a girl, and spotted Tommy Lee.

I saw Tommy Lee, he thought to himself.

Whoa, I saw Tommy Lee.

You did Pamela Anderson—and I watched.

Alcohol and celebrities aside, Reed spent much of the night wandering around the club by himself, separated from his friend. He wanted to look like he was having the time of his life, but as he stared at the twenty- and thirty-somethings who didn't notice him back, he realized they were old and he was young. Even the club itself looked different—dirty, sweaty, like any old club (or at least what he imagined any old club would look like, considering that this was his first one). Nightlife, he decided, would be better when he was older and had money to burn.

Meanwhile, back in the hotel room, Josh and Erica rolled around on the king-size bed. Even though he'd decided that he didn't like her, he couldn't dismiss the possibility of oral sex. He invited her back for a second night and made the first move, pushing his face between her thighs. *That is a lot of uncomfortable stubble for a face to take,* Josh thought. He had never gone down on a girl before. He wasn't motivated by love or respect; he did it because he hoped she would return the favor. He lasted roughly ten seconds, and he hoped it was enough.

I want to make sure that this is meaningful, Erica said.

Was she going to give him head? He had to say something, anything, to convince her.

We'll see each other all the time this summer! Let's just have some fun.

I don't want to do this if it's meaningless, she replied. *I want to make sure that I'm doing this for a guy where this is going to be a meaningful relationship.*

Don't worry about it, Josh said. *Just go ahead. Just kiss it a little bit.*

He didn't recognize himself but he couldn't stop, either. He was so close. Please, he thought, please. And then, just as suddenly as Erica had popped into his life, he felt magic. Her mouth was warm and wet. Her tongue swirled. Josh couldn't even grasp what was going on, but whatever Erica was doing, however well or poorly, it felt incredible. And then it was over. He came too quickly.

Only after his mind went blank with pure physical pleasure did the reality of his surprise set in: Erica had just swallowed his come. He was impressed and embarrassed. He felt like an asshole. Josh brought Erica a glass of water while she put on her shirt. He stared again at her overhanging stomach. Under the covers they courted opposite sides of the bed. Josh didn't want to cuddle. He didn't want to hold her or even touch her, but he knew he couldn't kick her out. He embraced the reality of his situation: girl, big bed, the W in New York City, blow job, acting like an asshole. *This is pretty sweet,* he thought, knowing that he had finally gotten what he wanted—oral sex, an orgasm, and, most important, his first good story.

What is he doing? Isabel, Jillian, and Phoebe whispered as Reed boarded the bus and sat down next to Josh. Isabel couldn't believe what was happening because Reed promised he'd sit with her during the trip home. He wasn't seriously going to ignore her—not after what had happened Friday night, right? But there he was, sitting with Josh. She had no idea that all Reed really wanted was to listen to his iPod, not talk, and maybe fall asleep. He didn't want drama. He didn't want to discuss his feelings and whether he wanted a relationship. He wanted to wonder why now, after all the girls who had practically begged him to sleep with them, he hadn't really felt ready for sex until Isabel. But Reed's conscience took hold, and he agreed to swap seats. He put his arm around Isabel. Talk eventually slowed. Sitting silently became easier, and eventually he felt her soft body snuggle into him. Then they slowly fell asleep.

Jillian sat behind them, mulling over the drama of the weekend. She hated seeing Isabel so vulnerable and full of self-loathing. Jillian knew exactly what it felt like to look in the mirror and hate what she saw. She did it almost every day, though lately she'd been feeling thinner and happier. Just before the trip to New York, while Jillian was at tennis practice, her mom had called and told her she'd been accepted into college, an eclectic and competitive liberal arts college in New England.

How did your match go? a teammate asked Jillian.

Oh, I lost, she said. *But I don't care, 'cause I just got into college!*

And then, while in New York, she and a senior guy on the trip had flirted all weekend long. Friday morning he wanted to sit with her on the bus and play her music from his iPod. Friday night, when she saw him after leaving Isabel at the W, he told her she looked hot. For the first time in a long time, Jillian felt pretty. She wondered what might have happened had she not had to play chief mediator with Reed and Isabel. She could have had her own hookup, but Jillian knew this guy also had a crush on Caroline, who'd just broken up with her longtime boyfriend. And what boy didn't like perfect Caroline?

Jillian wrote in her journal:

went to new york . . . which was really fun . . . hookah bars, fake LV purse . . . the apartment which made me want to have sex constantly, in like a really trendy and artsy way, and then marry into their family so i can live there . . . i like a boy but he likes someone else. it's painful. had a breakdown.

A few rows ahead, Josh stared out the window listening to a CD mix. Earlier that morning, he woke up to Trevor asking, *Why the hell did I sleep on the floor if you didn't sleep with her?* Josh couldn't admit the truth—that getting head from Erica was the most exciting sexual moment of his life; that all those times he'd said girls had gone down on him were lies. No, the truth wouldn't work, because Trevor and Reed were real guys. They had girls and sex and at least a dozen blow jobs in their repertoire—or so it seemed. Josh felt he was now just barely on the map.

He thought he'd feel different. But it was like waking up on your tenth birthday, running to the mirror, expecting to look older because you were now in the double digits, and then discovering that you were exactly the same. A blow job may have felt great at that moment, but it hadn't happened without consequences. Josh knew oral sex would be even better with a girlfriend, or at least someone he liked. Even Reed understood that what had happened with Isabel was mostly physical attraction. As the bus barreled down the highway, both boys headed back to Boston as men, sexually charged, liberated, able to be assholes and pull it off. The problem was that neither one felt particularly proud.

chapter fifteen

waiting up for you

Whitney posed for pictures on a beach in the Caribbean. Her long brown hair was slicked back, exposing small stud earrings, and her skimpy bikini showed off her muscles, abs, and shapely legs to perfection. She was the kind of girl any woman would look at with envy and any guy would look at and then want to look at some more. With one leg crossed in front of the other, Whitney turned her torso to the left and stuck out her butt. She held her drink up to her mouth and raised an eyebrow at Michaela, her best friend from skating, who held a camera. Click. The girls scrambled up the beach to the outdoor shower. Michaela stood under the water. She closed her eyes and ran her fingers through her hair, like the woman in the Herbal Essences commercial. Whitney steadied the camera. Click.

Whitney was an avid fan of picture posing, and her spring-break trip with Michaela and their moms was no exception. When she wasn't in a bikini, she wore a little outfit that exposed her tummy, like a miniskirt and short tank top. One night the girls met Church and his brother, who was an older and equally hot version of Church. The girls had been trying to reach the boys for a few days because the implied assumption was that Whitney and Church would hook up. Both had significant others (Nick was still in the picture), but that had never stopped Whitney before.

She covered her face in makeup and put on one of her cutest outfits, a pink-and-white tank top with a short black skirt. The girls met the boys at the bar. Whitney and Michaela sipped Smirnoff Ice through straws. Church drank Corona. He smiled at Whitney as she leaned into him, wrapping her slender arm around his neck and pulling his head close to hers. They looked at Michaela, both of their noses red from the sun, and smiled for the camera. Whitney picked up her Smirnoff Ice and put the straw in her mouth, pursed her lips and raised her thin eyebrows. A strand of wavy brown hair fell into her cleavage. Click.

Later that evening, while Michaela went off with Church's handsome older brother, Whitney and Church went back to her hotel to swim in their underwear. They kissed, and she had the distinct sense that one thing would eventually lead to another. She and Church had hooked up before, during their junior spring when she and Nick had taken a break. Now Whitney was on vacation. The weather was hot, and she looked amazing. So did Church. They were on the verge of going all the way when a hotel employee kicked them out of the pool. Whitney, dripping wet, climbed out, thinking yet again how she was somehow always saved from herself. She hadn't had sex, and this time it really mattered, because what Tripp and Nick had done for her on Valentine's Day a few weeks earlier, right before the five boys were expelled, was so incredible, it was one of the most memorable days of her life.

Whitney arrived at school on Valentine's Day wearing a brown shirt, a headband holding back her hair. She wasn't one of those girls who wore pink and red in every hue, as though the holiday had vomited all over her outfit. But she was sentimental about the day because Tripp gave her a thong and a scented gift from Victoria's Secret. He also handed her a card, which she read in front of him while they sat in her car, Whitney looking at the card and then at his face, then back at the card.

You've changed my life, he wrote.

She could hear the words as though he was speaking to her in his sexy Southern accent.

I've never met another girl I have more in common with.

I feel like we're meant to be.

I've never felt I could love a person as much as this.

I love you.

Whitney started to cry.

Shit, she thought to herself, *this guy really loves me, he's the kind of guy I want to be with.*

They hooked up, but deep down inside, in her vault of untold truths, she knew she would never be Tripp's girlfriend. After school, Whitney walked to her car in the ACC parking lot and found another present—a rose and a letter from Nick. *I can't wait to see you later tonight,* he wrote, *it's going to be the most special night of our lives.* She held the flower up to her nose. Usually students gave and received flowers on Valentine's Day. But that year the administration banned the practice because the girls' varsity field hockey team, which had always organized the fundraiser, was making money for itself, not school or a charity. Roses became just another lost tradition.

Whitney read Nick's note again. She felt morally wrong about misleading both him and Tripp, but she didn't let herself get distracted by guilt. She wondered what Nick had planned and had no idea it involved dinner at a tiny restaurant in the North End, Boston's historically Italian neighborhood, flutes of champagne, delicious food and a night at the Radisson. They walked into the hotel like a couple in love. She looked gorgeous in her cocktail dress, a total DSG, and he looked as proper as a boy with a shaved head and a fake diamond earring could.

Nick told her to wait in the lobby and then, a little later, he called to say she could come to their room. Whitney fixed her hair and straightened her dress on the way up.

Clutching her bag and holding her jacket, she opened the door to their hotel room.

Ohmygod, she said, dropping everything on the floor.

Oh. My. God.

In front of her was a runway of rose petals in pink, red, and white leading from the door all the way inside. With one step she was surrounded by petals, their edges cupping inside one another. As she walked through the hallway and entered the bedroom, she saw the words *I love you* spelled out in the flames of what looked like a hundred candles. The flames flickered in the breeze she'd created, *I love you* momentarily in motion. It was as though one version of the rest of her life began.

Come here, Nick said from the bed.

A slow, sexy rap song played in the background. She saw strawberries and champagne. She saw a boyfriend who loved her. And she saw a diamond promise ring in his hand. Whitney and Nick spent the night talking and crying, professing sentiments of love and commitment, as though it was their last time together. She put the ring on her ring finger and stared. Suddenly, two and a half years of life and love and sex converged, the past slamming against her future, now no longer mysterious but suddenly graspable: Whitney and Nick. Together.

Whitney could have had no idea that a few weeks later, on an island in the Caribbean, in a pool with Church, she would betray Nick again. She couldn't outrun her history. Even in paradise, it was impossible to escape the past because she was who she was, and she brought her flaws and urges with her no matter how far away she went or who she tried to become.

Spring break is about possibility. It's a universal signifier—momentary freedom from classes, adults, and homework; from the everyday social pressures that seem so defining in their consequences. The stereotype is obvious: stretches of white beach, kids gyrating to music, boozing all day, girls kissing girls and guys watching. Those staying at home can tune in to MTV to watch raw footage of sexually charged contests and bars bulging at the seams. Anything is possible away from school. Primarily the domain of college students, such vacations now extend to some high-schoolers, including those at Milton. For many, this is a time of indulgence, lenience, and abandon. The social boundaries that existed inside the student center evaporate; being someone else for a while was liberating. There was no one to answer to except, perhaps, oneself.

Brady had been hooking up with one of Emma's friends, then had sex with another DSG at a party, and almost had sex with a random girl in the Bahamas. While on vacation, he and his buddies partied on booze cruises, bought a packaged deal that got them into bars and nightclubs, and stayed out until morning. Josh heard rumors and wished he could've been there.

Jillian overlooked her general distaste for warm climates and the fear of exposing her body to go to Florida with Phoebe. She'd already spent the first week of spring break trapped in hell, otherwise known as tennis camp with the Milton team. She hated it more than she hated the special exercise program her mother had made her do the summer before senior year; the trip meant being around the girls from her team all the time, which was bad; playing tennis, which was worse; and hanging out in a ritzy golf town, which was the worst. But Jillian did it anyway, because the prospect of staying with her parents was even more unbearable than going to tennis camp.

The past few weeks:
—vacation doesn't feel like vacation
—got depressed because i'm fat
—magically lost seven pounds
—blaaaaah.

Reed sat at home over spring break, clowning around with his brothers and text-messaging Isabel, who was on vacation with her family in Europe. A buddy called him out on the indiscretion; texting a girl over spring break meant he was heading toward a relationship. Reed and Isabel officially going out? Impossible. She was a pastime, a name on his list. He never meant for anything serious to happen, because Reed wasn't looking to be anyone's boyfriend. Senior spring was meant to be the best time of his high school career. He had expectations of girls, parties, and irreplaceable times with the guys. There wasn't room for a girlfriend.

With each text message Reed sent, Isabel's regret over New York City faded. She'd been preparing herself to be devastated, because she believed guys like Reed weren't looking for relationships senior spring. But then he decided to stay over at her house the weekend before school started again after spring break. He could have spent his last few days at home in Farmington Hills or crashing with Brady, but no, Reed wanted to visit her.

He performed the obligatory greetings when he finally arrived at Isabel's house—hi, I'm Reed, here's my steady handshake, it's nice to meet you; you probably think I'm a dumb jock, but I'm actually smart; did you know I took your daughter's virginity? After having dinner at a sushi restaurant and staging their bedtime rituals, Isabel sneaked into the guest room, where Reed was supposed to sleep alone, and brought condoms. They had sex for the second time, passed out for a while, woke up, had sex, passed out, and did it all over again. Isabel was happy; she was with a guy who liked her (texting meant liking, right?), and sex was so much better in her house than in a hotel room. Reed was happy, too. The second time he slept with a girl, he got to have a sexathon.

Before spring break ended, headlines like "Depraved Society Lures Kids" and "Academy Sexcapade Had Prelude" reminded Reed of his tumultuous February. He followed some of the developments as they came out in the papers. The public learned that Zoe's family history had been problematic. According to the *Boston Globe* and the Associated Press (as printed in the *Concord Monitor*), her father was accused and acquitted of indecent exposure at a private school when Zoe was a young girl. Around the same time, her mother took out a restraining order against her son (Zoe's half-brother) because of threats he made against his stepfather and the family. On March 15, the Department of Social Services, responsible for monitoring schools and ensuring the safety of minors throughout the state, cleared Milton of any blame, stating that *these students are busier than any other students who have come under our jurisdiction. . . . There's only one hour after dinner that they are not supervised or involved in something,* the DSS spokeswoman told a *Patriot Ledger* reporter. *Unfortunately, with all of the supervision sometimes things still happen.*

Letters to the editor appeared in the editorial pages of the *Boston Globe.* Readers questioned Milton parents: *Where is the shame and embarrassment? Where is the support for the administration from the other parents?* Another reader argued that *the reaction by the school is the real scandal.* And a Milton graduate invoked support, explaining that *we're all confused. Nobody has a good explanation for why this happened, and everybody is starting to understand that this sort of thing probably happens a lot more than is realized.*

Reed rarely spoke at home about the incidents. He preferred to pass the time sleeping—rejuvenating himself—and boasting about getting into the Ivy League. *I told you you didn't have to apply to safety schools,* his mother said when she learned of the news. Reed told his friends back home in Farmington Hills, who still remembered him as the hockey jock, not the student who had ranked sixteenth in his class at his old high school. He bragged when he got back to Milton as well, especially when he learned that the smartest girl in his class didn't get into her top-choice Ivy (he also heard she'd made a bet with her father; $1,000 if she didn't get in).

Some students nicknamed Thursday, March 31, *Bloody Thursday,* because that's when many Ivy League schools' decisions went public. Most of Jillian's friends, including Isabel and Caroline, had already been accepted as early decision candidates. Phoebe got in almost everywhere, but even then she complained, because Milton was a place where ranking Ivy League schools was part of the college process.

Josh wasn't accepted to a single school he liked. As if his shortcomings with girls weren't enough, now he was wait-listed everywhere he wanted to go, even at his second-tier schools like Emory and Johns Hopkins. Brady didn't talk much about how he scrambled over December break to not only come up with an essay topic (football dinners at Wendy's), but to write it coherently, too. Months had passed since he'd mailed in his applications, but finally it happened: Brady got into college. The small liberal arts school in New York had a competitive football team. The school wanted him. With Brady's legacy connections, his acceptance to Milton had been expected; college was a monster he actually toppled on his own.

The week Annie vacationed in Aruba with her family, a group of girls from her class was doing the same thing—with little supervision. These girls weren't DSGs, but they were cool, and they invited Annie to hang out with them at night. They went to clubs like Carlos'n Charlie's, drank gigantic margaritas, and pretended to be freshmen in college. They got past the bouncers by sharing fake IDs or, if they were old enough, like Annie, using their own. She was relieved she was eighteen and could legally drink and get into bars, though once a bouncer kept staring at her ID and then at her face, back to her ID and then her face. She stared back, smiling, probably playing with her long blond hair, saying, *Yeah, it's the same person,* because it was a real ID, after all.

Annie entered the club and passed sketchy guys who huddled at the entrance, whispering *hey there* and *hey, mama* as she walked by. She glared at them with disgust, yet still wished she'd packed something more seductive than her black ruffle skirt. Her friends wore short miniskirts, see-through lace tank tops, and bandanna shirts that rarely covered belly buttons. They danced on tables and kissed several boys a night. Just when Annie had resigned herself to a night without attention, a cute guy picked her up while she ordered a drink at the bar.

He went to college in New England, was training to be a firefighter, and wanted to be a hero. Annie wished high school could be just like this. Away from Milton, she found it easy to meet guys, especially since they didn't know anything about where she hung out at recess or how many Milton guys she hadn't hooked up with. The firefighter looked like one of the cute fraternity boys who invariably appeared on MTV's *The Real World* each season—brown hair, dimples, an amazing body. He made Annie feel like the only girl in the world. She was her old self again. She smooched with the firefighter and then teetered off with her friends, giddy, filled with teenage hope, finally getting to be the kind of girl she'd idealized.

Then her mother called.

Are you safe?

Annie looked at her watch. It was 4:30 A.M. Before going out that night, she had promised her parents she wouldn't go anywhere alone, and said she'd slip a note under their door when she got home.

Are you safe? her mother asked again.

Yeah, Annie yelled into the cell phone, screaming over the music because she was still in the club. *We were just waiting for a cab.*

Okay, her mom said. *I will be waiting up for you.*

No, Mom, you don't have to do that.

I'll meet you in the lobby.

When Annie got back to the hotel, she felt guilty for making her mom worry. But partying was such a novelty, and not having to check in with a dorm parent or get parietals was like tasting freedom for the very first time. Had her parents known that going out in Aruba involved scandalous outfits, drinking, hooking up, and coming home at some horribly early hour in the morning, they would have made her stay home. Her mom and dad weren't "cool" parents. They imposed rules and didn't condone underage drinking. Yet they were surprisingly amenable to the idea of Annie going out, as long as she stayed with her group. Had their family vacation occurred later that year, her parents never would have let her go to Carlos'n Charlie's, the hot nightspot chain that earned national notoriety a few months later, in May, when Natalee Holloway, a high school honors student from Mountain Brook, Alabama, tragically disappeared while on vacation. The attractive eighteen-year-old blonde was last seen at the club, where she was probably drinking and dancing with friends, just like Annie did that night.

At the time, Annie considered herself a responsible Milton student who rarely drank. Years later, upon reflection, she amended this perception. She first drank the summer after sophomore year. Over the next two years, she threw back countless shots of Irish whiskey from her parents' liquor cabinet before sneaking out to meet Scott. And senior year, she drank once in the dorm, once on New Year's Eve, and now in Aruba. Annie thought alcohol tasted like nail polish, but she drank it anyway, at least on these particular occasions, because alcohol made everything easier.

The girls went back to Carlos'n Charlie's a few more times, and one night Annie spotted the firefighter. She panicked immediately. *Ohmygosh. There he is. Does he see me? Does he like me? He totally thinks I'm fat. His friends think I'm ugly. Look at all these gorgeous girls. Look at their skinny bodies. Ohmygosh, ohmygosh!* Annie steadied herself and started walking toward him, brushing against body parts until she was close enough to speak. *Hi,* she said, looking him in the eyes and then walking by. She thought she was being flip. She thought she was being brave. Inside she was filled with self-doubt, because the idea of actually talking with him was terrifying.

Time passed. The girls drank and danced. Later, the firefighter's friend found Annie.

Why did you ignore him?

She didn't know what to say.

He like, came back here because of you.

She didn't believe a word he said. Usually guys only wanted to get in her pants and look at her without a bra on. She glanced over at the firefighter and saw him talking with one of her friends. Had they been at school Annie might have felt intimidated, but this was Aruba. This was spring break. That girl had already hooked up with two guys in one night, and Annie was not going to let the firefighter slip away. The moment her friend disappeared to the bathroom, Annie asked him to dance.

The firefighter held her and kissed her neck. He made her feel sexier than she'd ever felt during the past three years with Scott. And when he asked her to come back to his hotel, she looked into his eyes and thought about his soft kisses, wondering how she would justify spending the night with him. It would be so different from her nights with Scott, but her girlfriends didn't let her leave. *You're not gonna go,* they insisted, pushing her into a taxi. She acquiesced, glaring at them, thinking how hypocritical the situation was; these girls had been hooking up with random guys all week.

Before driving off, the girls traded phone numbers with the firefighter and his friends. Everyone scribbled their information on a small piece of paper, which Annie put in her back pocket for safekeeping, though not for long, because one of the girls asked to see it, promised to hold on to it, and then lost it.

When spring break ended and Annie went back to school, the girl who lost the note came up to her one day, right before math class began.

I got a call this weekend from this guy who was asking for you, she said.

Ohmygosh! Annie said.

I think it was one of the guys from Aruba.

Annie knew it had to be the firefighter. She wasn't sure which was cooler, finding out he'd called looking for her, hearing the news in front of the popular guys who were in her math class, or getting to brag to Scott over IM.

> Scott: sup?
> Annie: just got back from Aruba
> Scott: oh yeah how was it?
> Annie: unreaaaal.
> Scott: So what did you do?
> Annie: my parents were actually really cool, i went out to this club like
>   every night.
> Scott: Oh i see . . . so how were the boys there?
> Annie: awesome I hooked up with a really hot guy
> Scott: oh I see
> Annie: yeeeeeah he was a firefighter too

Usually she replied to his questions with fibs like *I'm hooking up with somebody* or *We're kind of dating.* This time she didn't have to lie, and when Scott called a few weeks later, toward the end of March, she was still riding the success of having her own story, the proof that she could get a guy.

While Annie was browsing the shelves at Sephora with two friends, her cell phone rang.

What are you doing? Scott asked.

Oh, I'm at Copley, she said.

Well, we're going to be hanging out with some of my guy friends. We're probably going to be drinking, you guys should come hang out.

Um, I don't think so. I'm with my friends. We're probably going to have a girls' night in.

Okay, talk to you later.

'Bye, she said.

Annie's two friends, Beth and Macy, stared at her.

What? Annie asked.

Who was that? they asked.

Oh this guy from Northeastern, she said. *He was like, inviting us to do something tonight.*

Beth and Macy looked at each other.

I told him that we were going to be doing our own thing, Annie added.

Why? they exclaimed. *Why did you tell him that? We really want to do something! We really want to go!*

Oh no, Annie thought, not saying it out loud, just thinking it, because the last person she wanted to see was Scott. She couldn't show up in her boring daytime outfit and see him for the first time since the mall, in the winter. And she was genuinely excited for a girls' night of TV and gossip at a Boston hotel, where they were staying with one of their parents.

We really want to go, Beth and Macy said again.

I don't really want to go, Annie said.

It would be so fun to, you know, go to a big college party. Please can we go?

Annie called Scott back.

Actually, she said, *we might come to Northeastern later. We'll go but we won't get there until later. We're only going if there's alcohol.*

Annie, Beth, and Macy headed back to the hotel to primp and pass the time. While Beth and Macy played around with different outfits they had in their bags, Annie faced herself in the mirror and assessed the damage that was her daytime outfit: black pants, a white polo, and a pink sweater. Her hair fell neatly down her back, but she couldn't believe she had to go to her first college party looking like such a preppy dork.

The girls took the T to Northeastern and waited for Scott to show up. When he finally appeared, unshaven and scruffy, Annie looked at him blankly.

Do you have the alcohol?

You're being really rude, her friends whispered.

Annie didn't care. Scott probably just wanted to make sure he'd get to hook up with her that night, but the empowerment and happiness she'd felt on her spring-break trip had stayed with her. It was time to use Scott for something back.

He took the girls to his dorm room and introduced them to his friends.

That was George.

That was someone else.

And that was Dan.

Oh wow, Annie thought, looking at Dan. *That guy is really, really cute.*

She and her girlfriends sat down on Scott's bed while he mixed concoctions of raspberry vodka and Coke or Sprite. Annie downed hers in a few gulps.

Wow, you drank that really fast, Scott said.

Oh, she muttered.

Scott sat down between Beth and Annie and rubbed Annie's back.

Ugh, this is gross, she thought.

He held her hand.

Ugh, I am NOT going to do anything with him, she thought.

He simultaneously slid an arm around Beth's back, too.

Annie couldn't believe what she was seeing. She didn't want Scott that night, but she didn't want him to have anyone else, either, especially her good friend, especially right in front of her. She got up and moved to the other bed to sit next to Dan. He said he liked art history. Annie liked painting. Dan liked graphic design. Wow, she thought to herself, we're having an actual conversation. The more Annie flirted with Dan, the more Scott stared.

Where's the bathroom? Beth and Macy asked Scott when they were the only others left in the dorm room.

It's up—

Can you show us where it is? they asked, because they knew Annie wanted to be alone with Dan.

Sure.

Annie and Dan stayed behind and kissed on the bed. This was exactly what she wanted. Scott was jealous. She was tipsy. A boy liked her. Scott walked in with Beth and stuttered something as Annie pulled away from Dan. She massaged her blond hair back into place and waited awkwardly while Scott and Beth sat down on the other bed, which was partially hidden by a bookshelf that probably offered the standard freshman-year fare: Psych 101, Toni Morrison, European history textbooks. Annie heard them kiss, so she pushed herself against Dan and kissed him again, unsure of which was worse, listening to Scott hook up with another girl or having that other girl be her friend.

What are you doing? Annie finally asked Scott.

Well, you hooked up with my friend first, he said.

Beth and Dan quickly fled.

Annie looked at Scott. He was so gross. He was so mean. Why did she still care about him? Why did she—

Scott kissed her.

No, Annie said, pushing him away.

Yeah, Scott said, *because I don't want to be sloppy seconds anyway.*

Annie wanted to leave. It was three-thirty A.M., and she and Beth had been hanging out with the guys for hours. But they couldn't find Macy. Last they remembered she was standing on her tiptoes in the hallway, sucking face with an older guy simply because someone yelled *I dare you to kiss him.* Macy wasn't in the bathroom and she didn't pick up her cell phone. The girls left messages. The boys looked around the dorm. Scott said they should knock on George's door. A few minutes later Macy poked her head out.

Now's not a good time, she said.

We want to go, Annie said.

Macy stalled, then disappeared back into the room.

Let's leave, Beth said to Annie.

We're not leaving her, Annie replied. *Where have you been?* she asked Macy, whose head reappeared through the crack in the dorm-room door. *We really want to go.*

Okay, I'll be a second, Macy said.

She emerged five minutes later. The boys walked the girls outside. Annie kissed Dan, making sure Scott could see, and then hopped into a taxi.

Where were you? the girls asked Macy. *We were worried about you. We couldn't call you.*

Oh, Macy started.

Where were you? they asked again.

Macy said it: She'd been giving George head. For thirty minutes straight. Just because.

Ohmygosh, Annie said.

I can't believe I did that, Macy said.

Why did you do that? Annie asked. She instinctively knew the answer to her own question. Each time Annie went back to Scott, she did things to him that she often vowed she'd never do again. She appeased him, went down on him, and let him touch her body. And why? Because she wanted him to like her. This time, at the Northeastern party, something had empowered her—the firefighter, regret, possibly even the will of a survivor. Annie finally fought back.

The drama of Annie's spring break settled down very quickly when she got back to Milton. Her mom drove her to campus the night before classes started, and they stopped at the student center on their way to Pryce so Annie could check her mail. The first floor was calm at night, devoid of the crowds of girls and boys. Annie headed down the stairs, past the ghosts of hockey boys who usually stood there watching, and hurried to her mailbox.

Thank God I didn't find out at recess, she thought as she stared at her rejection letter from Barnard. She would have been mortified had she opened the letter there, in front of hundreds of students. Thank goodness her mom was waiting outside in the car. She took Annie to Starbucks for hot chocolate, but nothing eased the bitter news that she wouldn't be going to New York City for college next year.

She didn't understand what went wrong. College was where girls like Annie—smart girls who were involved and talented—were supposed to get revenge upon girls like the DSGs. Over the next few days she watched her boarder friends move back to campus, check their mailboxes, and hear from schools. To Annie, it seemed as if everyone was complaining.

Oh, I really don't want to go to this school.

I would rather go to a better school.

He got into Georgetown, but his parents wanted him to go to Yale.

All Annie wanted was Barnard.

chapter sixteen

the best feeling of my life

BEEP BEEP *BEEP BEEP BEEP BEEP BEEP.* A hand emerged from underneath blue-and-white-pin-striped sheets and flailed toward the noise. *BEEP BEEP BEE—* Silence. The hand disappeared. Blond hair rustled on a pillow. A sigh. Annie tossed the covers off in one decisive movement and pulled herself out of bed. She put on a sweatshirt, grabbed her Hervé bag, put her flute inside, and walked into the usual commotion of a school morning in Pryce House. Girls traipsed in and out of the bathrooms, knocked on friends' doors, and rushed to grab breakfast before assembly at eight A.M. Had any of them been Annie, they might still have been asleep, because she had first and second periods free. But it was April, and Annie needed every free hour she could find to prepare for her solo in the orchestra's spring concert at the end of the month.

As she walked across the main quad toward Kellner, the performing-arts center, she noticed spring had suddenly arrived. Daffodils cropped up behind the library. Buds sprouted on tree branches, like light green cotton balls. Grounds crews were already preparing the lawns for graduation in June, and students had become a permanent fixture on the steps outside buildings and on the smaller quads around Wigg, Ware, and the dorms. In the afternoons, sunbathers, Frisbee players, couples, and dorm parents' children soaked up those precious hours after classes but before Forbes dinner. Annie hoisted her Hervé higher onto her shoulder and walked into Kellner, preparing to begin yet another day cooped up in a claustrophobic practice room.

Once Annie found a vacant room, she emptied her bag. She took out her music tuner and sipped her water, skimming over the notes her teacher had made in her notebook during their last lesson. She arched her back and stretched her arms, forcing the muscles to expand and contract until the pain lessened. After weeks of intensive practice, the discomfort was familiar. Any time she prepared for a major orchestra concert, she spent at least three hours a day in one of the tiny practice rooms. Sometimes a girlfriend visited, though never for long. *I'm leaving*, Ida would say, *have fun for the next two hours*. Other times Annie commiserated with another girl who also had a solo in the spring concert. Most of the time, though, her breaks were spent walking around Kellner alone.

Her practice room that morning was sparsely furnished: a piano, a bench, a chair, a music stand. Daylight trickled in through a narrow window carved into the wall. Annie fit the three pieces of her flute together, connecting the mouthpiece to the body without squeezing the keys. She blew hot air into the instrument and licked her lips. Standing erect, she faced her sheet music, lifted her arms above her right shoulder, and brought the flute's mouthpiece to her bottom lip. She took a breath and began to play.

Annie's entire music career had been building toward her senior solo. Every year, the full orchestra and chamber orchestra performed in two concerts, one in the winter and one in the spring. Mr. Graham, Milton's longtime conductor and head of the music department, chose the best senior musicians as soloists. The concerts were their big days, and those soloists selected were like the hockey team's starting line or the football team's quarterback. Family and friends sat quietly in the audience, waiting to clap when the music stopped and give flowers after the concert.

As an underclassman, Annie had watched these elite seniors rehearse with their accompanying group, either the full orchestra or chamber orchestra. She peeked over the top of her music stand, watching them improvise cadenzas without even having to look at their music. When she got to Milton, she was one of many flutists and resented sharing the spotlight with the older girls. Now, senior year, her time had come. She'd been part of the school's legendary musical tradition for four years. In the past, Milton students had performed at Carnegie Hall and the White House, and shared the stage with well-known musicians like James Taylor, Poncho Sanchez, and Abdullah Ibrahim. She'd traveled to Hawaii and Ireland to perform. She'd given up sleep and weekends to practice. For one night, she was going to perform her Mozart solo and be a star. She'd been waiting for this event since she first got to Milton. Now all she wanted was to get it over with.

On the night of the spring concert, parents arrived on campus in droves. They dropped grandparents off at Kellner's side entrance, then circled around to the far reaches of campus in search of empty parking spots. The walk back to Kellner was long, and once inside they merged with the other moms, dads, siblings, teachers, and friends who constituted a gigantic crowd in the main entryway. Parents schmoozed with other parents, asking questions about college and sharing impressive stories about their own children. A bake sale usually appeared in the corner. Packs of boarders showed up. As seven thirty P.M. neared, a steadily growing cacophony of indecipherable noise blasted from the orchestra room.

The musicians warmed up. Usually the space was undecorated and organized. Folding chairs and music stands created a semicircle around Mr. Graham's podium. Violins to his left, cellos to his right, and violas in front, followed by wind, brass, and percussion spread out in rows in the back. On the night of the concert, though, this traditional setup was wiped clean. Instrument cases lay open exposing crushed velvet linings and extra reeds and rosin. Spring jackets and sheet music littered the floor, as though the orchestra had suddenly become a communal bedroom. Students left instruments unattended to go to the restroom or traded with friends just for fun. The girls and boys looked deceptively like grown-ups in their black-and-white clothes, huddling around someone's tuner and practicing difficult runs.

At some point Mr. Graham appeared in the doorway, his round, disheveled physique belying the delicacy of his craft. He took pride in his musical constituencies, and his presence alone commanded the players' attention. The din lessened as students waited for his instructions.

Get your music.

Get your instruments.

Alex, tie your tie.

Janie, give the trombone back to Steven.

The concert is about to begin!

Are you excited? friends asked Annie. She forced a smile, not realizing just how beautiful she looked. Her long lavender gown shimmered, setting off her blond mermaid hair. The full skirt balanced out her breasts, and pinned prominently in front, in the center of her halter top, was a small brooch. Annie hadn't even planned to wear a gown until her flute teacher told her she couldn't possibly wear all black for her solo. *Ohmygosh, I need something nice to wear!* she told her mom, who took her to Jessica McClintock on Newbury Street to find something dazzling.

Out in Kellner's main entryway, guests slowly filed into King Theatre, one of Milton's most prestigious gems, designed and built as a modern adaptation of Shakespeare's Globe. The three-story space boasted an adaptable stage, catwalk, and sophisticated lighting and sound equipment. The audience waited in their seats. Boys' legs rocked nervously while girls braided their hair. Younger siblings played hangman on the backs of the professionally printed programs, bugging their mothers for gum, because they were already bored and wanted to go home.

But then there was movement onstage. The chamber orchestra entered. These gawky-looking boys and attractive-looking boys; these gangly-looking girls and delicate swanlike girls—they were poised and ready, instruments at hand, fingers anticipating the rush of notes, trying to look like an orchestra. Mr. Graham acknowledged the audience, because this was his big night, too, and then he turned to face his musicians.

The first soloist began. Backstage, Annie held her breath. She could hear his performance. It was perfect. And long. Ten minutes went by. Twelve. She didn't understand. Why was he taking so long? Annie ran her fingers through her hair and shimmied around in her gown, making sure all the seams and straps were in place. She visualized the first few bars of her solo. All she had to do was play the first note; the rest would happen naturally. Without her even noticing, the first soloist finished. It was Annie's turn.

On stage, Mr. Graham waited. There was little movement, little noise, just waiting. From out of nowhere an angel appeared. Annie was blond and curvaceous, a splash of lavender against the traditional black-and-white orchestral attire, a firecracker darting in the sky. The audience clapped and chamber orchestra members tapped their feet. She walked to the front of the stage, her flute clutched in one hand, and adjusted her music stand. She looked out into the packed theater, trying to find familiar faces—relieved, too, that she couldn't.

Ohmygosh, she thought, feeling the cellos behind her.

I am so squished.

I really have to keep my focus.

She felt the lights beaming down from the ceiling. Her cheeks flushed. Just start playing. Just start playing. *You will do a great job,* her mother had said. And so this angel, this soft vision of lavender and blond hair, cradled a flute between her fingertips, swept in a breath, and began. Almost immediately, Annie felt a cellist's bow jabbing her from behind. There it was again. The edge of the stage was only inches away. She was moments from tumbling into the laps of those who'd snagged front-row seats, her gown flying, ripping. But eventually the jabbing stopped. Annie focused. The first few measures were always the scariest. They set the tone, captivating the audience or putting them to sleep. Annie quickly slipped into autopilot. She looked and sounded exquisite on stage. There she was, a girl performing in a woman's moment, enticing a crowd not because of her breasts, face, or willingness to hook up but because of her talent.

Eight minutes later, Annie filled her final note with a rich vibrato. The chamber orchestra hushed. Mr. Graham made his closing dip with the baton. Silence. And then the audience erupted in applause. *Oh, I'm done!* Annie thought as she bowed. She tried to make out the faces in the audience. There were so many people! Her family was somewhere. Her teachers, too. She was disappointed that her flute teacher couldn't attend, but Ida was right there in the front row.

Annie walked off the stage and then returned for a second bow. Her mom brought her a bouquet of yellow roses, and so did a friend. Mr. Graham handed her flowers, too. She had everything she wanted— attention, respect, awe. *This is the best feeling of my life!* she thought. This was being the center of a very good kind of attention. The only problem was, it was at an orchestra concert—an *orchestra* concert—not at a party or a dance, not even at recess.

Like a good Milton student, Annie woke up the next morning to catch up on her homework. She knew she should have been celebrating; the concert marked the beginning of senior spring, and she wanted to relax with friends and do something commemorative. But April's assignments had piled up because of her solo, and though she wasn't an A student, not caring about school was not in her nature. Yet as she flipped through her homework, she could hardly focus. Outside waited possibility.

What do I do next? she wondered.

Where do I go from here?

How do I start my senior spring?

These questions hovered like rainbows, as though letting loose was a conscious and obvious choice, like going to the library rather than Forbes for lunch or leaving class to use the bathroom. Annie wanted to suspend her Milton life. Usually she headed into Boston, but this time she needed something more than shopping on Newbury Street. Her momentary solution: She called Teresa, a friend from Lenox.

You know, I'm just in a kind of odd mood, Annie confessed.

Come home! Teresa said. *Come to my house!*

Perfect, Annie thought. She didn't want to go to her own house, because she'd just seen her family the night before, and she didn't want to stay at Milton because that's what she always did. She packed an overnight bag, contacted Scott, and arranged to meet at Teresa's. During her trip out to western Massachusetts, Annie wondered why she wanted to see Scott that night. He had no idea what she'd just accomplished at the orchestra concert. She'd mentioned the solo only in passing, possibly online. She assumed they would inevitably hook up, but making out wasn't her primary motivation. Knowing he still liked her and seeing that he wanted her, these were justifications enough unto themselves.

Once Annie got to Teresa's, preparations for Scott's visit began. Teresa explained that she would turn off the alarm system so Annie could let Scott in through the garage. They'd have to go straight to the basement, which Annie understood, and she promised to be quiet.

You can turn on the TV, Teresa said.

Do you want to say hi to him? Annie asked, fiddling with her starfish necklace.

No, I'm just going to be resting. I'm going to be up here if you need anything.

But Annie wanted Teresa to stay. She wanted her to come down-stairs and hang out—to do anything so that the night would feel more like a celebration and less like a last-minute hookup scheme.

When Scott came over, Annie took him to the basement. She sat down on the faded orange pull-out couch, feeling surrounded by child-hood: framed pictures of her friend's family, artwork from elementary school, a box overflowing with toys and stuffed animals. This was not romantic. This was where she and Teresa sat as little girls, their backs pushed up against the couch cushions, legs sticking out, too short to reach the floor.

Can we turn on the TV? Scott asked.

Annie said yes, and moments later, he leaned over and kissed her. Their routine was familiar. Her shirt and bra came off. So did Scott's clothes. At one point they heard Teresa from the top of the basement stairs.

Everything okay? she asked.

Annie blushed, but no, everything was not okay. Scott was naked. He was hairy and ugly and so totally all over Annie in the middle of her best friend's basement. Right there was a picture of Teresa as a little girl. And there, not far from her face, was Scott's white and fleshy body. His chest lowered onto hers. The brown fuzz made him look dirty. Ev-ery inch of him wanted sex, ached for orgasms, and Annie was the one who was supposed to make it happen.

This is all about hooking up, she realized.

This is all about sex.

This is just so animalistic.

Almost three years of hookups came crashing down in the dimmed light of Teresa's basement. There on the couch, tangled up between Scott's limbs, Annie knew he would never give her what she wanted. He would never be—and had never been—anything more than some-thing physical. Her orchestra performance the night before represented a massive accomplishment, the culmination of Annie's high school career. Scott might have complemented the success. He should have been the supportive boyfriend. He should have known the real Annie—kind, demure, beautiful in her awkwardness. Instead, he was the guy she hooked up with, the sum total of her high school sexual experience. And still she was going to college a virgin.

Scott quickly dressed after Annie's passive attempt at a hand job. She redressed, too, threading her arms through her bra and hooking the clasps behind her back. She wanted Scott to leave, and when he did, she watched him walk out the garage door, wondering if she would ever see him again. Maybe they'd run into each other next year on the T. Maybe she'd have a boyfriend in college and they'd be in Boston, holding hands, acting like a couple in love, and Scott would suddenly appear. He'd see how happy she was—how beautiful and, at last, unattainable she was. She'd say *I'm over you* and *I'm better than you* and throw it in his face. For the moment she watched him disappear, remembering this relationship that spread out between childhood and womanhood, teetering between fantasy and reality. Annie watched him, hoping that she was done with him.

chapter seventeen

bobbing for apples and beer

isabel was home alone, in a big house, her parents out of town. She was still hooking up with Reed. She felt brave. It was time for something big. It was time to make an impression. At Milton, students anticipated several rites of passage during the last two months of school. For athletes it was a final varsity dinner, held in the ACC to honor the spring season's finest players. For artists it was their final art exhibition. For Jillian it was the annual Persky Awards, which celebrated the year's best writing in student publications. For Reed it was his induction into Milton's cum laude society, which honored top students in the graduating class (thirty-one students in 2005), as well as two juniors. *Who are you here with?* a classmate asked Reed at the ceremony. *I'm here because I'm being inducted, too,* he said, pleased that he, the hockey jock, had earned a spot at the top. Graduation would be the ultimate event, when seniors sat in fold-up chairs on the main quad and faced a sea of proud, weepy, bored family members and friends. Grad parties would follow, and then supposedly the best summer of their lives. But for now, all that loomed on the horizon, so Isabel decided to throw a party.

A few friends had come over the night before with alcohol and extra hands. They hid an antique table, laid a shower curtain over a beloved carpet, and locked a room or two. Isabel wasn't planning an *Animal House* evening. She expected only about twenty friends, and had originally thought some cheap vodka and a bag of limes would do. But for a first-time host, twenty was a nerve-racking number, so the precautions were necessary.

After her friends left, she looked around at her empty house and the kitchen that was now stocked with booze, and sensed she'd made a horrible decision. Her house was not a "party house," and her mom and dad were strict. They were the kind of parents who avoided conversations about drinking and sex, and reacted to the hockey incidents with outright shock. Twenty friends might have been passable, but she couldn't throw a rager. Isabel felt guilty before the party even began. How could she do this to her parents?

She made a plan. Her girlfriends would come over first, and then Reed would show up later, after he and his buddies went to the Sophomore Semi, a formal date dance for the sophomore class, with a crew of young DSGs. The problem was that Reed mistook Isabel's party for his party. He had ambitious ideas. They would move out all the furniture (not just the antique table), bring in a wading pool, and fill it with ice and beer. He wanted to invite all of his friends, but even Reed knew there were some places where Brady wasn't welcome.

Dude, you can come over if you want, a party host would say, *but like, no Brady.*

All right, gotcha, Reed would say, and then promptly call Brady, because even if Brady came with a carload of young DSGs and liked hiding empties in the host's microwave for some parents to find, how could Reed exclude one of his best buddies?

Meanwhile, Jillian worried about Isabel.

You can't let Reed like, take over your life, she told Isabel. *He's totally manipulating you with this party.*

No he's not, Isabel said. *No he's not, no he's not.*

Fine, you're right. You can do whatever you want. I'm sorry that I inter-fered.

Jillian had grown tired of helping Isabel. She never listened. It was as though she wanted to be disrespected. Yet Isabel was only part of the problem. In truth, Jillian had been feeling alienated from her girl-friends for a while. In the fall they were cliquey. In the winter they had boy dramas. Now Isabel, Caroline, and Phoebe spent all their time with the Pryce Girls, organizing weeknight TV dinners, going to Starbucks, and acting as though they'd been friends for years. Jillian didn't under-stand. High school was about to end; why make new friends? What was so great about the Pryce Girls? While her friends seemed suddenly en-amored of their new crowd, Jillian would escape to the *Paper* office to read one of her three books or write in her journal. Her latest crush, Oliver, also worked in the office, and the possibility of something hap-pening with him was so much better than stupid chitchat with the Pryce Girls and pretending she still adored her girlfriends.

Still, Isabel remained a problem she couldn't ignore, because Jillian knew more about Reed than she let on. She'd already heard dirt from a girlfriend, who'd divulged the details of a recent conversation she'd had with Reed. According to Jillian's friend, Reed thought it was cool that he and Isabel were having sex, but he wasn't sure he really liked her. He thought she was chubby. He thought about breaking up with her. Jillian wanted to run straight to Isabel, but how would she even begin to repeat the horrible things Reed had been saying?

Then, just hours before Isabel's party, another friend revealed more disturbing news.

Isabel is driving me crazy, she said.

Oh my God, me, too, Jillian confessed. *Tell me. What happened?*

She just won't listen to me about Reed. I think he's like, totally manipu-lating her with this party. You should hear the things he says about her.

What does he say? she asked.

He goes around telling people he doesn't really like her. And he's just in it for kind of like, free sex.

Jillian's friend took the information as fact because it had come directly from her friend's boyfriend, whom Reed knew well. Apparently the story Reed told was that after he and Isabel randomly hung out in his dorm, a buddy said, *Someone should try and fuck that fat bitch.*

And so I did, Reed supposedly blurted to the guys. *And at first Isabel was cool, but then she got kind of clingy. So I was like, fuck that.*

Jillian's friend looked at Jillian with as much shock and frustration as she felt herself.

I don't know what to do, Jillian sighed. *She already won't listen to anything I have to say. She's mad at me. I don't know what to do.*

I'll talk to Isabel, her friend offered.

Okay, Jillian said, *but don't tell her the stuff he said.*

Don't worry, I won't.

Jillian wasn't surprised when Isabel called her, crying about Reed. Through tears, Isabel recounted bits and pieces of a watered-down version of the gossip Jillian knew. Something about Reed accepting a bet with a friend to hang out with her.

Yeah, that's pretty much what I heard, too, Jillian lied.

She couldn't bring herself to tell Isabel the truth, because everything she learned about Reed that day was appalling and unforgivable. And Isabel was already beside herself. How could he do this to her? How could he be so cruel? Jillian thought Isabel should have seen it coming. Getting used was within the realm of possibility when a hockey player was involved, and Isabel should have known that. Everybody knew that.

Oh my God, I'm so upset, Isabel moaned. *The party's off. The party's off!*

Good, Jillian thought. Now the whole mess with Reed could finally be over. She wanted to get Isabel a breakup basket to cheer her up, because that's the kind of friend she was. Usually chocolates and sappy movies were perfect, but the grocery store was limited, so she bought magazines and Lucky Charms, fully prepared for an evening of tears and regret. When Isabel answered the door, she looked surprisingly all right. Jillian handed over the gifts.

Oh this is like, so sweet, Isabel said, *but why'd you bring this over?*

Because you and Reed like, had that fight, Jillian said.

Oh, everything's better now.

Reed had gotten to Isabel first. After receiving a series of angry voice messages from her, he explained that the whole situation was a silly misunderstanding. His words were misconstrued; the bet to hang out with her was more of an encouragement, and no, of course he wasn't using her for sex. Besides, talk with the guys was just that, talk. Reed didn't mean half the things he said, especially when it came to girls. He liked Isabel. He said it again and again until she believed him and he almost believed himself, too.

Jillian wasn't going to try to convince Isabel not to be with Reed, so she helped set up for the party. Phoebe, Caroline, and a few other girls arrived early. Over dinner, Caroline dropped possibly the biggest news of her life: Innocent Caroline, the one who said *ewww gross* when sexual matters came up, had just lost her virginity to her new boyfriend, the same guy Jillian had flirted with that weekend in New York City. And now she was telling her friends, albeit with her eyes squeezed shut, stumbling through her story while Isabel guessed what happened as Caroline flashed a thumbs-up or thumbs-down until the correct details emerged.

Caroline and her boyfriend were on the floor of her living room, the film *Almost Famous* playing in the background. Everything had been perfect, Caroline said, except that she spontaneously cried halfway through. What if her parents walked downstairs and the stair that usually creaked didn't? What if they came in without warning? What if the pain (which she expected—and felt) got worse and she bled everywhere? Blood stained, didn't it? What if it ran all over the floor and her parents saw it the next morning?

Her boyfriend asked if she wanted to stop.

Caroline said no.

They kept going.

Wow, she thought to herself. *This is happening. This is nice.*

Caroline told her friends she was so in love. She'd found someone who made her feel comfortable in every way. She was fascinated by the idea that a life-changing moment could leave her looking exactly the same and yet feeling so infinitely different. She couldn't wait to do it again.

Jillian wasn't too bothered that she'd lost her New York City crush to Caroline, but now Caroline had lost her virginity after hanging out with him for only a month? *Insane,* Jillian thought. This meant Caroline, the same girl who dated her previous boyfriend for a year without having sex, had more sexual experience than Jillian did. Great, she thought. Now she was that much closer to being the last one of her friends to lose her virginity.

Jillian made a hasty exit before Reed arrived, but by ten thirty P.M., Isabel's house was still empty. The girls joked that they'd worried about the number of people for nothing, but Isabel now felt disappointed at the prospect of a night spent only with her girlfriends and Reed. Finally he called. He and his friends were still at the Sophomore Semi, but they wanted to stop by.

You can come over, Isabel said, *but you realize that it's not a party. It's like, me and my friends.*

Can I bring my date? Reed asked.

Was he serious?

No! Isabel said.

Before Reed arrived, a random kid from school showed up at Isabel's door looking for a party. She invited him in, not entirely sure what was going on. Then a phone rang; another group was on its way over. Isabel was beginning to feel as if things were spinning out of her control.

When Reed finally arrived—with his date—he had young DSGs in tow because he thought the idea of spending Saturday night with the Hysterics was just plain scary. After he and the girls crammed into Brady's Volvo for the forty-five-minute ride from Milton to Lexington, Reed's cell phone rang constantly.

We have a pack of junior girls, two guys said.

abigail jones and marissa miley

Dump those off first, then come back, Reed replied.

We want to go, others said.

Don't. Don't show up. Don't do anything until I get there and call you back.

Someone else called to say cars were literally circling Isabel's house.

Don't worry about it, he said to Isabel when he finally arrived. *I'll be the bouncer.*

Park your car around the corner! he shouted.

Get the fuck off the lawn! Isabel added.

Reed felt like Van Wilder, from the film of the same name, who, after spending seven years in college, becomes a professional party planner when his father decides it's time for him to get a job. Reed saw a future for himself as a PR person. Organizing the party, inviting friends, coordinating parking spots—he was a boy on a man's mission, and his only true moment of weakness came when he spilled beer on his pink Purple Label tie. He thought his night might actually be ruined for good.

Isabel looked around her house in utter disbelief. Her friends were in the kitchen. Brady and the hockey guys had taken the basement. Other people were everywhere; walking around, sitting on the stairs, hooking up in Isabel's room.

This is my room! she thought. *Get out!*

When she went down to the basement, she found it foggy with weed, and there at the heart of it all was Nick—Whitney's Nick—getting high. Here she was hosting a party, with a guy she thought might be using her for sex, for his friends, who were clearly using her for an empty house. Isabel finally spoke up.

No more! she cried. *No more people.*

Don't be an asshole, Reed said to Nick. *Don't smoke.*

Isabel was so wound up, so absolutely stressed out, that all she could do was drink, throw up, and run around the house. Hours passed. From the outside, the house stood still. Inside, the girls and guys partied into the late-night hours. Reed took off with a few young DSGs and a friend who was too drunk to drive his own car. Phoebe defended the fridge against a drunk and hungry boy.

No you are not going to take the Lean Cuisine, she said.

His eyes were glassy. He was totally high.

What are you doing? she asked.

He was still going after the Lean Cuisine.

No! You're not getting that! she insisted.

Around six A.M., Isabel went to the store to buy carpet cleaner and Febreze. It was still dark outside, and Reed was already gone. He left her with three bulging trash bags filled with the beer cans she'd already collected herself. By morning, her house smelled of booze, smoke, and bodies. A carpet was drenched with beer. Cans were strewn everywhere. Someone had changed the password on her computer. Someone else had puked on a wall. Later, Reed would put the total number of people around fifty, Phoebe and Caroline sixty, but Isabel swore there had to have been at least a hundred and fifty kids. None of this ever would have happened had Reed not invited his friends. It was all his fault.

When she returned from the store, she saw that less than a dozen kids had slept over, most of whom were her friends. One of Reed's buddies remained, and tried unsuccessfully to reach his friends. *Come on, pick up. You have all my shit. Come back.* Isabel gave some leftover vodka to a random kid when he woke up, and then watched him empty the bottle into his orange juice. She looked around at the total destruction, at the evidence that was so blatant, and let reality crash back: How in the world would her parents not find out? What would they say? How did all of this begin?

Any Milton student who has been in this situation knows exactly how it began: with a rush of adrenaline and a desire to rebel. It starts when parents decide to go away. They trust their daughter for a weekend. She has her license; she's stayed home alone before; she's a respectable prep school student who knows better. They hand over phone numbers, addresses, and emergency contacts. Her mother leaves a good-bye note on the kitchen counter, signing it with a smiley face. When the daughter finds it, she closes her eyes and says *yes*, because now she knows they're really gone. So she calls her friends and spreads the word. This is what having fun in high school is all about.

Eventually her friends arrive. They come bearing gifts—more cases of beer, iPods with party mixes, food. She is pleased. Someone hands her a drink and makes a toast: *Seniors!* The doorbell rings again. Friends of friends. She gulps down her drink and grabs another. The doorbell again. She hears excited voices. Is that— It can't be— Is it? Is that the hottest guy in school? It is. He smiles at her and slaps his hand across her back as though the two of them go all the way back to kindergarten. She laughs nervously and grabs a third drink, even though she finished her second just five minutes ago. Time slows. She hears people laughing.

She turns. Some kid has wrapped himself in Saran wrap. His entire body is covered in see-through plastic. In the kitchen she notices empties perched in her mother's garlic basket. A full can sits in the banana hammock. A boy has his finger in the peanut butter jar, and on a shelf to his left is a picture of her family. She looks at it thoughtfully. Her parents. What will she do when they return? Someone walks by wearing her mother's goofy garden shoes. And her gloves. The girl wobbles. She takes a sip from the cup she's holding and realizes it's pure vodka. Ohmygod, her parents.

That afternoon, when Isabel's mom and dad got home, she met them on the porch.

Is everything okay? they asked.

It's okay, Isabel started, before her mouth started running with a combination of fact and fiction.

Word got out that you guys weren't around and that I was having a party.

But I really was only planning on having my friends come over.

And a lot of people showed up that we didn't expect.

I lost control of the door, and then everybody just kept coming in.

I was all over the house trying to keep things safe.

Her mother opened the fridge.

What are these? she asked, referring to the leftover bag of limes.

I don't know! People just brought stuff! People brought apples! They wanted to go bobbing for apples and beer. I didn't know what was going on!

Her mother was skeptical.

Her father was livid.

They had questions and Isabel fudged her answers.

It got out of control, Isabel said. *But Reed was really good and helped me get people out,* Isabel said.

I don't get it, her mom began. *You hated him, and now he saved your party?*

I don't know! was all Isabel could say.

She wanted to leave Reed out of her explanation. Just a couple of weeks earlier her mom had found Isabel crying. She had to have known it was about Reed. But how could Isabel's parents be sympathetic if they knew that he was involved in planning the party? They would never, ever approve. Sometimes it's hard to self-edit in front of parents. Some teenagers can be masters, and others, though beginners, cling to the art as best they can.

In the end Isabel's parents didn't punish her; they forgave her.

We think there are parts that you left out, they said. *We feel that you didn't tell us the whole truth, but we're glad you told us.*

The only thing we can ask you to do is to use better judgment and be the best person you can be.

To this day, Isabel still feels guilty about lying to her parents. But her mother wasn't finished. When her dad left the room, she told her daughter she had one more question. Isabel waited.

I know you had boys over. I just need to know if you are sexually active.

Yeah, Isabel said.

I want to schedule you a gynecologist's appointment.

Isabel nodded. It was one of the rare times her mom spoke about sex. This was different from the birth control pill, which had been a topic of conversation since freshman year, when she had to take it to regulate her periods. Isabel didn't necessarily want to talk with her mom about sex, but she didn't want to discuss it with a gynecologist, either. What girl wants to strip from the waist down, lie back on an examination table, place her heels on stirrups, and spread her legs while various cold medical instruments are inserted, cranked, poked, and moved around inside? Treacherous fears lay in waiting: an irregular pap smear, herpes, chlamydia or any other STD, or, God forbid, a baby. Having a doctor's head between the legs, touching, looking, moving through folds of skin, can be oddly reminiscent of private moments, especially to girls like Isabel who were just learning about their sexuality.

Besides, she already had her girlfriends for answers to all her sexual curiosities. That spring they'd started imitating *Sex and the City* conversations, dishing out advice they'd just barely discovered. Have you had an orgasm? What positions do you like? What do you think, spit or swallow? Caroline blushed, but Isabel didn't. She watched *Sex and the City*. Her father did, too, and made the same disclaimer with nearly every episode: *This is not what the real world is like.* Isabel understood what he meant, but if she stripped the show of money and glamour, the lives of Carrie, Charlotte, Samantha, and Miranda resonated with those of Isabel and her friends. When it came down to it, they were all searching for love and sex, though rarely for orgasms.

All Isabel had wanted in the beginning of the school year was a hookup, and now that she had it she wasn't planning to let it go. She fell for Reed's deep-set eyes, his pale skin that matched her own, even the way he played with her heart. Her friends didn't see what Isabel saw. They thought Reed was a player by association, because of Brady, no doubt, and a wise guy by definition, if not a little sketchy. They played along, though, knowing how much Isabel wanted a boyfriend—or someone. But Jillian, who usually refrained from judging her friends' relationships, thought Isabel was blatantly being hurt, used, and ignored.

chapter eighteen

a lovely girl

Senior spring was a state of mind, a fantasy that existed for all Milton students, promising that rare life opportunity to enjoy the present. For some, the experience began with the early decision acceptances in December. For others, it began after regular decision acceptances trickled in at the end of March. By late April, every senior was free. College had finally been decided. A vigorous high school career neared its end. Summer was not far off. Seniors were on top of the world. Over the span of four years, they had survived the daunting U.S. history term paper; their class IV talk, in which every freshman wrote and performed an original speech in front of the entire grade; the infamous honors physics lab involving the electromagnetic charge challenge; and mandatory ethics and English workshop classes. The college process was a distant memory. Regardless of the results, seniors had weathered SATs, APs, college applications, and getting in—or not—and then getting over it. And they did it all while surviving high school.

Since Isabel's party—actually, since before Isabel's party—her mother's refrain had gone like this:

So, is Reed your boyfriend yet?

I don't know, Mom. It's really complicated.

Now that her mom knew she and Reed were having sex, Isabel's answer became even more urgent. As April went by, Reed took Isabel out to dinners. He held the door and paid, but at school he breezed by her in the student center, saying, *Hi, how are you?* as though they were lab partners. He blew her off and refused to commit to plans until the very last minute—until he called her cell phone and told her to pick him up at Hanley House in half an hour. Isabel tried to orchestrate chance encounters. When recess began, for example, she'd sometimes rush to the first floor of the student center and park herself at a computer near the jocks and DSGs, pretending to check her e-mail until Reed arrived. She hung around campus after school waiting to see if he'd text. She drove him wherever he needed to go.

Her efforts didn't go unnoticed, but Reed still didn't want a girlfriend. He'd been giving up his Friday nights to watch movies like *The Notebook,* which seemed to be, at least at this school and among these students, a clear favorite. Sure, he had sex while his buddies drank and bonded, but he always felt he was missing out on something grand. Yet even as he limited their daily contact to text messages and IM conversations, he defended his nonrelationship.

Are you together with Isabel? Like, hooking up? Whitney asked one day.

Yeah, Reed said.

Well, what are you doing? she pressed, her thin eyebrows arched in doubt, as though her relationship with Nick made sense.

She's a lovely girl, Reed said, and left it at that.

Brady wasn't one to question his friends, and Cush lent support now that he and Ava were together again and he'd finally (hesitantly) let Reed back into his life.

You're not being that big of an ass, Cush said. *She's still dating you.*

But of course Reed was being an ass. He couldn't commit to being a boyfriend yet he wanted the benefits of being in a relationship. At first those advantages had come in the form of sex and companionship, but when senior projects started in May, Reed's justifications for spending time with Isabel grew practical: He needed a place to stay. Every year, seniors proposed month-long independent projects to pursue in lieu of class during the month of May. The class of 2005 found there were new requirements for getting their projects passed. Now students had to demonstrate prior experience or interest in their topic; slacking off and procrastinating became more difficult. Suddenly cool ideas like growing a garden, making a Claymation movie, and filming a Red Sox documentary might not make the cut.

Reed's business internship with a friend's father offered access to the usual suspects—wealth, power, adults, an office, the city. Waking up was the hard part. On his first day, he dragged himself out of bed at five A.M. to meet his friend's dad in Boston. They exercised at a private club before going to work, which gave new meaning to Reed's locker room experiences. As his friend's father stood naked before him, Reed thought about the seasons he and the guys had spent cavorting unclothed in the varsity hockey locker room, slinging friendly insults and sharing advice on how to shave pubic hair. Reed was in the professional world now.

His mornings began at ungodly hours, when he got a ride into Boston with a dorm parent's spouse. They left campus at six fifteen A.M. and Reed arrived at his office with more time than he wanted to read the *Wall Street Journal*. Then one day, not long after the projects began, he signed out to Isabel's house and slept over. Then he did it again. And again. He hoped the sleepovers didn't signal commitment, but he also thought there was nothing better than waking up to Isabel's freshly made breakfast and getting a ride into Boston—*not* at six fifteen A.M.

Soon he called her each afternoon from Hanley and told her he'd be ready to go home in about twenty minutes. She'd show up twenty minutes later, and he'd materialize some time after that. They'd eat out, order takeout, or rent movies. Sometimes they cooked dinner with her family and played board games. At night they hung out on the couch until after midnight, crept to the same bed, had sex, and woke up with enough time for Isabel to return to her bedroom or Reed to the guest room.

At first Isabel's parents didn't understand how to sign out Reed from school. His dorm parent asked about alcohol and supervision, and they took the questions seriously. Milton's rules aside, most parents are uneasy about letting their teenage child share a bed with a significant other. A son's or daughter's sex life becomes too obvious when a girlfriend or boyfriend sleeps over, as though blow jobs and doggy style are flashing in neon lights, illuminating the baby pictures on the walls. Isabel thought she was lucky; her parents eventually allowed Reed to sleep on her trundle bed. He and Isabel, like most seniors in relationships during the months before graduation, saw themselves as grown-ups. They were mature. They were eighteen years old. They were about to go to college, where they'd get to do whatever they wanted. They also believed they were sensible about sex; Isabel was on the pill and Reed used a condom.

Reed quickly adapted to his day-student lifestyle. How he convinced his dorm parents to permit the scenario to go on was past the point; he was having sex, bending the rules, and loving every minute of it. Isabel presented a challenge he'd never found in a girl before, but she was, nevertheless, one of the Hysterics, so he downplayed his feelings for her. She sensed his ambivalence. *I wake him up,* she reasoned to herself. *I drive him to work and pick him up. I drive like, twenty-five minutes each way, twice a day, to get Reed.* Of course she wondered if she was being used.

One afternoon she sat in her car waiting for Reed to walk out of Hanley. Tears fell over her freckles. She sobbed. Yet again she'd been parked in front of his dorm for what felt like hours. When he finally strolled up to the car and sat inside, he saw that Isabel looked miserable. Her lips were thick. The skin around her eyes was reddened. She didn't understand: Reed had told her he'd be ready in twenty minutes, and that was much more than twenty minutes ago. Why couldn't he ever be ready on time and follow through when he made a promise, not to mention say something more than *hey* at recess or, God forbid, come down to the Cave to acknowledge that she had her own friends, she wanted to know.

Reed studied Isabel from the passenger seat of her car and found her rant endearing. Concession: He was late that day, but he was always late if he was coming to meet her from his dorm. Concession: He knew she had friends, he just didn't like them. They'd been seeing each other since March break ended, avoiding their obviously dissimilar definitions of what exactly they were doing. But there in the car, as Reed watched Isabel cry, he felt something.

Don't worry, he said, *you can cry in front of your boyfriend.*

Isabel's eyebrows shot up to the sky. Did Reed just call himself her boyfriend? Her real live boyfriend? He said it. He said it! Reed was her first real boyfriend! This was the beginning of the rest of her life. Isabel never expected Reed to actually date her. She accepted her fate as his springtime hookup. They'd be going to different colleges next year, and besides, they had such different friends and hung out in such different circles that a real relationship hardly seemed possible. But those few words—*you can cry in front of your boyfriend*—changed everything. She looked at him with a cute smile, her cheeks bulging like small balloons. The tears stopped. She grabbed his hand, trying to mark the moment with touch.

Fuck ass, Reed thought to himself, *I can't believe I just said that.*

Faces and bodies hung out the windows of Brady's Volvo wagon as he drove with haphazard caution through campus on Centre Street. Behind and in front of him were more cars, all crammed with seniors, all according to social group—DSGs, baseball guys, football guys, lower-level kids, and so on. Music blasted from open windows. Horns honked obnoxiously. Seniors threw water balloons and candy. Reed and his friends chucked stale bagels into the crowd. Underclassmen and faculty members watched the scene from the sidewalks in front of academic buildings, cheering or staring with terror as the seniors defied the administration's embargo on Senior Drive By, the springtime ritual that graduating classes loved.

Senior Drive By celebrated the carefree recklessness of senior spring, but it was also a potential safety nightmare, and the class of 2005 continued to suffer the consequences of an administration in panic. There'd been enough public tragedies that year. Did they need seniors driving wildly through campus, packed into cars, probably without seat belts, hurling objects into the crowd? Absolutely not. The administration proposed a compromise: Campus police cars would escort seniors down Centre Street, slowly and cautiously. Was the administration serious? Seniors were insulted, so some secretly planned Drive By on a different day, coordinating over e-mail until that warm May morning when roughly a dozen cars, each packed to the brim with seniors, took the student body and faculty by total surprise.

Annie stared at the cars rolling down Centre Street from a window inside Pryce. She wasn't the only senior who'd missed the staged event, though her absence reminded her that she was a boarder without access to friends with cars—as well as the inside knowledge about what went on in her class. She watched the caravan loop around campus and take a second turn on Centre Street. Milton security tried to gain control. Faculty members shot dirty looks at the drivers. The cars bulldozed forward, taking another left onto Randolph Avenue, preparing to make the loop yet again when they ran into a roadblock. At the corner of Voses Lane and Centre Street waited the Milton police. Game over. No matter how empowered Milton students became, the administration was always lurking, ready to reinforce its control.

When Reed got back to Hanley that day, he heard that Mr. Carr, his dorm parent, had been looking for him. Reed assumed he was going to get in trouble for clocking a girl with one of the stale bagels, but the real reason was decidedly worse. Reed had committed a whereabouts violation when he'd signed out to go to his internship in Boston and remained on campus for Drive By. The typical punishment was an appearance before the Dean's Committee, but Mr. Carr, neither oblivious nor a pushover, handled the breach confidentially to keep Reed's record clean, and revoked Reed's sign-out privileges for a week.

Isabel was devastated. Those precious liberties that she and Reed had been abusing—that seemed to make their relationship possible by getting him out of the dorm, away from his friends, and into Isabel's world—were now gone. A whole week without Reed in her bed? What if he stopped liking her? What if he found another girl? What if his buddies convinced him to dump her? Isabel's fears were reasonable, because, quite recently, Reed had tried to rescind the whole "crying in front of your boyfriend" statement.

Can we erase that word? he texted not long after he made the momentous declaration in her car.

No, Isabel replied in a display of assertiveness.

Is it okay if we keep it ambiguous for a while?

No!

Isabel was adamant, and besides, she'd already told her mother the good news. Not seeing Reed for seven nights in a row would be torture. She baked Mr. Carr a batch of cookies in a gesture of both apology and plea, but Mr. Carr gave the dessert to the Hanley boys. Reed was upset, too. Now he had to wake up before six A.M. to get a ride to his internship with the dorm parent's spouse. But he saw a silver lining to the situation—a week back in the dorm with his buddies, pulling pranks, living like a senior should. He'd already given up so much of his senior spring to spend time with Isabel, and the stories his friends told only reinforced the realization.

Brady was up to the same mischief. He chose not to do a senior project. Attending a couple of classes a day—in comparison with forty hours of project work a week—was definitely the way to go. And so Brady did what he did best; he socialized. He and the guys spent afternoons in Emma's basement playing beer pong when her mother wasn't home. Somehow Reed had missed the T-shirts Brady and the guys made for everyone who'd been attending Caitlin Lane's basement parties that year. The yellow tees said "The Basement" in black letters on the front, with a beer pong ball flying into the cups, and listed the girls' and guys' names on the back. Reed also missed the night, later that spring, when Brady kissed Church in order to get two girls to make out with each other. And then there was the story of Singer's party, which Brady recounted to Reed with all the amusing details.

We just went balls to the wall, Brady said, *and just invited everybody.*

I heard it got out of hand, Reed said.

Singer was like, The cops are coming, the cops are coming, so everyone started running and tried to leave.

Reed was already amused, because Singer was the type of kid he liked to call a *cock block,* meaning he never knew when to step aside and let a friend get the girl. The guys didn't dislike Singer because his father had connections all over Boston. They disliked him because they thought he sucked at hockey and at life. Still, Singer was always good for a laugh.

Some Milton parties—not all, but some—were held in large, imposing houses with acres of land, private roads, and stashes of cigars Reed and his friends liked to steal. Even if the wealth and grandeur wasn't their own, they still showed up for parties at the host's expense. All that seclusion meant one thing in particular: protection from local police. But if the cops did show up, and they did from time to time, the kids ran for their lives, because if they got caught for acts *prejudicial to the academy,* they would, at the very least, make an appearance before the Dean's Committee. They sprinted into the wooded areas or across lawns, darting as fast as they could behind some kid who was smart enough to wear sneakers and jeans, not the flip-flops they had on or the shorts that barely protected their own legs from the poison ivy that was most definitely thriving among the trees.

On the night of Singer's party, all the kids emptied out of the house. About twenty minutes later, Brady realized that the police had never arrived.

We were like, Forget this, he said to Reed, *so we just went back. And the party was going. And Singer comes down and he's like, Everyone shut up, shut up, shut up. Dr. Robertson just called.*

I was like, What are you talkin' about?

He was like, I gotta call back in twenty minutes. She called and was like, I hear you're having a party. You gotta get everyone out, or everyone's gonna get in trouble.

I was like, Singer, shut up. I thought, this is something you do to get people out of your house.

But then ten minutes later Singer got on the phone and called someone back. And I was listening on the other line.

Reed chuckled.

It was Dr. Robertson, no question, Brady said. *If the school had found out about any other party, everyone would've gotten in so much trouble. But [his father was important].*

Yeah, that's true, Reed said.

So then we left with the girls and we went to IHOP to kill time and get food. And we were like, just for kicks, let's all go back to Singer's.

So we go back to Singer's, and Frank's car is outside, and we're like, Frank's inside, we'll give him a call, he'll let us in.

So we call Frank and we're like, Frank, what are you doing?

He's like, Ah, I just got home, I'm just going to bed.

We were like, Oh really Frank? Brady said, laughing like a girl.

He's like, Yeah, yeah, I'm just going to bed. Singer's got broken up. I'll talk to you tomorrow.

So we were like, Oh, okay, Frank we'll talk to you.

So we all get out of the car and start pissing all over Frank's car. And Church gets up on the hood of the car and just took a shit.

Yeah, Church is a shitter, isn't he? Reed said.

He loves to, Brady said. *He loves to.*

Reed should have been there. Nights like this one were what senior spring was all about, and now that hockey season was over, Reed didn't see his teammates every day. He ran into Brady at parties on the weekends, but Reed's world was largely comprised of his senior project and Isabel—and surviving a pregnancy scare. Reed remembers that their condom broke while they had sex in the bath. Even though Isabel took the birth control pill, he was still worried, and lay there afterward, sipping a glass of wine, thinking, *I don't want a baby, I don't want a baby*. Isabel got the morning-after pill the next day, just to be safe. Meanwhile, Brady hooked up with a young DSG to end his fling with another DSG, and then had to take this second girl to Planned Parenthood because they forgot to use a condom. In the last month of senior year, he hooked up with Emma. This time it was just the two of them. Again and again. Brady didn't think of Emma as his girlfriend and he certainly didn't consider himself to be her boyfriend, but as the weeks went by, the general consensus among his friends was that they were in a relationship, and had to accept his fate.

Despite the brazen behavior associated with senior spring, Milton's seniors were still cautious about the weeks ahead; no one wanted to end up in front of the DC committee just before graduating. The year had been an exceptional one, plagued by the very public sex scandal. No one doubted the power of the administration or the police, whose investigation was still ongoing. And then Zoe returned to campus not long before senior projects began.

Ohmygod, today's the day she comes back, students said. Teachers felt the waves of resentment, and some worried about what their classes would be like with Zoe sitting at the table. Brady saw her prance around campus with a small pack of girls, wearing oversize sunglasses as though nothing had ever happened. Girls saw her at breakfast wearing short shorts and an indecently revealing top. Reed saw her in passing and, once or twice, out of pity, tossed out a casual, *Hey, how are you doing?* The same divided opinions persisted. Zoe was innocent. Zoe was a slut. The expulsions were all her fault.

In early May, the *Globe* reported that police filed statutory rape charges in juvenile court against the two younger boys, both sixteen-year-olds, involved in the locker room incident. The school expressed shock, claiming it knew nothing of the police's plans to press charges. One night Isabel, Caroline, and a few Pryce Girls were watching *The O.C.* when a news preview came on at a commercial break. There in front of them was a shot of three male students walking on Milton's campus.

That's my boyfriend! one of the Pryce Girls squealed, pointing at one of the boys.

Oh, our guys are on TV! the girls yelled.

What are they doing?

We should not be on television.

This is so weird!

Brady stayed on top of the developments and in constant touch with the guys who'd been expelled. He didn't know what to think when charges of statutory rape were officially filed in adult court at the very end of May against the three older boys involved in the third incident.

It's so ridiculous, Brady thought.

It so wasn't rape at all.

There's got to be an exception to the law.

He realized that the course of his life would have shifted had he participated in that third incident. Senior spring, the prom, and his college acceptance would have disappeared, and the charges might have meant registering as a sex offender, or worse—going to prison.

Whitney spent her weekends getting drunk and high, choosing Captain Morgan over Bud Light because she liked getting it over with. Specific nights and events were committed to memory only later, after looking through photographs of scenes that would, nevertheless, become a single blurry memory of smiling faces. When Whitney wasn't partying, she went to class high. She was convinced that Milton teachers were naive when it came to students' social lives, as though the oral sex incidents hadn't happened just a few months before, as though the repercussions weren't still echoing around campus.

What do you think about the ending? Whitney's English teacher asked one day.

She looked up at her teacher, who, in return, stared back at her, waiting for an answer.

He died, Whitney said, grateful she'd overheard classmates talking about the assigned book, which she hadn't even read.

What do you feel about the way he died? the teacher asked again.

So how do you feel about this? Whitney asked a friend sitting next to her. *Why don't you take over?*

Rather than read her assignments, Whitney spent the last month of school hanging out with the DSGs. They blasted Mariah Carey's "We Belong Together" and the Backstreet Boys' "Incomplete" in the car, stayed in for nights of chocolate chip cookies and TV, and prepared for the prom. The beautification process alone was extensive. Whitney tanned, worked out, got manicures and pedicures, and shopped for the perfect dress. But her primary pastime was to help organize the event, because she wanted her prom to be done her way, especially given the school's restrictions.

At Milton, there'd never been a prom king or queen, but now limos were banned as being too ostentatious, trolleys were the required mode of transportation, and bags could be searched at any moment. After-prom parties were forbidden, too, because, as Phoebe believed, the school didn't want a repeat of what had happened two years before, when three students were hospitalized during an out-of-state party. The class of 2005 would return to the student center for a required, up-all-night, alcohol-free party with live entertainment, movies, food, and adult supervision. Whitney wanted the night to be amazing, and she made sure that the money the school put toward the event included every luxury and garnish possible.

The prom was the sort of event that Jillian rolled her eyes about. DSGs flitting around the dance floor with thin bodies and stand-out dresses, lining up for pictures they would later place in their Milton prom picture frames and hang above their beds—no thank you. But

Jillian's romance with the event wasn't entirely defunct. She had been doing yoga all spring and actually felt positive about her body. Plus, she thought she'd found the perfect boy to be her date.

Oliver was captivating because he was funny, liked to write, and played in a band. Jillian's friends thought he was a certifiable loner and unconventional looking, but Jillian was intrigued. He was on the *Paper* staff with her, and they became friends. They flirted. They hung out after school. One day, from out of nowhere and yet not surprisingly, Jillian asked him to be her prom date. *Hey, Oliver, do you want to go to prom?* she typed on Milton's online intranet system. *Okay,* he said, with the enthusiasm and spirit of a true teenage boy.

Before the prom came the boat dance, the juniors' annual end-of-year dance held each spring on a boat in Boston Harbor. Jillian had already been twice before, once with a girlfriend as a sophomore and once as a junior when, yet again, she'd had to invite her own date. A friend invited her senior year, and, as it turned out, Oliver was going, too. They spent the night making fun of people from a corner, saying things like *oh, look at them* and *they're funny looking.* Jillian felt relaxed and beautiful, because she'd heard rumors that Oliver thought she was the hottest senior girl. Rewind: the *hottest* senior girl? That was a highly competitive demographic. DSGs were hot. Skinny girls with Burberry scarves and tight jeans were hot. Jillian was Jillian. She had flaws. She wasn't fat, but she wasn't skinny. They were only rumors, but rumors usually stemmed from truth.

When the boat docked in Boston Harbor around midnight, Jillian, Oliver, and about twenty of their friends headed to someone's house for the afterparty. Jillian and Oliver got lost on the way and didn't arrive until three A.M., but they got roaring drunk in no time. Jillian had plans: They were going to hook up.

Ohmygod there's a spider in the bathroom! she yelled from the bathroom. *Oliver, come kill it!*

He walked in and closed the door.

I don't see a spider, he said.

The spider wasn't the point, because now Oliver was in the bathroom with Jillian. They sat down on the floor and talked.

I mean, there's dental floss on the floor, he observed.

Jillian giggled.

What are you laughing at?

You say I mean before every sentence.

He paused. *I mean, can I kiss you now or what?*

Over the next few weekends, as senior projects continued and graduation neared, Jillian and Oliver hooked up. In her mind, an emotional connection didn't come before a physical one, and a physical connection didn't come before getting drunk. As long as alcohol and a party were involved, they remained a couple. At one party they migrated to the laundry room. On the linoleum floor, immersed in the smell of detergent, they kissed, made out, and then eventually passed out. Days passed uneventfully or were filled with excitement, depending on whether or not Jillian saw Oliver at school. As the weeks went by, she had a stunning realization: She and Oliver had never hooked up sober.

Then a friend mentioned something about Oliver having another girl at another school. Jillian confronted him in the library stairwell. Closed in by the claustrophobic cement walls, she leaned in and kissed him.

What was that all about? he asked.

I'm sorry, she said. *I just had to see what that was like when we're sober.*

Oh, Oliver said. *That's a good one.*

I just want to talk to you, Jillian started. *This is really weird. We need to talk about this.*

Yeah, I'm really sorry. It's just that—

Well, I totally understand if you don't want to be together. But just so you know, I'm not going to hook up with you if you have a girlfriend.

Okay, Oliver began. *I'll take care of it.*

Well, you don't have to, Jillian said. *I'm just telling you I won't hook up with you if you have a girlfriend.*

I know, Oliver began. *I really like— I'm going to break up with her.*

So does that mean you want to be together?

Yes, he said.

The boy actually said yes.

I can't believe this is really happening, Jillian thought to herself, realizing she now had a boyfriend who was also her prom date. She felt like the luckiest girl in school.

chapter nineteen

one really, really pretty dress

et's play a game, Whitney's friend said as they scanned the racks in Caché, a part-stylish and part-tacky dress store in the SSP.

Okay, Whitney said, because she always liked games.

Find one really, really ugly dress and find one really, really pretty dress, and try them on.

It was senior spring and they'd decided to go shopping for the prom during their free periods. Whitney grabbed a pale pink silk dress with subtle beading down the front. This one looks nice, she thought, and took it into the dressing room.

I need to have this dress, Whitney told her friend when she put it on. *Like, this is my dress for prom.*

The pink silk dipped into a deep V and gathered beneath her breasts, extending over her shoulders in an elegant X against her back. She loved the low back and floor-sweeping length. She looked like a classic Hollywood movie star, and this time it wasn't all in her mind; she truly looked sophisticated.

The problem was that neither of them had brought any money.

Whitney would have asked her mom, but she knew the answer would be *no;* she'd already worn the first prom dress they'd bought that winter in the Caribbean to Nick's prom. She couldn't possibly ask for a second gown when she had a beautiful gold dress hanging in her closet at home. Whitney knew exactly what to do. She called Nick.

Nicholas, there's this dress, she began. *If you saw it on me you'd make me get it.*

That was all she had to say, because the next weekend he took her to Caché and bought the dress himself with his grandfather's credit card. (Her mom, dismayed, later paid Nick back.) Whitney bought gold heels and wanted a classy blow-dry, because this was her prom and she thought she had it all—a boyfriend, the best group of friends, a hot dress, and a prom she herself had helped plan.

A prom invitation arrived in every senior's mailbox. Inside the Milton Academy envelope was a plain card with a tuxedo bow at the top. *The Milton Academy Class of 2005 cordially invites you to the Senior Prom,* it began in cursive writing. Annie read the invite with dread. There would be pre-prom photos at school, an open-air trolley ride to the Radisson Hotel in Boston, and an overnight afterparty in the student center; none of it would be fun without a date. She was almost relieved when seniors started moaning about the strict rules and chaperoned afterparty. Spending the night locked up in the student center with over two hundred kids? No thanks. The prom was the one night all year when shit was supposed to go down and stories were made. Did the administration actually believe a group of seventeen- and eighteen-year-olds would enjoy a night spent with comedians, food, teachers, and sleeping bags? What was this, middle school?

Annie heard rumors that a girl might throw her own party instead. Reed and the guys discussed alternatives. They could go to the Cape or rent a hundred-foot yacht with captain and crew (it was only $1,500 a night). But the chatter eventually died down, because it was the prom, after all. Annie's friends paired off quickly. One had a boy-friend, another had a best friend, one had a guy she was hooking up with, and Annie had no one. She could have taken a girlfriend to the dance, but that was always a last resort, and it invited an unwanted question: Why couldn't she find a guy? When Annie learned that an-other dorm mate planned to skip the prom, she realized it might be okay for her not to go.

You're not going to go to your senior prom? friends asked. *You should take Scott.*

No way! she said.

You're going to regret it.

I don't think I am.

And so Annie decided not to go.

Jillian found herself in a precariously similar situation, because Oliver decided not to go to the prom. He told her the news a week be-fore the event, not offering a clear explanation, simply not wanting to go, as though they hadn't been officially hooking up for the past couple of weeks. Jillian didn't get it. Only after she'd bought her ticket ($65) and her dress (considerably more), and let herself imagine the night in all its perfection, did everything get taken away. As a middle-schooler, she assumed she would go to the prom with her steady boyfriend, have the best night of her life, and lose her virginity. It never occurred to her that life wouldn't turn out as she expected. In the end, for this prom, she invited a younger girlfriend so she wouldn't have to go alone.

On the night of the prom, Jillian rushed from her tennis match to the shower, shoved herself into the strapless dress she'd bought with her mother, who insisted on having a mother-daughter bonding expe-rience, and then quickly brushed makeup across her face. Her thin hair looked thick, swept up into a nest on the top of her head. A silver oval pendant glinted off her olive skin, drawing attention to her chest. She prepared herself for what came next—being surrounded by her girlfriends, all of whom had real dates, most of whom had recently lost their virginity. And so she headed to campus for the pre-prom pictures, elegant in silver, dateless, dumped by Oliver, doing her best to smile, taking it all like a true beauty. She handled the situation with poise until her friend dumped her, too.

so [this girl] was going to come with me and i thought i was being way nice or whatever cuz i wasn't going to make her pay for the ticket and i bought her a corsage and everything. but then a half an hour before the trolleys leave from school for the hotel, she calls and is like "will you be really mad if i ditch . . . i have a lot of work." and obviously i caaaaant be mad at her. so i go, one hundred percent dateless, and the only person i know who doesn't have a date.

A crowd of gowns and tuxedos clustered in front of the student center around six thirty P.M. The trolleys parked on Campus Road and the overnight bags dropped in the student center were a blatant reminder of the jailhouse night ahead. Students' parents milled about, oohing and aahing while taking pictures, intermittently shocked by what they saw—a girl's chest overflowing from her dress, a boy's hand on his date's butt. Cameras flashed at posing couples, at rows of girlfriends aligned like models, their bodies contoured by the lines of their dresses and each other, breasts more visible than ever before. A fuchsia gown, gathered with a jewel in front. A sexy black V-neck, deadly low. Polka dots, blue floral, a lady in red. Guys smirked or beamed, trying not to look like little boys playing dress-up. Some wore traditional black. Others stood out in white tuxedos.

In the middle of the crowd, Isabel stood alone holding Reed's red rose boutonniere and her own white orchid corsage. She'd made her father pick up both, because she refused to be seen buying her own prom accessories, and because Reed insisted he couldn't possibly get the flowers since he was a boarder. Isabel looked absolutely radiant. Her red hair was pulled back in a sleek updo, and her freckles were softened by makeup she'd had professionally done (most of which she'd already wiped off). Her dress—green, empire waisted, Grecian, flowing—made her skin and eyes pop, and her gold shoes matched her gold earrings, which matched her gold clutch. She looked statuesque, or at least as statuesque as a short girl could look.

Reed was late. Again. Isabel wasn't mad yet, because prom was supposed to be their announcement party—the first time they'd be seen by the entire class as a couple, arm in arm, belonging together for an entire night. If, of course, he showed up. They'd planned to meet at school because they'd each gone to separate pre-prom events. While Isabel went to a friend's house, Reed was at Church's house with Brady and the rest of the guys. He'd invited Isabel to come, but she had no desire to stand in pictures with DSGs who didn't know her, like her, or treat her as an equal. Hanging out with Church would also have brought back memories of middle school, when they used to be friends, and then freshman year, when he stopped acknowledging her existence. Reed understood. He didn't want to take pictures with the Hysterics, either.

He was ambivalent about being Isabel's date. After weeks of sleeping at her house and having sex—after letting the "boyfriend" statement finally set in—he still didn't know what he wanted from her. Time went by, and he stalled about asking Isabel. Asking meant committing, and while he'd accepted the idea of a relationship, going to the prom was a very different and public declaration. Two weeks before the event, Isabel finally intervened over IM.

Isabel: So are you going to prom?
Reed: I don't really know.
Isabel: Okay, well if you do go, are you going with me?
Reed: Yeah yeah, I'll go with you.

Just to be sure, she asked him to be her date again at school, in person, in front of one of his friends. Reed said yes, and when she walked away he looked at his buddy and cracked up.

The girl had to ask me, he said, laughing.

I'm not sure if I am going to go.

But I am not going to say no to her.

The moment Reed spotted Isabel waiting for him in front of the student center, he felt like a million bucks. He already looked handsome in his traditional tux, his body fitting perfectly inside the crisp black fabric. But there was Isabel, gorgeous, soft, and all his. *Oh, my, God,* Reed thought, noticing her green eyes because he loved her eyes, but then there were her breasts looking so big and beautiful, so edible the way they were pushed up in that dress. *Oh, my, God,* he thought again, which was exactly what other guys told him they were thinking, too.

Isabel saw him walking toward her and smiled to herself, admiring the bow tie that he'd worked so hard to acquire. His tux had initially arrived with a necktie. *This is bullshit,* Reed said, because he refused to be seen in a tux with a necktie. Bond would never do that. He made (not asked, but made) Isabel take him back to the store to get a white bow tie. She clutched his boutonniere, staring at his sharp white shirt that made his springtime tan look even deeper. She was ready for the best evening of her life, and as he walked closer, then closer still, he didn't smile or even wink. He breezed by without saying a word, disappearing into the student center.

Isabel was about to die. This was the prom. This was her fucking senior prom and Reed, her date, her supposed boyfriend, had just ignored her. She stood there, an undiscovered beauty, thinking the entire time that she was absolutely going to kill him. The problem, of course, was that Reed didn't get it. The prom was an event where having a date meant something. A boy promising to take a girl was like signing a contract. He will stand next to her, in front of a flowering bush, and smile while her mother takes thirty-seven pictures of them. He will compliment her on her dress while trying not to stare too obviously at her body. He will ask her to dance, hold her tight, breathe in her perfume, and, if he isn't her boyfriend, jerk his torso back the moment he feels himself rising in his pants.

Reed's contract was of dubious value. He didn't *have* to take a picture with Doc Robs, which he did while Isabel watched. He didn't *have* to ask another girl to dance, which he did later that night, and he didn't *have* to ask a teacher to dance, either. Looking back on the prom, Reed insisted he spent the majority of the night with Isabel. He probably did, but all it took was a compliment to another girl, or ten minutes spent with someone else's date. Isabel wanted to be Reed's world, at least for one night, and prom, she believed, should have been that night.

Reed eventually emerged from the student center and crept up behind Isabel.

How does it feel to have the best-looking date? he asked.

Isabel couldn't believe him. She'd dressed up for him (because girls dress up for boys, even if they deny it), and all Reed could do was compliment himself? Typical. It was so totally typical.

Around seven P.M., girls raised their dresses and climbed the stairs to the trolleys in their stiletto heels. Boys trudged behind them. Everyone prepared for the blustery highway ride ahead. The trolleys were in lieu of limos, which the administration deemed too showy and divisive among students. Still, one group of friends rented a stretch limo to drive them from pictures at one girl's house to pictures at another girl's house. On the way some of them took shots of alcohol, and when they got to school a boy stashed the bottle in a drop-down panel in the bathroom ceiling, ready to be retrieved at the afterparty. Most students, however, boarded the trolleys stone-cold sober, including Brady, who realized that even if he got drunk before prom, the alcohol would wear off long before midnight, hours before going back to the student center to sit through a night of obligatory entertainment. Like most of his classmates, he decided to be practical and follow the rules.

When Whitney made her entrance at the Radisson Hotel, she couldn't believe what she was seeing: Church's date, the same girl he'd been seeing over spring break when he and Whitney hooked up, was wearing a nearly identical dress. *That's so mean,* she thought to herself. *Whatever. I look better. You're really pale. And you don't have the best body. You're a bitch.* Her dress and hairdo made her feel like Audrey Hepburn, and, except for Church's date, Whitney thought everything about the prom was perfect. The Radisson's ballroom looked nothing like the drab meeting space it usually was. The hideous patterned carpet was hardly visible, and balloons shot up from the center of round tables covered in white tablecloths. The Radisson didn't compare to some of the prom locations from years before, like the Boston Harbor Hotel and the Boston Park Plaza. But the committee eked out a deal from a senior's father, who owned a number of Radisson hotels.

Students checked in at the master list outside the ballroom, received disposable cameras with their names on them, and arranged themselves at the tables by clique, in the usual fashion. Reed sat with Isabel's friends and, surprising himself, had a good time. Josh sat with his basketball buddies, Brady with the boys and their dates. There were hors d'oeuvres, smoothies and sodas, and a chocolate fondue fountain. Dinner arrived late. Chicken and vegetables prepared for over two hundred can be only so appetizing, but Brady thought it was a decent meal. Some students picked at their food while others scarfed it down, and when the music started up, everyone hit the dance floor.

Jillian did the electric slide with her friends and serenaded couples as they slow-danced to "Total Eclipse of the Heart." She realized that not having a date could actually be fun; had Oliver been there, they would have spent the night sitting in a corner being negative and talking shit about their schoolmates. Still, the evening was what she called *a cheesy eighties teen movie in that absolutely everything went wrong.*

i felt so stupid getting all dressed up and wearing ladey underwear, shaving my legs, spending mad money on shit, wearing uncomfortable shoes, putting on makeup when i had no one to look pretty for. i also felt stupid when slow songs came on and i'd either go sit down by myself, or dance

around jokingly with a [friend] . . . also, everytime someone told me i looked
pretty . . . i felt like they felt sorry for me.

Whitney and Nick seduced each other on the dance floor. Tripp was there with another girl, and when Jay Z's "99 Problems" sounded from the speakers, Nick pushed Whitney in front of him and yelled the opening lines in Tripp's face.

> *If you're havin' girl problems I feel bad for you son.*
> *I got 99 problems but a bitch ain't one.*

Nick danced with Whitney in front of Tripp, and when another provocative song came on, Nick did it all over again. He claimed Whitney as his territory, feeling her body with his eyes, knowing exactly what it looked and felt like underneath her dress. Later that night, when she waited for Nick in the hallway outside the men's restroom, he stormed out, pushed her up against the wall, and pressed his body against hers.

Why are you all of a sudden so aggressive? she said.

Nick kissed her in response, and a moment later Tripp walked out of the same bathroom. She knew right away that Nick had planned the entire scene, and when Tripp confronted her she felt bad about it and immature. Still, she wasn't embarrassed; it was cool having two guys fight over her, even if she instinctively realized that all of it was pure high school drama.

So far, Josh's night had been the complete opposite. He danced with his date once, made small talk at his table, and tried to be charming. After spending hours with a girl he didn't like, who, he was almost positive, didn't like him back, he was done with keeping up appearances. His date was a fairly random girl. He'd asked her only after he'd turned down another girl, as though saying *no* to a first offer would somehow make his life, which had been relatively tame since his weekend in New York City, exciting again. Initially the moment was invigorating. A girl asked *him* to prom. She wanted *him* to be her date. But not long after he turned down this first offer, he realized that available girls were dropping like flies. Less than a week before prom he asked the girl who became his date. When he shared the news with his mother, her questions morphed from *Who are you going with?* to *What is she wearing; we have to get her a corsage!*

Josh's date wore a turquoise dress, a white corsage his mom picked out, and probably looked pretty, though he doesn't remember ever thinking so. Taking a girl he didn't like was hardly how he imagined his senior prom. He had fantasies of having a girlfriend and being in love; of taking Diana, the girl he'd pined for since freshman year. He didn't want a date just to have a date. He wanted a date he was actually dating.

When the trolleys returned to the student center after the prom, Josh stepped off the bus like all the other boys who'd had mediocre times with mediocre dates: ill prepared for the dreary night ahead. There was a mad rush for couches and chairs in the student center, because everyone wanted a soft place to sleep. Girls went off to the girls' changing area to hang their dresses on racks, slip into pajamas, and pull bobby pins from their hair. Boys changed too, and then everyone reemerged to begin the second half of the night.

Some students were too tired to notice the elaborate scene before them, care of the parents who headed up the prom committee, devoted their free time to the afterparty, and couldn't help but live vicariously through their children. White Christmas lights twinkled everywhere. A large glittery CONGRATS 2005 was suspended in the air, just above a gigantic arch of gold balloons. There was even a painting of the Boston city skyline, designed so that students felt they were looking out into the city, not the main quad.

Three different movies played in three different rooms. Two comedians performed (Milton censored them to such an extent that one of them apologized for his lack of humor). There were cookies, popcorn, Dippin' Dots ice cream, and hot chocolate. Yearbooks were passed out late at night, and everyone received a goody bag with a silver picture frame that said *Milton Academy Prom 2005*. Adults monitored the scene, reinforced the rules, and made sure no one did anything inappropriate or illegal. Brady remembered a roped-off doorway in the student center with an amusingly threatening message, something to the effect of *Before you cross this line, think about all the money your parents have spent on you, and how awful it would be if you didn't get to walk with your class-mates at graduation.* No one dared, but most people were too tired to do much of anything.

Except, of course, for Josh, who suddenly made eye contact with Diana. Courage embraced him. This was prom, the last night before the rest of his life, so he squeezed into a tiny space right next to her on a couch. As the night wore on they readjusted (she leaned against his body, her legs extended next to his), listened to the comedian (she leaned against his body), and talked (she *leaned* against his *body!*). The scenery was anything but romantic, yet there he was having his very own midnight romance with his longtime crush.

He and Diana watched the sun rise in that fuzzy half-awake state that makes you feel like something is about to happen. He wanted to kiss her, but the student center was heaving with bodies. The smell of sweat, hair spray, and food permeated the air. The floor was filthy. The couches probably were, too. Still, no amount of grime diminished the fantasies rolling through his mind.

Eventually, inevitably, something did happen: The afterparty ended. Before six A.M., a breakfast of bagels, doughnuts, muffins, fruit, and coffee began upstairs. The lavish spread came courtesy of Dunkin' Do-nuts, where one student's father had connections. Josh assumed he and Diana would have breakfast together, capping off a perfect end to a suddenly perfect prom. But when she abruptly stood up, she didn't wait for Josh or even walk upstairs with him. She bulldozed across the room and chatted up her ex-boyfriend. The irony was nauseating: Elsewhere in the student center, Josh's prom date sat on a couch talking with her own ex-boyfriend. Josh was left without his date and without Diana. He headed upstairs alone.

Outside, parents waited to collect their children. The school required that all students attending prom be picked up the next morning, any time after six A.M., because no one wanted the sleep-deprived girls and boys driving home and getting into accidents. Seniors thought the rule was ridiculous. They'd been driving since they were sixteen and a half. They weren't children. They were adults. They were about to graduate. Yet they tumbled from the student center in a mob of exhaustion—from a night of dancing and celebration without alcohol and drugs, with constant supervision. Sex was contained. The myth of innocence lived another night among these students, who for the most part had lost their naiveté long ago.

chapter twenty

you never really graduate

One of the Pryce Girls held up a pair of pink bunny ears and spoke.

There was this boy that I really liked, she said. *He bought them for me.*

She looked at a younger girl in Pryce House, who waited among all the other girls on the floor of the dorm's computer room. It was a hot night, and the girls sat cross-legged in pajama bottoms, T-shirts, and spaghetti-strap tank tops. They were themselves that night; no makeup, messy hair, and ponytails.

These bunny ears, the Pryce Girl said, *I want you to have them and remember that you are so so beautiful, and someday you will find some boy who thinks that you are the most beautiful person in the whole entire world. I hope that the rest of your time at Milton goes well. No heartbreaks.*

The younger girl reached for the gift, beaming, because this cool senior Pryce Girl had just handed her a coveted item at the wills ceremony. Every June, this tradition was carried out on the night before graduation, and lasted into the early hours of the morning. Freshmen, sophomores, and juniors squished into the cheery room as though they were having one gigantic sleepover party, circa sixth grade. Annie and the rest of the seniors in her dorm were the honored guests. They sat with boxes and shopping bags filled with personal treasures they'd been collecting over the years for precisely this night, for precisely one purpose: to pass them down to younger girls in the dorm.

Annie was so excited about her final wills ceremony, so in love with her new blond highlights, and in such a happy mood from a day spent with her grandparents and family, that when the evening finally commenced, there hadn't been time to panic about the flower ritual. One at a time, the adults held up a flower in front of the entire group. Ribbons hung from its stem, each with telling adjectives written on the fabric, and when a dorm parent read them aloud, the underclassmen had to guess which senior that flower represented. Annie listened as the younger girls guessed which seniors were *fashion forward* or *confident* or *poised*. She was nervous: What if no one could tell which flower was meant for her? The year had passed too quickly, and in the end she was neither a straight-A student nor a popular girl nor a girlfriend. But of course the girls in Pryce knew that Annie was the *caring* senior, the one who spent all her time helping them manage their stress and survive homesick nights, fighting back her own tears in order to dry someone else's. She'd been recognized not for being pretty or cool, but for being herself. Nothing had changed since the morning of Senior Walk In, and yet everything had changed.

After the dorm parents left, wills officially began. One by one, the senior girls bestowed their cherished gifts upon the underclassmen, exchanging posters, stuffed animals, and clothing, sharing stories that the younger girls would remember until they, too, became seniors. One senior willed a vibrator. Another passed down a key to the yearbook office to the girl whom she'd caught having sex in Pryce's common room after check-in. *Make good use of this with your boyfriend,* the senior said.

When it was Annie's turn, she reached into her cardboard box and gave away an Anne Geddes poster of babies in sunflower hats she'd had since freshman year, and a snakeskin skirt she'd had since middle school. She and Alexa also had a few joint wills from freshman year, a sour reminder of a friendship that had failed. Then Annie relinquished her bumblebee headband. It had rested in her closet all year, a reminder of belonging and loss—of being a Pryce Girl at Senior Walk In even though the title didn't actually include her. Giving the headband to a young girl was like passing on a tradition of artificial acceptance, and by the end of the night, after bequests had been exchanged and memories relived, all the girls were a mess, sleeves wet with tears and cheeks stained from crying.

Annie looked around the room at her dorm mates and realized she'd never see some of them again after graduation. Younger girls would eventually become seniors, go on to college, and lead lives that had nothing to do with hers. The Pryce Girls would diminish in importance, replaced by other cliques of girls wherever Annie went. Ida would always be there for her, but she, too, was setting off on a new life in a different city. If she hoped to change as much as Annie hoped to change, how would Annie ever truly know her in the future? The significance of the moment shook her by her rounded shoulders. She *had* made an impression on her school, on these girls who looked to her for guidance and support. Yet in a few more months, another girl would move into Pryce for her senior year, ready to fill Annie's role as a leader in the dorm. Wills had only just ended, but Annie already felt memories pale, the past sliding further away even though all around her, through her dorm mates' tears and hugs, a group of girls rallied together, yelled *Flagpole run!*, took off varying amounts of clothing, and did a seminaked run to the chapel, Forbes, and back.

The morning of graduation, Annie woke up in Pryce for the very last time. Her dorm room already looked different as she peeked out from beneath her blue-and-white-pin-striped sheets. Posters no longer covered the walls, and her desk drawers were empty. Clothes and makeup lay scattered, half packed in boxes. Annie walked to the bathroom, her hair touseled. She brushed her teeth at the sinks she'd used for four years. She showered. She examined her skin in the mirror, checking for blemishes. Her eyes were still puffy from crying the night before, but she smiled at herself, knowing that graduation—the end of high school—was only a few hours away.

Annie dressed quickly. Foundation, black mascara and eyeliner, hair, strappy silver sandals, and then the white halter-top dress she'd picked out weeks ago. It was Lilly Pulitzer (DSG to the very end), and had white flowers embroidered on top. She put on her silver starfish necklace, recalling the day her mother had given it to her as a middle school graduation present. Annie looked tired when she walked into the common room to meet Ida for breakfast. The girls ate muffins and fruit and debated whether they would participate in the seniors' pregraduation walk around campus. The annual march was informal, disorganized, and early. Some seniors thought it was a waste of time and others wanted the extra sleep. But it was part of graduation, and Annie wanted to savor every single moment.

The walk commenced outside one of the dorms on the main quad, and when Annie got there she found her classmates looking like a flurry of doilies and blue inkblots. The senior girls were like springtime snowflakes in their variations of white—eyelet skirts, strapless dresses, capped sleeves, all of them fresh and delicate, almost virginal. They mingled with the senior boys, who were dressed like budding yachtsmen in navy blazers, khaki pants, ties, and loafers. The dress codes were a tradition at Milton's graduation, and applied to both seniors as well as underclassmen, but seniors individualized their looks. Reed and the Hanley boys wore matching orange ties from Brooks Brothers. The DSGs pinned pink rose corsages to their dresses. One girl wore a cowboy hat. Another a wreath of purple and white flowers in her hair. Another a long necklace wrapped around twice.

The group marched along the exterior of the main quad, past Pryce, Hanley, and Jessups. It was the second week of June, and the air was hot. Some of the boys were overheating. They pulled at their long-sleeved shirts and regretted their long pants, unaware that their looks were part of that studied prep school mystique, a watercolor of well-ironed whites, blues, and beiges. That morning, the main quad was dotted with white graduation tents pitched like giant peaks of whipped cream. Grass spread out like green velvet, every inch bright and perfect after being mowed, mulched, watered, and nurtured for the past few months. Rows and rows of fold-up chairs surrounded the graduation stage in front of Apthorp Chapel, and behind it rose the brick and columns of dormitories, lending grandeur and New England elegance to the scene. Cars crawled down Centre Street, turning onto campus drives that meandered toward the parking lots. Families and friends arrived with cameras, water bottles, and sunscreen, dressed for the occasion, lugging umbrellas in case of rain, barking in slightly frantic voices—those seats have already been saved!

Isabel didn't notice any of it. Her eyes filled with tears as she looked around the campus. Beyond the tents was Straus, where she and Reed had art history class. Behind her was Hanley, where she'd run into Reed that random night in December, and the Hanley parking lot, where she'd waited for him nearly every day that spring—where he'd made her the happiest girl when he told her she could cry in front of her boyfriend. Isabel looked around her, feeling extremely pale in her white dress, and couldn't stop sobbing.

Her time at Milton was actually over. Thinking back on her years there, she realized that her high school experience was really a collection of often melancholy memories, until senior spring. Somehow, almost miraculously, Reed had come into her life. Regardless of his uncertainty and occasional asshole behavior, he erased all the bad times she'd had before. At last Isabel had a boyfriend, a sex life, friends, and the college of her choice. Now that she finally had everything she'd hoped for, high school was about to end. It wasn't fair.

Isabel approached her future with tentative hope. She knew she played a significant role in Reed's life and he did the same for her. But they didn't know how to approach the future, so they planned to take one day at a time. Isabel was convinced they'd break up before they went to college. Her Ivy League college was hours away from his. A long-distance relationship wasn't realistic. They weren't even sure what they were going to do that summer.

The senior walk ended inside Straus, where, under the tiered chandelier, each senior received a gerbera daisy in bright orange, red, pink, or yellow. As part of Milton tradition, girls also received blue irises and boys received small white flowers to pin on their left breast jacket pockets. Thick sunlight poured in from tall windows, lighting up the bookshelves and paintings on the walls. The school's history surrounded the seniors, but their own Milton stories did, too. Here was where the seniors had gathered every week for class assemblies. Where they met with their college counselors and watched friends perform senior projects. Where they heard the school's first formal announcement about the oral sex incidents.

Reed didn't know what to feel as he stood with Cush inside Straus. Reed's ambivalence wavered between wanting to stay at Milton and itching to get away. Senior spring had disappeared just as quickly as it had begun, and now he was graduating—with a girlfriend. Despite all his efforts to avoid commitment, he wound up in a relationship with the last girl he'd ever expected. But Isabel was right there in Straus, across the room, looking adorable and emotional. As she talked with the Hysterics, Reed wondered if he'd still have to be nice to them after graduation. In a couple of weeks he'd be in St. Tropez with a friend. By September he'd be in college. There would be new girls at every turn, but as he watched Isabel fuss with her dress, he made possibly his greatest realization of high school: He didn't want to lose her. That night he'd endure yet another test, a celebratory dinner with Isabel's family at one of Boston's finest restaurants, on Beacon Hill. Her twin sister, the genius, would be there, and their entire family would joke that he and Isabel were like Romeo and Juliet.

He knew he had to play the part, but suddenly, quite unexpectedly, he didn't feel he was acting anymore. While waiting in Straus, Reed didn't yet know that he would act like a real boyfriend that night, not a hockey player, not a jock, and not a guy's guy. He would respect her. He would be a true man.

Somewhere nearby, Brady joined the hockey guys. He must have been tired, because the night before, they had gone to a party with friends from a nearby prep school. It was one of the only times in his entire life that his mother called to find out where he was. *You're graduating tomorrow,* she said in her voice message, *get home.* He eventually did, and the next morning, as he and the guys waited in Straus for graduation to begin, Brady felt something tugging inside. It was sadness. High school had been one big amazing time. He remembered the pep rally that fall and hockey practices. Senior spring with the guys. The comfort and ease of hooking up with Emma over the past few weeks. Even the oral sex incidents brought the team closer together. He would have done it all over again, from the very beginning, and loved every minute. There wasn't much he would have changed, except for that one weekend back in January, when he would have made sure his friends didn't get in trouble.

The sex scandal was faint yet ever present that morning. The *Paper*'s graduation issue featured the latest development: "Resolution Reached as Milton Boys Avoid Trial, Jail. End of Tribulation Leaves Questions for Community." Surely Brady and Reed felt their friends' absence. They absolutely adored Milton, but it was hard to love a school that had expelled some of their best friends while protecting a girl who, in their opinion, was equally to blame.

On the morning of the Milton graduation, while the five boys involved in the incidents could have been sitting in the audience whooping for Reed, Brady, and the rest of their senior teammates, they were nowhere near campus. Ten days before, on June 1, 2005, the three older players sat in a courtroom inside the District Court of East Norfolk County, in Quincy, Massachusetts. If the boys hadn't yet realized how real their situation was, they knew it now, because instead of spending the end of the school year in class, on the quad, driving with friends and preparing to be a whole year older, they were charged with statutory rape. These were real kids facing real consequences. The boys were no longer Milton Academy varsity hockey players. They were defendants.

The district court rises from its surroundings like a fortress of sharp, modern edges and dark redbrick. The building squats in an ambivalent suburban environment, much like Milton Academy emerges out of its own local melting pot of class, wealth, and opportunity. Nicknamed the City of Presidents and the Birthplace of the American Dream, Quincy draws much of its image from the second and sixth presidents, John Adams and his son, John Quincy Adams, who were born and lived in Braintree, which later became Quincy. Businesses bear names like Presidents' City Inn and Presidents' Golf Course, and street signs in red, white, and blue are perched at corners, like immobile flags invoking national pride. Vestiges of the nineteenth-century village remain, but the city is a mixture of old and new, and the new isn't always so nice. The underside of Quincy reveals run-down houses and sidewalks, a blue-collar world that clashes with the romance of its stately flourishes.

Two worlds collided on the morning of the hearing. Here was Milton Academy, elite and privileged. And here was a courthouse with hallways, stairwells, and employees that proved to any *Law & Order* viewer that the television show truly resembles reality. There was no doubt that there was power in the law. Inside one of the courtrooms, the three boys stood next to their lawyers, dressed as though they were about to go to a high school dance. They wore suits and ties and looked like the guys that girls have crushes on—like the guys they used to be at school. But the hearing that day would finalize the terms of the pretrial probation agreement reached between the three boys and the district attorney, thereby avoiding a trial. Over the next two years, the boys were to complete counseling programs, undergo and participate in one hundred hours of community service programs, make statements accepting responsibility, and have no direct contact with the victim or the victim's family. If they succeeded, the charges would be dismissed in May 2007.

Zoe's parents sat in the front of the courtroom. Regardless of their daughter's involvement in the incidents, which remained questionable and debatable, they probably regarded the three boys with anger. The scene was familiar to them. When Zoe was a young girl, according to the *Boston Globe,* her family sat through her father's trial for indecent exposure (he was acquitted). He cited family problems and depression as an explanation for his incident, but what were these boys' explanations? What was his daughter's explanation?

The three defendants stood, each in turn, and read the statements they were required to present in court. One of them spoke quickly, almost without breathing. Another sounded exactly like what a teenage jock was supposed to sound like—raspy, slightly accented, casual. The third sounded sincere, honesty spilling from his mouth.

I want to tell you how sorry I am for what happened on January 24, 2005, one began.

I want you to know that I understand that nothing I can say can ease the pain, but I hope that you know that my regret is sincere.

Not a day has passed since the incident that I have not wished that I had showed more respect for you, myself, and everyone else involved, another said.

Since then, I have reflected on what happened every day. I understand that by taking part I put myself in a very dangerous situation with consequences none of us had dreamed of.

My irresponsibility, immaturity, and selfishness has put so much pain to you, your family, and my family that I'm sick over it, the last said.

These statements, in conjunction with the probation agreement, were supposed to have been enough. But the attorney for Zoe's family surprised everyone in the courtroom by standing up and raising questions. Were the boys truly sorry? *The problem with the statements,* he said, *is that they don't sufficiently recognize the victim or accept the consequences. . . . The statements before you trivialize the seriousness of the matter, and have the unfortunate result of leaving the victim still penalized, and without a clear statement that she was a victim.* Perhaps even Zoe's family doubted she was truly a victim, and needed it to be affirmed in court.

One boy rolled his eyes. The boys already appeared in court, read their apologies, and accepted two years of probation; now they had to apologize again? The judge accommodated the lawyer's request but kept the hearing moving, asking the three defendants to express their regret again. One at a time, the boys turned toward Zoe's parents, who knew more than they probably wanted to about their daughter's sex life, and bluntly, totally without feeling, muttered, *I apologize.*

And so the hearing ended. In a brick building of very different standards than those on Milton's campus, built for very different purposes, an ordeal that was characterized by sexual desire, adolescent abandon, legal responsibility, hubris, and pure stupidity, that was followed and scrutinized in the news, came to a legal end. Whether or not Zoe's parents were satisfied, the three boys had only one more question to answer.

Do you understand all [of the] conditions [of your probation]? the judge asked.

All at once, and for the last time: *Yes, sir.*

From inside Straus, Jillian looked out at the romantic scene on the main quad, wondering how she hadn't been picked to be a graduation speaker. Milton didn't have valedictorians. Instead, seniors chose one girl and one guy to represent their class and speak at graduation. Grades and academic performance were not factors; seniors wanted comedy, entertainment, and sincerity. Jillian was an incredible writer. She was witty and respected, albeit a little controversial. Her friends assumed she'd win. But then, of course, she didn't. Jillian glared at the girl-elect, who she found to be a cloyingly perfect specimen resembling Tracy Flick from the film *Election*—overly perky, nauseatingly accomplished, hungry for recognition. How was she chosen instead of Jillian? The disappointment was typical of a year of endemic frustrations.

From the moment she woke up on the morning of graduation, Jillian felt the presence of her entire life press into her from all sides. Her parents were being overly emotional. Her mother looked perfect. Jillian felt fat. In a few years, she'd look back on the pictures her parents insisted on taking and notice how miserable each family member looked. Oliver had written a painfully distant message in her yearbook, something to the effect of *Have fun in college*. And so far he'd ignored her all morning. Evan was somewhere in Straus, another reminder of yet another failed attempt at intimacy. Around her were the rest of her classmates, the boys and girls who had known her, ignored her, and competed with her for grades, attention, and college acceptances.

After what seemed like hours of disorganization, someone in charge said something about the seniors getting in line; graduation was about to begin. The seniors arranged themselves according to clique, standing two by two next to best friends and buddies, waiting to walk out of Straus and into graduation. Nearby, the bagpiper's skirl signaled the beginning of the procession. He wore a kilt and the traditional high white socks, and marched toward the grassy aisle that divided the audience and led up to the graduation stage. Behind him were the two incoming senior leaders, one holding an American flag and the other holding a Milton flag for the class of 2005. And behind them marched the trustees and faculty members. They entered much like professors do at college graduations, an army of intelligence (though without academic regalia), the distinguished educators who were just as proud as the parents watching from the audience.

Once faculty members were seated, Mr. Graham steadied his baton.

He listened to the campus quiet and raised his eyebrows at the full orchestra, which sat underneath the large tree in front of the Old Boys' Gym. With one dip of the baton, the first notes of "Pomp and Circumstance" rang out in adagio, inviting the seniors to their graduation. They snaked toward the aisle in two long lines of white, blue, and beige. Seniors clutched gerbera daisies in their hands and couldn't help but smile.

Jillian put on her oversize sunglasses and patted down her hair, making sure her two French braids were still intact. She saw the graduation stage up ahead. The familiar wooden podium blazed with the Milton Academy seal and the immutable school motto, "Dare to Be True." A gigantic blue-and-white sign that said 2005 leaned against the stage. The audience fanned out on both sides, standing and cheering as the seniors walked down the central aisle. Jillian passed the mothers and fathers, family members and underclassmen, letting emotion take hold. Milton, she knew, hadn't been about the multimillion-dollar additions or its students' latest newsworthy achievements. What she loved about her school began with her teachers, who had, over the past few years, treated her as an adult, challenged her to ask questions, and taught her how to think, not what to think. It dawned on Jillian that graduation might be symbolic and melancholy for them as well.

And now this place that had been her home for years was about to send her off into her future, prepared and thoughtful, thrilled and petrified. After all those days wishing high school would end, Jillian was now about to leave Milton forever. Suddenly she didn't want to. Caroline walked next to her. Isabel and Phoebe were nearby, saying things to each other like *You never really graduate* and *You'll always be close to Milton*. Jillian knew that her best friends loved her regardless of her flaws, and even those who had abandoned her had made her stronger than she ever knew she could be. She looked at Caroline, with her pretty face and blond hair, and listened to Isabel and Phoebe whisper excitedly, recalling the words she'd mulled over using on her yearbook dedication page to thank each of her friends. Caroline: *I love how I don't*

have to talk. There is no other way to say it except I love you like a sister.
Phoebe: *You are the most giving and heartbreakingly kind person I've ever met. Thank you for always having the sweet grandmotherly way.* Isabel: *I know I'll look back at pictures of you and remember how cool my high school friends were.*

Jillian would have thanked her mother: *for helping me with everything even when you used your [mom] voice.* Her father: *for being my biggest fan.* And now, as she slipped down one of the aisles arranged around the graduation stage for the seniors, she saw her school unfold before her: families in the audience, grandparents already snoring, underclassmen and alumni, photographers, white tents in the distance, all the gorgeous buildings. A breath of gravity and consequence filled the idyllic scene, and for a moment paradise was quiet. Jillian knew she'd miss Milton forever:

> *milton: for beatniks, for dance concerts, plays, [the paper], for english, for snow, for kisses, for knitting, for half moon cookies, for [tennis], for cemetery runs, for a cappella, for [creative writing], for freshman year, for crying in front of people, for lipton tea, for the library at night, for climbing trees, for headphones, for no sleep, for silent laughing, for dorks, for driving home at night, for broken hearts, for third team soccer, for swap it, for letting me change.*

Doc Robs's voice rang out through the microphone. There she was at the podium in her signature solid-color blazer and cropped brown hair. As she welcomed the students, faculty members, and guests to graduation, senior girls crossed their legs or, hidden by the rows in front of them, slipped off their shoes and spread their knees. Boys eased back into their chairs. Whitney tried to listen with genuine interest as the two chosen seniors gave their valedictory addresses. The girl walked up to the podium, two thick tan lines growing out of her strapless white dress. Jillian squirmed in her seat, knowing she could have written a better speech and delivered it with more punch, humor, and meaning than this girl ever would. But Whitney was content. She tried to listen again when guest speaker Bertha Coombs took the podium next. In past years Milton had attracted high-profile graduation speakers, and though Ms. Coombs could not rival former president Bill Clinton, who spoke in 2003, she held her own—until she cried.

"Thank you so much," Ms. Coombs began. *"It's quite a trip to be back here. It's a twenty-five-year round-trip for me. I graduated over there, from what used to be the girls' school. . . . Quite frankly, when I was at Milton I was the loneliest girl here."*

Reed was already bored. Brady probably didn't pay attention. Josh thought the woman had lost it. He reached into his pocket and felt the four cigars he'd brought with him, anxious to hand them out to his friends. He leaned forward to check out his prom date, not because he liked her but because it was graduation and seemed like the thing to do. Mostly he wondered when the diplomas would be given out, who would stand up and clap for him, and how obnoxiously his older brother would have yelled had he been there. Yet some ears perked up at Ms. Coombs's speech. Annie listened, overwhelmed by emotion, knowing that after graduation her best friends were going home to families who lived in faraway cities. None of them would be around for grad parties, which meant Annie wouldn't attend either.

"Don't be a stranger," Ms. Coombs said through tears.

"Take someone from here with you.

"Reach out to someone else or one of your teachers or someone who you met in the cafeteria.

"[Because when] you've had some big failure in your life and you think . . . 'Yeah, which of us is not forever a stranger and alone?' you can raise your hand and say, 'I'm not.'"

Whitney paid attention, though a year later she wouldn't even remember the gender of her graduation speaker. From her own perspective, she was hardly alone. She had Nick, who'd left a bouquet of roses on her car that morning, along with a note: *I'm so proud of everything you've done.* She had Tripp, now a best friend who loved her unconditionally. It wouldn't be until nearly a year later that she'd recognize how truly alone she was on the morning of graduation, estranged from her mother, barely communicating with her father, sitting with a cohort of best friends who didn't understand how she could love a boy she cheated on over and over again. Whitney didn't want to listen. She wanted to get her diploma, take her picture, and get out.

The moment before Doc Robs called the first senior's name, Whitney and her classmates sat with tense bodies, wondering who it would be. Diplomas were always awarded in random order, and the very last senior to be called received the traditional orange-and-blue Milton Academy sock filled with quarters, one from each classmate. The seniors were just as impressive as they'd been nine months before, when they sat in front of the upper school during Senior Walk In, only this time they boasted college acceptances. Forty-four were going to an Ivy League school, including twelve to Harvard, nine to Brown, and four to Yale. "Potted Ivies" like Bowdoin and Williams also did well.

A breeze pushed the warm air around. When the first student's name was called, the applause began, the noise rising and falling with the announcement of each graduate. Parents crouched near the front row to take pictures of their children. Girls hugged and interlaced fingers. Seniors stood up for each other, whooping for their friends. One boy walked across the stage, diploma in hand, arms raised and pumping, smiling the widest he'd smiled in his entire life. Another rushed into his father's arms. The moment was tender and public; his father taught at the school and, according to Milton tradition, was there to present his son with the diploma. Underclassmen watched the ceremony with bored or big eyes, knowing that, one June morning in the not-so-distant future, they would be the ones graduating.

Whitney wanted her name to be next. She wanted to graduate and get to college; nothing could be better than her own room, independence, freedom, and life without parents or rules. She wasn't emotional about leaving Milton, and as she sat there, twiddling her fingers, she finally heard her name. She bounced up, not even wondering where Tripp sat in the audience. The rising DSGs watched, waiting for the seniors' social privileges to be passed down in subtle yet certain ways. The younger girls' lives would change next fall, when the senior guys were replaced by a new pack; when they'd be one year older, facing a new crop of freshmen young things hitting campus like firecrackers, just as they had not long before.

Whitney stepped onstage and graciously accepted her diploma, then walked to the 2005 sign and slipped her gerbera daisy into one of the empty slots that perforated the numbers. She stepped back and glanced at the sign, which was now one step closer to total color, and then pranced back to her seat. There. It was official. She'd graduated. *That's over*, she thought to herself. *All that hard work paid off. I'm into college. I can officially get out of here. It's the next step in life.* Now she could go off and be with Nick. Now she was free.

After the final student collected the final diploma, the first notes of "America the Beautiful" rang purely across the quad. The audience erupted, descending into measured chaos: Graduates recessed down the runway, followed by school leaders and graduation speakers, then trustees and faculty. Girls received bouquets. Reed, Brady, and the guys smoked cigars. Parents met each other for the first or the millionth time. Mothers checked out boys, whispering questions like *He's cute, who is he?* to their daughters. The teachers formed a long line on the quad and said good-bye to the seniors, who walked by them slowly, hugging, shaking hands, beaming at the men and women who had taught them everything over the past years.

The white tents filled with people. Whitney couldn't be bothered with food. She wanted to take pictures with her favorite teachers. One in front of the 2005 sign, which was now a confection of pink, red, orange, and yellow. One with her skating coach. Lots with the DSGs. Boarders watched the time, knowing they would eventually have to drift back to their dorm rooms to finish packing and officially move out.

This was a day of loss and rebirth. The students were not the same as they had been nine months before, when Senior Walk In signaled the beginning of the end. They'd survived, and were leaving Milton's cloistered world with raw expectations and new hopes—with the academy's pedigree and promise forever stamped on them.

epilogue

ilton weathered the sex scandal. Two years later, the school continued to do its thing. Seniors went off to great colleges, incoming students vied to fill their shoes, and life at the academy found a new equilibrium. The school added another graduate to its list of famous alumni when Deval Patrick became governor of Massachusetts, with Milton students working for his campaign. And the hockey team survived. The five boys involved in the oral sex incidents moved on. The two youngest players transferred to a boarding school with a particularly strong boys' ice hockey program. They graduated and one went on to play competitive hockey. Two of the three oldest boys also continued playing hockey in prominent leagues. The fifth boy graduated from another prep school, and a year later, the three oldest boys' pretrial probations ended.

One of the three older boys filed a lawsuit with his family against Milton Academy in the winter of 2006. The suit argued that the school did not do its job in preventing sexual acts among students and fostered an environment in which students could easily break rules. Like most other developments in the oral sex incidents, the lawsuit made headlines in the newspapers, but the judge dismissed the case later that year without it ever going to trial. Milton was victorious once again. In the aftermath of the 2004–2005 school year, the academy may have floundered in the public eye, but the school still attracted exceptional students. Doc Robs remained vigilant as ever.

The summer after Whitney graduated, she taught skating lessons and continued to wage war with her mother. She also talked about marriage with Nick. One day he took her to Tiffany, walked up to a salesperson behind the counter, and announced that he wanted to spend $1,000.

Nick, what are you doing? she asked.

You are the most important person in my life, he said.

Don't do that. Like, I love you, and that's sweet of you, but don't spend that on me. Husbands are supposed to spend that on wives. We're just in high school.

This is just a token. I would spend everything on you.

So she chose a diamond solitaire necklace.

The gesture came with an offer that he made to her mother, an attempt at peace that he may not have understood in full at the time: *I think I want to marry your daughter. I want her to go to college and experience other guys. But if in four years, like, if we end up still liking each other, I really want you to like me. And I want you to want me to be with her.*

Little did Nick know, Whitney had found, yet again, another guy to see on the side. He was eventually replaced by someone else in college, and then another someone else, and so on until she met Luke. She walked up to him in the gym because he was wearing a T-shirt from another ISL school. They talked for five minutes, and then, a few days later, he sent her a message on the online website Facebook: *so, were you the girl?* referring to Zoe and the oral sex incidents. This wasn't the first time someone in college made such a comment to Whitney after learning she'd graduated from Milton. But Luke was the opposite of Nick: attractive, clean cut, preppy, an athlete, a hard worker. He came from a good family and challenged her as an equal. Luke breathed new life into Whitney. She started skating again. She went to the library, tried theater and dance, and discovered how important it was for her parents to like her boyfriend. And on Valentine's Day in her freshman year, she sat across from Luke at Friendly's eating a gigantic ice-cream dessert, realizing that this was the kind of celebration she never knew she'd been dreaming of.

Now two years into college, she and Luke are still together. He graduated, so she visits him on the weekends, and although college is no longer the same without him there, the impact of meeting him remained life-changing. With Luke came clarity. In ten years she wanted to be married, living in Dedham, trying to get pregnant or already a mom armed with rules and discipline. Looking back on high school, she regretted how much she'd hated her mother, blamed her father, and mistreated her body and her talents.

A dark cloud just came over me when Nick came into my life. . . .

He ruined my family life.

He made me do things that I never wanted to do, like smoke weed.

I quit skating.

I became lazy.

I stopped doing my homework.

That was Nick who did that to me. . . . And at that time I thought [my relationship with Nick] was great. But now I look back and I'm so happy. And I feel happy because I'm not lying. I'm not sneaking around. I'm honest. It's a genuine happiness. I'm truthful. It just feels so good.

I have something to tell you, Emma said, looking up at Brady's long eyelashes and little-boy eyes.

They were standing on the lawn outside a friend's house a month after graduation. Brady waited, thinking how amazing his summer had been so far, and how great college would be once he finally got there, a football player, single, ready for everything new.

I love you, Emma said.

It happened fast. Brady was unprepared. Love? Brady in love? He'd never even thought about saying those words to her, much less anyone else. He looked at this adorable girl and, for the hell of it, or because it seemed like the right thing to do, said the same words back.

I love you, too.

Brady continued being Brady in college. He and Emma broke up at the end of the summer, and he became *the man* among a new group of guys, collected stories from a new group of girls, and excelled in all his areas of expertise—social life, sports, just being cool. He learned to be a student and decided to major in government. And two years after graduating from Milton, he still had not had a girlfriend and was quite happy about it, too. In high school, Brady never tried to be anything other than who he was, and after graduation he never had to change, perhaps because once you're the guys' guy, you're always the guys' guy. Brady will always be *the man.*

Reed pursued the title in all its incarnations. While vacationing in St. Tropez with a friend after graduation, he flew on private jets, went as a VIP to exclusive clubs, saw celebrities, drank with billionaires, and stared at their women. Girls were everywhere, giving him their phone numbers and wanting to take him home, but Reed had one problem: He was now a boyfriend. The whole situation seemed to have happened to him. After all that time he'd spent avoiding commitment and asserting his independence from Isabel, Reed discovered that he actually liked being in a relationship. Away from Milton, it was easy to dote on her. He spoiled her at restaurants and learned to be attentive. He handled their second pregnancy scare with calm. Reed's image of *the man* was being transformed.

Had someone told Isabel that she'd graduate from high school with a boyfriend, she never would have guessed he would be a jock, much less a hockey player, much less someone like Reed. But there she was, an actual girlfriend, sporting a handsome boy on her arm. As graduation parties ended and summer went on, she saw a new Reed. He stopped playing games, showed affection, and shared parts of himself he'd kept hidden from others. They spent hours in bed together and went out to restaurants. They stayed at each other's houses and realized that their parents were nothing alike. Reed's mom and dad were traditional and raised a brood of boys who constantly made a ruckus. Isabel's family was liberal, and enjoyed reading, talking, and playing intellectual board games. But they learned how to be part of each other's families.

Reed loved Isabel and he also loved having a relationship. As a boyfriend, he could be tender, caring, and sexual. At his Ivy League college, girls made him their guy friend and turned to him for advice. To pass the time between his and Isabel's weekend visits, Reed dreamed up business ventures with equally ambitious friends. He studied English and art history, and realized he didn't want to go into finance. *I don't want to be in a world where everyone thinks they're God's gift to the world,* he said, *and there's no actual social value to it.* He also decided not to try out for the varsity hockey team. His mother wondered what had happened to her son, but Reed knew exactly what he was doing. Isabel had shown him that he didn't always have to train, study, and be perfect; there were so many other ways to spend his time, and finally, after months of agony and deception, he made her a top priority. A year after graduating, Reed and Isabel were still together, defying the odds and, at times, still not entirely believing it themselves.

But sometimes Reed wondered what would happen if he didn't have a girlfriend. Everyone told him how difficult long distance would be. Couples never lasted; the distance was too hard; someone always cheated. In time his and Isabel's differences prevailed. She didn't want to hang out with his Milton friends whenever they were in Boston, and Reed still viewed her girlfriends as the Hysterics. She was embarrassed when he showed up at her arty college wearing his salmon Polo sweater. His college buddies had always expressed surprise that he'd dated a girl like Isabel for so long. They both began to look around. During their sophomore years in college, Isabel and Reed tried having an open relationship.

There were rules. No sex. Hookups were okay, but they had to tell each other everything. The confessionals were nauseating, because neither one really wanted to hear the details about the other person's hookups. Soon their open relationship became a break, and then their break became official. The relationship was over.

I'm divorced, Reed told a buddy from Milton.

It's about time, his friend said. *You're way too beautiful to be locked up.*

In some ways Reed agreed. Now he could spend nights in the basement of his fraternity, a can of cheap beer in his hand, a room of girls to chase. Reed had more free time than he'd ever had before. He played club hockey. He did what he wanted, not necessarily what he thought he should do. With Isabel's absence came realizations about how he'd treated her. Even if he didn't want to jump back into a serious relationship, he knew he could never do that to another girl again.

Isabel was surprised by how casual relationships could be in college. She felt liberated and empowered. She could go home with a guy and never speak with him again. She could go home with him and not sleep with him, or not go home with him at all. For the first time in her life, she realized that she was the one with the power, and learned to demand respect from guys. Looking back on her years at Milton, Isabel saw herself as an insecure girl. Reed helped to make her more confident, but it wasn't until they broke up that she became truly independent. She would never compromise parts of herself for a guy again. She would never tie her happiness to a boyfriend or a hookup. Reed had changed her, and she'd changed him. *I don't know if our breakup is final,* she thought, *but for now it's what we need.*

Of all the disappointments Josh experienced at Milton, nothing rivaled the fact that he graduated from high school having never been a Boyfriend. His experiences with girls were limited to embarrassing dates or flirtations that did not end well. Diana had been a fantasy, a girl who may or may not have liked him for a brief period freshman year. And his sexual experiences were tied neatly into three brief nights from eighth grade and senior year. Josh saw Erica only once more after that weekend in New York City. She showed up at a friend's party, and when she walked in, Josh froze. He didn't smile. He didn't even try to hide. He just watched silently as she walked by him. *I'm an asshole,* he thought, and actually felt bad, too.

A few weeks after graduation, at a party at his family's Cape house, a girl asked Josh if he wanted to have sex. *If you turn this down now,* he thought to himself, *what the hell are you doing?* He got a condom, played it cool, and fumbled his way out of virginity. In that single night he discovered a new side of himself—passionate, animalistic, selfish. His high school career was such an embarrassment. He realized he'd always held himself back, taken the easier route, and avoided risks. It dawned on him: He'd been a pussy.

And so when he arrived at college for his freshman year, he wanted to become the kind of guy who could go to parties, get drunk, and hook up. Now that he'd had sex, he could finally keep up with the guys. Technically he was a "man," but even Josh realized that he had no idea how to actually be one. Getting the girl remained a mystery, and he'd lost his virginity only because someone else made the first move. Random hookups and stories about girls without names weren't enough for him. Having sex, he realized, didn't make him *the man*; it made him less of a boy, and this boy realized that he wanted to be a "man" in every way. He wanted love, a relationship, and trust. Something enchanting and surprising, like holding hands, personal jokes, and flowers on Valentine's Day. The smallest, simplest thing: romance his way. That's all.

In the six months after graduating from Milton, Jillian lost her virginity twice. The first time was at her own graduation party, which she threw at her family's summer house, against her parents' wishes. She could only imagine their reaction had they found out.

You lied.

You jeopardized your future.

You put us in a terrible position in terms of liability.

But throwing a grad party was just something Jillian had to do. The night was fantastic, somewhere between an intimate get-together and a kegger, but then Oliver showed up and ignored her. Jillian was furious, so she dragged him into a bedroom. Despite questions and fury, however many drinks into the night, she found herself down to a bra and hooking up with Oliver, who was in a T-shirt and socks. The condom was on. He entered. Four seconds later, he withdrew.

We shouldn't do this, he said.

Jillian didn't get it. She thought every guy wanted to have sex. Why did he stop? Didn't he want her? Feeling rejected was so much more of a reason for regret than having sex with someone she wasn't in a relationship with. Jillian thought she was ready to have sex, and now that she'd committed to the task, she found herself somewhere in between. Did four seconds count? Was she still a virgin? She decided that she was, because having sex was supposed to be a physical and emotional experience. The next day, when Oliver rose early and hugged her good-bye, she knew she would never see him again. Months later she learned he was dating another girl from Milton. Jillian was jealous until she learned that he never even hooked up with the girl unless they were drunk. In the end, Jillian thought she was the only girl he'd ever kissed sober. She still considers him to be the one who got away.

In college, Jillian discovered that she was a likable girl. Guys paid attention to her. They called her attractive. She felt attractive, even though she was the same size she'd been senior year. She made new friends—not a clique, but friends. She hated her parents less. They were about three hours away by car, and she loved her arty school with its eclectic and impassioned students. She got two tattoos. She continued to write, and played tennis at her father's request. She also lost her virginity. Again. This time it was with the cute guy from Starbucks, and this time it counted. As with Oliver, Jillian sensed she would never hear from the guy again. She knew instantly that she'd compromised her values, giving in to pressures she'd watched her friends give in to throughout high school. The next day, and every day after that, she tried to approach her mistake practically: She'd expected it to be a one-night stand, and she knew he didn't want to date her seriously.

I am a sexually liberated person, she told herself, *not in a slutty, promiscuous way, but I am not prude. . . . I am excited that I can have all the sex I want . . . but on the other hand I am afraid that I will not have sex in a loving, caring, monogamous relationship. That it will never happen, so I don't want to do it again with someone that is . . . random until I have done it in a relationship. I just don't have any idea of when that is going to happen.*

Annie walked onto her urban college campus with a new hairstyle (she'd dyed it brown) and suitcases filled with preppy outfits, anxious to become a young woman. Scott was her past, and college was her future. She took time away from the flute. She worked just as hard as she always had, and was shocked when, by the end of her first semester, she had real guy friends. But the Scotts of the world slipped back into her life, and she hooked up with them out of habit and obligation.

History started repeating itself one night at a party the summer before she went to college. While flirting with a guy she'd liked back in middle school, he cornered her in a room and pushed her onto the bed. He'd always been so nice to her when they were younger, but on this night he flipped up her short white skirt, pried her legs open, and squeezed her breasts so hard bruises formed the next day. He pushed his mouth onto hers, and Annie kissed him back. She didn't know how to stop the situation, because she couldn't just beat up a guy she'd always liked.

Let's go watch a movie! she tried.

I don't want to do anything with you.

No. No. No!

She ran from the room yelling for her girlfriend. He stormed after her, and when he finally relented, slouching outside, drunk, raging, getting into his car, she ran after him despite her rage and fear, hoping to stop him, always the caretaker.

Am I always going to be seen as somebody that guys can just use? she wondered. *What is it about me that attracts these people or makes them think they can do this to me? Even though I know it's wrong and I don't want to do it, what is it about me that, to some extent, goes along with it?*

A year after graduating from Milton, Annie was still searching for answers. But she found in her mother an empathy she'd been yearning for. This woman who'd raised her and taught her to be good, wise, and hardworking knew her daughter well.

What's the matter? her mom asked.

Tears rolled from Annie's eyes as she told her story about nearly being raped.

I'm really proud of you, her mom said, loving her daughter with the same fierceness and love that Annie felt for her dorm mates and friends.

Still, Annie had yet to find a guy. She continued hooking up with boys she met, but she never stopped hoping for something better. She had the ability to look into her future and trust that there would be happiness and love in her life. Mistakes she'd made in the past were exactly that—mistakes. *What happened is what happened,* she realized. *I did really feel like the only way I could get a guy to like me was to please him in certain ways. And that's sad to me. But at the same time, it's good that I don't feel that way anymore.*

At some point during her first year at college, Annie learned to be single without feeling lonely or desperate. Being herself, and just herself, was enough.

acknowledgments

During the two years that we worked together on *Restless Virgins,* we relied on the advice, encouragement, and support of many people who believed in two first-time authors.

This book had its origins in the kitchen of the *Atlantic*'s Boston office, during a conversation we had with Scott Stossel. Scott first suggested that the Milton Academy incidents had the makings of a fascinating book. He encouraged us when the project was little more than an idea, and gave us our first lesson in proposal writing. Michael Curtis offered invaluable guidance along the way. He lent his keen eye for a good story, reminding us that something must always *happen.* We were fortunate to have the encouragement of Cullen Murphy at both the beginning stages and completion of this book. We thank him for his support.

Our agent, Brettne Bloom, helped us nurture the idea and was our constant cheerleader, friend, and adviser. There's no one else with whom we'd rather discuss teenage sex over meals in crowded restaurants.

Our editor, David Highfill, patiently guided us through the process of writing and rewriting. He had a compassionate vision for this book, and helped cultivate each story, striking the balance between advice and direction.

Beth Silfin lent her critical eye to our manuscript. Dee Dee De Bartlow was our enthusiastic publicist. Jill Kneerim was a true supporter. Gabe Robinson, James Houston, and the rest of the William Morrow team were always there to help. Maggie Lange walked us through our first encounter with contracts. We appreciate the hard work of our transcribers, Chris Chamberlin, Lynda Loebelenz, Kellie Congdon, Julia Garafano, Maria Fraser, and Maria DeBiase. They waded through fast talkers and noisy backgrounds, turning hundreds of hours of interviews into transcriptions in record time.

This book would not have been possible without Annie, Whitney, Jillian, Isabel, Reed, Brady, Josh, Caroline, Phoebe, and the dozens of other members of Milton's class of 2005. They believed in our book and devoted themselves to it wholeheartedly. They met us in coffee shops, classrooms, and park benches, and indulged our questions about everything imaginable. Their honesty, candor, and accessibility made *Restless Virgins* possible. By sharing their most intimate stories, they have added to a larger story about coming of age in America.

We also want to thank the other Milton graduates and adults who spoke with us. They helped us gain greater insight into the school, its students, and adolescent culture. A special thank-you to that certain graduate who was the first to respond to our e-mail and meet with us. You helped introduce us to the students who now appear in this book.

All the girls and boys of *Restless Virgins* inspired this book and filled it with life. And they inspired us, as well.

Personal Acknowledgments

I have been incredibly lucky to have mentors throughout my life who have encouraged me to write. John Demos has been gracious with his time, reading my work since I was in sixth grade. I thank him for introducing me to the power of narrative nonfiction, and teaching me to ask a very significant question: *Where does the story begin?*

While at the *Atlantic,* Michael Curtis patiently read my work and taught me what made a story artful, meaningful, or a candidate for the reject pile. He has remained a challenging and critical reader these past few years.

Among my many wonderful teachers at Milton, two captivated my imagination and launched me on my way as a writer. Mark Hilgendorf opened doors to new ways of thinking about culture and narrative. Walter McCloskey didn't know what he started whenever he kept me after English class to discuss my latest article for the *Milton Paper;* when he let loose an *Oooh Abba!* I knew I had something. I am also grateful to Michaela Steimle for her wise and thoughtful guidance, and David Britton for introducing me to "shelf sentences."

Professor Bruce Nelson of Dartmouth College indulged my desire to think creatively in each of his history courses. Professor Patricia McKee helped me understand the mysteries of writing an English thesis. I benefited from Dartmouth College's Reynolds Fellowship, which supported my graduate study in creative writing at the University of Edinburgh. My mentor at Edinburgh, Alan Jamieson, taught me that there's a story in everything. Tony K. saved this book from more three A.M. computer crises than I'd like to admit. And my friends at the Harvard Club gym helped me escape for that hour each day.

Marissa was my coauthor and coworker during this wild ride. I appreciate her many talents, warmth, and compassion, and thank her for reminding me of how important it was to stop and breathe. I will never forget the journey we shared.

Two years spent working in an apartment with a laptop could not have been done without my dear friends. Thank you to Hillary and Jason Chapman, Lynne Frappier, Alyson Goldberg, Rosi Kaiser, Rich Quincy, Morgan Rowe, Louise Sandberg, and Elizabeth Vadasdi for always being there for me.

In more ways than I can possibly express, my family helped to make this book possible. My grandmother has been my most faithful fan. My grandfather, who I miss every day, taught me to reach for the stars.

My sister and best friend, Eliza, lived with me while I wrote this book. She became my social coordinator and chef, accepted the plot diagrams I hung on our living room walls, and provided crafty acrobatics when a hundred pages of interview notes flew out the window and onto the fire escape. Thank you for keeping me happy and sane.

I grew up watching my parents, Virginia Drachman and Doug Jones, write and place books of their own on our shelves. They raised me in a home where ideas and conversations coexisted with support and love. I am a better writer because of them. They know everything that they've done, and most important, they have always been there for me.

A.D.J.

Boston, MA

This book took over two years to lovingly craft, research, and write, and I owe my success during this time to the unconditional support of my family and friends.

I am most indebted to my parents and sister, who cheered me on as I carved my own path. Mom and Mark, you believed in me always, even at times when I doubted myself, and patiently stood by me every step of the way. Danielle, you were my rock and best friend. You graciously permitted my papers, books, and ideas to fill our tiny apartment and, in turn, filled me with warmth. Dad, you shared your ethusiasm for reading and writing. My entire family—all the Harmons and Mileys—stayed excited about this project for a very long time.

My gratitude goes to my best friends from Milton. Danny, you were my go-to expert and avid fan, always there to answer questions over e-mail or by phone. Thank you for being utterly convinced you were contributing to an amazing feat, long before there were words on the page. Ellie, Leslie, and Margaret, you shared your thoughts, stories, and questions, and in doing so, helped this book come alive. You understood from the start that this was much more than a Milton story, and encouraged me to push forward. Thank you for hours upon hours of patient listening and sound advice.

I would not have enjoyed these two years as much as I did if Emre had not been by my side. Thank you for calling me one fateful morning and insisting that I do this. You were my confidant day after day, coffee after coffee, draft after draft, and I am incredibly grateful.

Thanks also to the many others who carried and inspired me along the way: friends who assured me I could do it, coworkers at Harvard who sent me on my way with applause, and mentors at Milton and Penn who shaped my writing. Special thanks to Michael, my forever adviser.

Finally, thanks to my coauthor, Abigail. We made a book out of an idea, a tangible reality out of a dream. I admire your tireless strength and creativity, and I am so appreciative of the incredible trip we've taken together.

M.L.M.
New York, NY